Therapeutic Recreation:

Cases and Exercises

Second Edition

Therapeutic Recreation:
Cases and Exercises

Second Edition

Barbara C. Wilhite, Ed.D., CTRS
M. Jean Keller, Ed.D., CTRS

Venture Publishing, Inc.
State College, PA

Production Manager: Richard Yocum
Manuscript Editing: Richard Yocum, Deborah L. McRann, and Michele L.
    Barbin
Cover Design and Illustration: ©2000 Sandra Sikorski, Sikorski Design

Printing and Binding: Precision Book & Litho Inc.

Library of Congress Catalogue Card Number 99-67811
ISBN 1-892132-12-5

Contents

Chapter Two 65
Individual Therapeutic Recreation Program
Planning ....

Table of Contents

Preface

The idea for *Therapeutic Recreation: Cases and Exercises* was born one day in conversation between the two authors. We were lamenting the fact that most therapeutic recreation students had limited working experience. Without such experience, principles and theories abstracted from the literature had little reality for them. We needed a way of socializing students into the complex therapeutic recreation process prior to an internship, and establishing further the link between philosophical and theoretical knowledge and practice. Investigations have identified basic competencies needed by therapeutic recreation specialists. One example is the 1997 Job Analysis Project, sponsored by the National Council for Therapeutic Recreation Certification, which resulted in a revision of the knowledge base for entry-level practice in therapeutic recreation and, accordingly, a revised certification exam. However, such investigations rarely explain how these competency areas relate to each other and to professional practice (Parr, 1996). We realized that successful therapeutic recreation specialists were challenged daily with situations that demanded the ability to go beyond "this is how it is done," and from this, we began our search for connections to the existing body of knowledge and creative new practice alternatives.

As the second edition of this text was being prepared, the need for creativity and innovation in therapeutic recreation was even more apparent. While therapeutic recreation is growing and maturing, it is, inevitably, changing. Because of changes in health and human services, we have opportunities to serve a more diverse group of consumers in more diverse settings than ever before (Landrum, Schmidt, and McLean, 1995). In response to present changes, and in anticipation of future changes, students, professionals, and educators continue to need opportunities to develop and refine applied aspects of the therapeutic recreation process such as assessing, planning, implementing, and evaluating (Austin, 1999).

Thus, the text and cases included in this edition are intended to provoke discussion and provide guidance as our profession moves forward in the new millennium. However, we attempt to do this in a way that acknowledges and respects our past—the foundation upon which the continued development of therapeutic recreation rests. The cases included in this edition attempt to portray the rich tapestry of therapeutic recreation by illuminating common threads woven through our known past connecting us to our desired future.

This text grew out of notions that therapeutic recreation specialists emerge as effective practitioners by developing, in addition to knowledge, a particular way of thinking about people and a belief in the role of therapeutic recreation in the rehabilitation and habilitation of people with mental, physical, social, and emotional disabilities. A process of discovery is a critical part of effective learning and, consequently, an important teaching device. Case method is a useful vehicle for discovery and offers an opportunity to think about people with disabilities and therapeutic recreation processes and techniques.

The Cases in the Text

The cases and issues presented in this text are real and dynamic. Therapeutic recreation is a profession fraught with stress, change, reward, and above all, challenge. Some of these elements emerge from our interactions with clients, professionals, administrators, institutions, and communities. Some come from within therapeutic recreation specialists themselves as they struggle to define their role and to be the best they can be. Obviously, there is no shortage of challenges for therapeutic recreation, as we have witnessed an increase in the use of harmful substances, a growing number of people with AIDS, a rapid expansion of people with depression, a more diverse society with an increasing divorce and suicide rate, a growing population of older adults, and indeed, an ever-increasing need for therapeutic recreation.

The cases of *Therapeutic Recreation: Cases and Exercises* are based on actual situations. Forty new cases are featured in this edition representing a diverse group of people and situations. Because aspects of some cases are featured in more than one chapter, readers can discover the complexity of therapeutic recreation. Some of the cases are virtually complete reports of therapeutic recreation situations, while others are partial reports to show open-endedness and to stimulate alternative lines of discussion. The cases are short enough to avoid discussions that bog down in a confusion of detail, and yet long enough to enable precise understanding of problems.

The Case Study Method

The case study method is an accepted way of helping inexperienced students to gain a mature, broad outlook. Case study requires the use and application of substantive content, technical and general knowledge, relevant information, creativity, and common sense (Bannon and Busser, 1992). Therefore, the cases in this text are to be considered in conjunction with other textbooks, articles, and resources that provide information about therapeutic recreation and its practice.

The specific questions at the end of each case are intended to stimulate initial inquiry into issues or topics related to or prompted by the individual case. In almost every instance the listed questions should be followed by additional questions such as "Why?" "Why not?" and "What then?" In no case do the questions exhaust all possibilities for discussion.

Many of the cases, particularly those with personal exchanges, lend themselves to effective role-playing. While preparation for role-playing outside of the learning environment may produce beneficial knowledge, spontaneous role-playing may produce even more meaningful learning experiences. Other experiences such as simulations, panel discussions, interviews, field trips, invited presentations, video tapes, and Internet resources are suggested to challenge readers. In this way, *Therapeutic Recreation: Cases and Exercises*, can serve as a supplemental text to all therapeutic recreation courses.

The Challenges of Case Study Analysis

A common hazard for readers is the rejection of a case due to what is perceived as insufficient information. Seldom is all desirable or useful formation available for analyzing and resolving therapeutic recreation issues. Therapeutic recreation specialists must use the information available and do the best they can with what they have. Furthermore, the main issue of many situations is to determine what additional information can be obtained before adequate analysis can be made and appropriate action taken. Therapeutic recreation specialists must decide whether additional information is worth getting, whether it would be meaningful and relevant, and whether it can be secured in time to be useful.

Learners may also conclude that two cases are identical, not just similar. Since many factors affect the behavior of people and the circumstances within which they react and interact, no two cases are identical, although they may be similar.

Beginners in case analysis should be cautioned to recognize their feelings and prejudices. Sifting case facts through one's feelings and prejudices (knowingly or unknowingly) tends to slant and bias the facts. Learners occasionally search for the "right" answer or solution to cases. Although some answers or solutions are better than others, there are no "right" ones.

Readers recall children's puzzles with little animals hidden in branches and foliage of a tree, contrived in such a way that they had to study the drawing, turning it at all angles to find the hidden, camouflaged creatures. They clung to the branches, disappeared in the foliage, or, in extremes, were etched in the sky and clouds. The artist may have placed as many as 15 camouflaged creatures in a sketch. If one was able to find them all, one was indeed perceptive. These puzzles encouraged intellectual freedom and individual creativity. So too, *Therapeutic Recreation: Cases and Exercises* encourages readers to apply what they already know, discover the unknown, seek new solutions, and enjoy the delightful challenge of analyzing and synthesizing the known and unknown into the practice of therapeutic recreation.

Sincere Thanks

This text would not have been possible without the contributors of the various cases. These individuals, both practitioners and educators, shared their experiences so that others may learn to be successful therapeutic recreation specialists. Their names are listed on the pages following this preface. Appreciation is also extended to Drs. Gerald O'Morrow, Radford University, Radford, Virginia, and Marcia Jean Carter, University of Northern Colorado, Greeley, Colorado, for their critical review, feedback, and assistance. Their comments and suggestions are reflected in this edition of *Therapeutic Recreation: Cases and Exercises.*

The authors wish to extend their appreciation to those individuals and agencies who provided pictures for the text. These include Dana Dempsey, CTRS, Texas Scottish Rite Hospital for Children; Ed Supina, CTRS, Bachman Recreation Center, Dallas Park and Recreation Department; Amy Docteur, CTRS, Denton Park and Recreation Department; and Marcia Jean Carter, CTRS, University of Northern Colorado.

The authors also wish to thank the University of North Texas for its support and assistance. Appreciation is extended to Michael Lioy for his attentive editing. Nadine Sevrain is credited for thoroughly compiling the references and resources. Appreciation is extended to Richard Yocum, Kay Whiteside, and the entire Venture Publishing staff for their encouragement and patience.

Barbara C. Wilhite
M. Jean Keller

Bibliography

Austin, D. R. (1999). *Therapeutic recreation: Processes and techniques* (4th ed.). Champaign, IL: Sagamore.

Bannon, J. J., and Busser, J. A. (1992). *Problem solving in recreation and parks* (3rd ed.). Champaign, IL: Sagamore.

Landrum, P. K., Schmidt, N. D., and McLean, A. (1995). *Outcome-oriented rehabilitation: Principles, strategies, and tools for effective program management.* Gaithersburg, MD: Aspen.

Parr, M. G. (1996). A cognitive approach to understanding the conceptual structure of the parks, recreation, and leisure services field. *Schole, 11*, 9–22.

Contributors of Case Studies

Jennifer Brown
Dallas, TX

Susan E. Lynch
Farmville, VA

Lorraine J. Brown
Carbondale, IL

Sylvie Wagnon
Euless, TX

Joanna L. Burns
Arvada, CO

Sharon M. Malley
Washington, DC

Marcia Jean Carter
Greeley, CO

Amy Massingill
McKinney, TX

Timothy T. Dodd
Richmond, VA

James E. Neville
Atascadero, CA

Cindy Flowers
Ft. Pierce, FL

Mason Peebles
Denton, TX

Amanda Green
Denton, TX

Karen S. Perkins
Bethesda, MD

Frederick P. Green
Hattiesburg, MS

Kathy Morris-Ritz
Jackson, WY

James L. Harlow
Ft. Pierce, FL

Don Rogers
Terre Haute, IN

Christine Z. Howe
Brockport, NY

Nancy Brattain Rogers
Terre Haute, IN

Susan D. Hudson
Cedar Falls, IA

Janet Sable
Durham, NH

Diane LaTourrette
Boulder, CO

Nadine Sevrain
Flower Mound, TX

Contributors of Case Studies
(continued)

Lynne K. Seward
Richmond, VA

Joseph Teaff
Carbondale, IL

Latee Shanda
Spokane, WA

Tom Turpin
Carbondale, IL

Marci Summer
Gainesville, GA

James Washington
Jefferson, LA

Alison Taylor
Plano, TX

Introduction
An Overview

Therapeutic recreation and the various settings in which it occurs is growing and changing at a rapid pace. On the downside, the effects of change are being felt by therapeutic recreation professionals in trends such as shortened lengths of treatment, loss of middle management positions, replacement of professional level positions by assistants and aides, increased client-to-staff ratios, replacement of traditional therapeutic recreation departments with "product line" or "program" models, increased paperwork (particularly in regard to authorization and reimbursement for services), a constant need to justify one's presence in an agency, and in general, a greater sense of "doing more with less." Moreover, clients may face reduced services, increased waiting times for services, limitation of client choice, and streamlined client assessment and evaluation.

On the up side, however, there are also positive trends in this new health and human services environment. For example, therapeutic recreation specialists are experiencing greater interdisciplinary cooperation between allied health and human service professionals, providing a more integrated way of thinking about and approaching service delivery; more comprehensive dialogue and planning with the client, family, and funding source; growth in less intensive settings such as outpatient, long-term acute, community, and home care; cooperative ventures with public and private agencies; a greater emphasis on health promotion and disease prevention; and creative programming trends.

In addition, the demand for therapeutic recreation services is growing as the population ages and as mortality rates for many conditions (e.g., stroke, spinal cord injury, acquired brain injury) decline, causing the number of people with functional limitations to increase. The achievement of relevant outcomes in this higher demand environment will be central to the evaluation of therapeutic recreation services by consumers, providers, and payers (Landrum, Schmidt, & McLean, 1995; PEW Health Professions Commission, 1995; Smith, 1995).

To meet present challenges, therapeutic recreation specialists must be able to apply theoretical, philosophical, and ethical principles to the design and implementation of therapeutic recreation programs and services. This case study text focuses on actual situations where therapeutic recreation specialists are challenged to translate principles and theories into practice and application. The study of these case histories and the exercises, role-playing, and structured field experiences may improve the practice of therapeutic recreation on a day-to-day basis. Additionally, the laboratory experiences these exercises provide, prior to or in conjunction with actual field placement, should increase the effectiveness of classroom learning and the professional preparation of therapeutic recreation specialists.

The goal of this book is to promote sound practice and application of therapeutic recreation principles, theories, and research findings in situations comparable to those experiences therapeutic recreation professionals and paraprofessionals encounter. Practice exercises, simulating realistic events, provide a safe environment in which taking risks, testing ideas, evaluating decisions, and comparing outcomes are encouraged. In this way therapeutic recreation specialists can learn from their mistakes without harming anyone. The exercises, however, are not limited to preprofessional education. They also provide a means to assess the skills of graduate students without therapeutic recreation undergraduate degrees. In addition, practicing professionals and paraprofessionals are provided opportunities to refine problem-solving and decision-making skills and continue their professional development.

This book focuses on the following aspects of therapeutic recreation and its practice.

Chapter One   *Assessment in Therapeutic Recreation* introduces readers to the philosophical orientation of the text, presents a definition of individual assessment, and examines the assessment process as applied to various populations. Assessment techniques and methods are highlighted, and characteristics of comprehensive interdisciplinary assessments are discussed. Information on protocol development has been added in this edition.

Chapter Two   *Therapeutic Recreation Program Planning* examines the establishment of individual goals and objectives based on comprehensive assessments and the development of individual program or treatment plans. A new feature in this chapter is the presentation of a model of therapeutic recreation service delivery developed by the authors that provides justification and direction for developing individual intervention plans. This chapter also covers principles for analyzing, selecting, and adapting activities and interventions with an increased emphasis on assistive technology. Intervention techniques that have been added in this edition include animal-assisted therapy, aquatic therapy, adventure therapy, and sports and fitness. Previously featured intervention techniques, including behavior management, sensory stimulation, reality orientation, remotivation, resocialization, relaxation, and assertiveness training are updated.

Chapter Three   *Implementing Individual Therapeutic Recreation Program Plans* presents a range of topics including documentation, the team approach, risk management, least restrictive environments, legal factors, outreach, and utilization of community resources. Staff development, working with volunteers, and technology are new sections that have been added in this edition.

Chapter Four   *Leadership in Therapeutic Recreation* presents guidelines for effective leadership and highlights techniques for improving communication and teaching skills and avoiding burnout. This chapter also presents selected teaching strategies, confidentiality, leadership concerns, and advocacy. Client motivation strategies, caregiver issues, and client diversity have been added in this edition.

Chapter Five   *Evaluation in Therapeutic Recreation* discusses the purpose of conducting individual evaluations and defines evaluation criteria. Approaches to formative and summative evaluation are also presented. An expanded emphasis on quality assurance is featured in this edition.

Concerns relating to management, ethics, and reform in health and human services are interspersed throughout the chapters. The chapters within the text are not definitive and should only serve as a means of review for the content and knowledge areas. It is critical for users of this text to supplement their preprofessional and/or professional development with outside reading. Cases are supplied with selected references. Learners will discover that references may not directly apply to a case, but will add insight into a situation or issue.

All five chapters focus on therapeutic recreation services and programming strategies with individual clients, and all present case histories and scenarios that incorporate a variety of disabling conditions in many situations and settings. Case histories and scenarios vary in length and complexity. Each case, however, describes a particular situation and includes information about the individual(s) involved, the setting, and other key factors. A series of suggested discussion questions and exercises follows each case study. Consistent with the multidimensional nature of therapeutic recreation, some cases are carried from one chapter to another. Learners will refer to the chapter where the case originated to review the complete scenario. Page numbers are indicated within the text (and in the index) to make this cross-referencing easier.

Discussion questions require learners to organize pertinent information; identify, analyze, and synthesize problems; determine indicators of successful experiences; identify possible courses of action; and develop action plans.

In-class exercises require learners to practice various skills highlighted in the scenarios.

Role-playing requires learners to represent key individuals in the scenario, simulating possible outcomes of a variety of problem-solving solutions.

Field experience exercises require learners to interact in particular situations with professionals and individuals with disabilities.

Learners will be required to observe situations, gather, analyze, and synthesize information about particular problems, and then present their observations and recommendations.

Although the methodological process of sorting, classifying, and analyzing case information may vary according to the preferences of learners and educators, diagnosing basic problems should be a common objective of all processes. Identifying and stating the basic problem of the case should generally be a starting point.

Some of the case histories and scenarios may necessitate a review of related literature that is pertinent to the case, but is not discussed explicitly in the text. For example, learners may want to review literature relating to such items as specific disabilities or illnesses, treatment interventions, and medications that are high-lighted in the case.

This book is action-oriented in that it requires interaction and active participation through analyzing, synthesizing, problem solving, formulating individual plans, and evaluating outcomes. Learners are asked to undertake a number of assignments related to completing leisure assessments, developing goals and objectives, conducting activity analyses, documenting, and developing evaluation and discharge plans. It is suggested that the text be used as a companion text with others throughout the entire therapeutic recreation curriculum to enhance the growth and development of therapeutic recreation specialists, and in training and in-servicing with therapeutic recreation specialists. For example, chapter topics and cases that relate to professional identity, philosophy, diversity, and inclusion practices could be used in an introductory therapeutic recreation course, or in an inclusive leisure services course. Topics and cases pertaining to assessment and evaluation, therapeutic recreation interventions, client motivation strategies, and working with volunteers would have application in courses and in-services with a primary emphasis on therapeutic recreation processes and techniques. Senior and graduate level therapeutic recreation courses might emphasize content relating to health and human services reform, ethics, management issues, protocol development, and advocacy. Critique of the model of therapeutic recreation practice presented in this edition could also be conducted by students and practitioners with a more advanced understanding of therapeutic recreation.

Learners should also consider developing their own discussion questions, exercises, role-plays, and field experiences to enhance

existing learning opportunities. The exercises
presented in this book
may be easily altered or
expanded to accommo-
date learners' and facilita-
tors' specific needs and
interests. Practicing
therapeutic recreation
specialists and individuals
with disabilities can
provide invaluable insight
into many situations and
problems encountered in
these exercises; hence, it
is recommended that they
be invited to participate.

Bibliography

Landrum, P. K., Schmidt, N. D., & McLean, A. (1995). *Out-come-oriented rehabilitation: Principles, strategies, and tools for effective program management.* Gaithersburg, MD: Aspen.

PEW Health Professions Commission. (1995). *Critical challenges: Revitalizing the health professions for the twenty-first century.* San Francisco, CA: UCSF Center for the Health Professions.

Smith, R. W. (1995). Trends in therapeutic recreation. *Parks & Recreation, 30*(5), 66–71.

Chapter One
Assessment in Therapeutic Recreation

Therapeutic recreation is basically about making a difference in the lives of clients as a result of specific intervention at specific points in time. The primary goal of therapeutic recreation is to enable clients to live in the least restrictive and least costly environment at their highest possible level of interdependence and quality of life. One characteristic of therapeutic recreation that distinguishes it from other health and human service disciplines is its focus on leisure as a necessary component of quality of life. Therapeutic recreation involves a knowledge of leisure as it relates to health and optimal well-being (Austin and Crawford, 1996). It is important to understand this philosophical orientation, to understand the "why" of therapeutic recreation service, before attempts to assess the needs of clients are made.

Leisure and Therapeutic Recreation

Kelly (1996) suggested that leisure is an element of life in which all people experience opportunities for expression, development, and relationships. Leisure's hallmarks include intrinsic motivation, self-determination, and enjoyment (Dattilo and Kleiber, 1993; Dattilo, Kleiber, and Williams, 1998; Iso-Ahola, 1980; Kelly, 1987). Opportunities to achieve a leisure effect are limited or excluded for some individuals who have certain impairments or vulnerabilities (Mobily, 1996; Sylvester, 1992) without "adaptation of the context or form of the activity" (Kelly, 1996, p. 401). Therefore, one aim of therapeutic recreation is to augment personal and environmental capabilities and resources, enhance residual functional (adaptive) capabilities, and advocate physical and social inclusion so that opportunities for experiencing leisure may be enhanced.

Kelly (1996) also highlighted evidence which suggests that "people can learn and develop through their experiences" (p. 401), including leisure and recreation. Paul Haun (1966), believed to be a seminal thinker on recreation and its relation to health and medicine, argued that leisure and recreation could potentially help create an environment for therapeutic change. Thus, a second aim of therapeutic recreation is to facilitate particular types of changes, whether in health or behavioral status, through enhancing cognitive, physical, social, affective, and/or spiritual development.

What Is Assessment?

Assessment is the process through which knowledge is obtained about clients, their interests, and their functional abilities related to school, work, leisure, and relationships. It is a multidimensional effort involving clients, therapeutic recreation specialists, family members, significant others, and representatives of professions and agencies committed to meeting clients' needs. In the process of assessment, therapeutic recreation specialists move from operating on the basis of general knowledge about diagnoses to specific knowledge of clients and their unique circumstances. Assessment leads to a definition of the problem, establishment of goals, and determination of possible solutions and interventions.

Purposes of Assessment

Therapeutic recreation interventions are intended to bring about changes in the function or health of clients (Carter, Van Andel, and Robb, 1995; Horvat and Kalakian, 1996; Stumbo, 1996, 1997). These outcomes may include changes in cognitive, social, physical, affective, or leisure domains (Carter et al., 1995). Thus, therapeutic recreation assessment must provide an adequate baseline or starting point and provide a foundation for identifying needs, determining interests, formulating goals, selecting appropriate activities, developing interaction strategies, and evaluating progress. Baseline assessment information is necessary so that the relationship between the therapeutic recreation intervention and the achievement of outcomes can be later established or "proven" (Stumbo, 1997).

Approaches and Techniques

Therapeutic recreation specialists should be prepared to participate in a client-centered assessment process that crosses and includes several disciplines. This approach to assessment allows the interdisciplinary team to integrate and coordinate care, delivering a consistent set of messages to the client and family or caregivers, and resulting in more efficient care (Gerteis, Edgman-Levitan, Daley, and Delbanco, 1993). Interdisciplinary assessment typically centers on functional skill areas and limitations, and how they impact disability (Landrum, Schmidt, and McLean, 1995). Interdisciplinary assessment may include areas such as physical status, cognitive abilities, affect and neuropsychiatric status, functional performance, behavioral symptoms, and psychosocial variables. The focus of the assessment is on discharge requirements and role resumption or attainment. Paramount is determining what will be necessary to achieve a level of functioning appropriate for discharging clients to a less restrictive setting (usually the home) and enabling them to resume or achieve desired activities (e.g., education, vocation, leisure) at an optimal level of functioning. From this assessment, individual treatment or program plans are developed.

Critical pathways may also be used as a guide for mapping out the progression of treatment activities and directing team members' behavior toward achieving desired outcomes within a specified period of time. These pathways identify the program components required to achieve desired client outcomes and the discipline that would ensure skill acquisition in a timely manner.

Areas of assessment may overlap with several members of the interdisciplinary team. Therefore, it is vital for team members to decide who is responsible for collecting that information, and to determine how access to all assessment information is provided. As mentioned earlier in this chapter, the point of departure for therapeutic recreation specialists in the interdisciplinary assessment process is in determining and implementing the appropriate therapeutic recreation interventions relative to desired changes (Horvat and Kalakian, 1996).

Often, therapeutic recreation specialists will use discipline-based therapeutic recreation assessments to supplement information gained through the interdisciplinary client-centered assessment. These assessments are usually specific to therapeutic recreation, and do not infringe on or duplicate assessments of other disciplines. Therapeutic recreation specialists must consider the unique role that therapeutic recreation may play in the achievement of global outcomes that have been identified by the interdisciplinary team. In the therapeutic recreation assessment process, therapeutic recreation specialists and clients are challenged to envision a preferred future. When these desired outcomes have been conceptualized, the necessary steps to achieve and maintain them can be determined. In other words, prevention and health promotion and problem resolution or treatment can be "reverse engineered" in relation to these optimal global outcomes (Landrum et al., 1995, p. 45). Therapeutic recreation specialists must then consider with clients which activities each client might enjoy and which are appropriate in relation to desired outcomes. Leisure pursuits should be chosen in conjunction with clients when possible, since personal relevance and meaning are central to developing one's leisure lifestyle (Ragheb, 1996; Richter and Kaschalk, 1996; Stumbo, 1996). As Stumbo (1996) pointed out, for some clients relevance might be related to achieving independence, living with dignity in later years, or simply learning to cope with a newly acquired health status.

Therapeutic Recreation Assessment

For leisure experiences to satisfy clients' needs and interests, these experiences should be designed based on accurate and comprehensive assessment of how clients actually function in various domains (e.g., physical, cognitive) and environments, what they hope to gain through leisure involvement, and what skills will be needed to facilitate full participation. For therapeutic recreation to be appropriate and meaningful, it must reflect clients' strengths, needs, and interests. Through assessment, therapeutic recreation specialists are able to identify therapeutic recreation programs that address clients' needs by supporting and utilizing their strengths and interests. Determining existing skills and behaviors enables therapeutic recreation specialists to identify and target behaviors that need maintenance or remediation to promote optimal well-being and enhance interdependent leisure functioning.

Essential components of therapeutic recreation assessment include clients' interests, skills and capabilities, aptitudes, needs and deficiencies, and life experiences (Horvat and Kalakian, 1996). Important questions to consider and discuss with a client during assessment are included in the following list (Fine, 1996; Horvat and Kalakian, 1996; Schleien, Meyer, Heyne, and Brandt, 1995). These questions may help obtain information related to four major areas of leisure functioning: leisure awareness, functional skills (including social interaction skills), leisure activity skills, and leisure resources (Peterson and Stumbo, 2000). Possible questions include:

1. How do clients currently spend their free time? What are their present leisure skills?
2. What do clients like and dislike?
3. Do clients appreciate the value of meaningful leisure experience? What do they see as the benefits of participation in recreation activity (e.g., making friends, being active, feeling useful, learning a new skill)?
4. What recreation activities appear to interest clients, even if they do not currently participate in them?
5. Of all the explored activities that appear to interest clients most, how much time do they spend partici- pating in any single activity or in utilizing a specific piece of recreation equipment? When presented with multiple leisure opportunities, how quickly do they respond to a particular activity or item?
6. What adaptations, if any, are needed to promote full or partial participation in clients' chosen activities?
7. What resources (e.g., discretionary money, equip- ment, materials) do clients have available that can be used during leisure?
8. What functional skills (e.g., cognitive, physical, social, affective, adaptive behaviors, independent living skills) can be maintained or developed during leisure?

The clients' need to acquire specific skills, or to make adaptations, should reflect both their activity preferences and the demands and opportunities of their community. Assessing environments, as well as clients, facilitates the identification of needed personal and environmental adaptations (Schleien et al., 1995; Schleien, Ray, and Green, 1997). The limitations of clients and the physical, as well as attitudinal barriers, within their communities, can then be reduced or eliminated so that maximum leisure functioning can be obtained.

Assessment questions pertaining to clients' environments might include:

1. What recreation activities do clients presently pursue in their homes?
2. What resources, such as recreation facilities, services, and transportation, are available?
3. What environmental adaptations are needed to enable clients to participate, at least at some level, in their chosen activities?
4. With whom do clients spend most of their leisure time?
5. What are the values and preferences of clients' nondisabled family members, peers, and other caregivers relative to specific recreation activities?

Because of the increased emphasis on consistently and reliably achieving desired outcomes through therapeutic recreation interventions, a need to develop common or best practices addressing the four areas of leisure functioning has emerged. Therapeutic recreation specialists are being urged to create and validate therapeutic recreation protocol guidelines designed to produce specific outcomes based upon assessed needs (Ferguson, 1992, 1997). Knight and Johnson (1991) defined protocols as a "group of strategies or actions initiated in response to a problem, an issue, or a symptom of a client" (p. 137). Teaching and activity protocols are oriented to client or family education and leisure skill development, and may include more than one discipline collaborating to produce the desired outcome (Ferguson, 1997). Development and use of therapeutic recreation protocols enables clients to achieve desired outcomes and demonstrates the efficacy of therapeutic recreation interventions.

Identifying Needs, Interests, and Skills

A variety of resources can provide useful assessment information. The information coming from clients is referred to as subjective information while that coming from others is referred to as objective information. In many instances, clients themselves are the most significant provider of assessment information. Various techniques are used to gather cognitive, social, physical, affective, or leisure assessment information from available resources.

Therapeutic recreation specialists can identify many clients' needs and interests by skillfully observing their behaviors in a variety of situations. For some clients, including those who are nonverbal, this may be the best assessment technique available. Therapeutic recreation specialists must know what to look for and how to observe significant factors in clients' general appearance and behavior (O'Morrow and Reynolds, 1989). Behaviors may be described according to their structure (e.g., appearance, physical form or patterning, posture, movement), the antecedents and consequences of the behavior (i.e., stimulus events that precede the behavior, effects of the behavior on the environment, others, the individual), and relation (i.e., the client's position or orientation relative to something or someone else) (Horvat and Kalakian, 1996; Martin and Bateson, 1986). Specific and accurate recording methods, such as frequency measures, response rates, interval recording, time sampling, and behavior duration and latency, should be used (Crawford and Mendell, 1987; Dattilo and Murphy, 1987; Fine and Fine, 1996). Recording mediums may include videotape, verbal description, and automatic recording devices (e.g., a device that measures miles walked) (Lavay, French, and Henderson, 1997; Martin and Bateson, 1986). Specific recording methods may include using check sheets (paper-and-pencil method) or using computer event recording software (Martin and Bateson, 1986).

Strengths, areas of need, and interests can also be identified by interviewing and listening to clients, family members, and other significant individuals. Interviewing family and other caregivers is particularly important when clients are very young (Fine, 1996) or unable to express themselves. Additionally, interviews with other professionals such as teachers, counselors, nurses, social workers, and vocational specialists can provide useful information about clients. Interviews can be conducted formally or informally, and formats will vary.

Assessment may also include the use of assessment instruments designed to identify clients' skills and behaviors. Many agencies use activity checklists, leisure interest questionnaires, and skill inventories designed to keep within the agency's operational framework and to present client profiles.

Standardized assessment procedures are valuable because they have been rigorously designed and include measures of validity and reliability. In addition, standardized assessment instruments help to reduce any biases therapeutic recreation specialists might have (O'Morrow and Reynolds, 1989). Numerous standardized instruments are available to obtain cognitive, social, physical, affective, and leisure information. Various instruments, such as the *Functional Independence Measure* and *Resident Assessment Instrument*, are widely accepted and used to determine functional and psychosocial status in rehabilitation and long-term care settings. These instruments will be described in the following sections. Of course, therapeutic recreation specialists must look beyond these measures and include those that focus more directly on leisure needs. *The Leisure Diagnostic Battery, Leisure Competence Measure*, and *Comprehensive Evaluation in Recreational Therapy—Psych/Behavioral, Revised* are also highlighted because they are frequently used by therapeutic recreation specialists.

Chapter One

The Functional Independence Measure (FIM) (Hamilton, Granger, Sherwin, Zielezny, and Tashman, 1987) provides a measure of functional abilities and skills clients demonstrate within their environment. This measure indicates severity of disability on a seven-level scale ranging from dependence to independence. Any trained clinician should be able to use the FIM, regardless of discipline. Therapeutic recreation specialists, however, most often assess items relating to comprehension, expression, problem solving, and memory. A child's version of the FIM, WeeFIM, is also available.

Long-term care settings adhering to regulations established by the Health Care Financing Administration (HCFA) are required to use the Resident Assessment Instrument (RAI). The RAI consists of two parts: the Minimum Data Set (MDS) and the Resident Assessment Protocols (RAPs) (Martini, Weeks, and Wirth, 1996). The MDS provides comprehensive ongoing assessment of clients' functional capacity, based on a uniform data set. Treatment plans or RAPs are developed from the needs "triggered" by the MDS (Martini et al., 1996). While several sections of the MDS provide useful assessment information for therapeutic recreation specialists, information pertaining to recreation therapy is recorded currently in Section T, 1.a, *Special Treatments and Procedures.* Recreation therapy is defined by HCFA as ordered by a physician, for a stated frequency, scope, and duration, provided beyond the general activity program, and provided by a certified therapeutic recreation specialist or a certified therapeutic recreation assistant. Sometimes therapeutic recreation specialists will also collect and record information for Section B, *Cognitive Patterns*; Section E, *Mood and Behavior Patterns*; Section F, *Psychosocial Well-Being*; and Section N, *Activity Pursuits Patterns.*

The Leisure Diagnostic Battery (LDB) (Witt and Ellis, 1987), one of the most comprehensive measures in therapeutic recreation, focuses on the leisure functioning of typical children, youth, and adults, as well as those who have orthopedic or cognitive disabilities. This instrument consists of a series of scales that measure indicators of leisure ability. Collectively, these measurements enable therapeutic recreation specialists to determine clients' perceptions of freedom in leisure and to identify factors that might limit their perception of personal freedom.

The Leisure Competence Measure (LCM) (Kloseck, Crilly, Ellis, and Lammers, 1996) is a behavior-anchored rating scale of leisure competence intended to document current levels of leisure functioning as well as changes in functioning over time. Designed to be consistent with the FIM, the LCM identifies specific skills, knowledge, and behavior necessary for independent and successful leisure functioning (Kloseck et al., 1996). Seven subscales assess the domains of leisure awareness, attitude, skills, social appropriateness, group interaction skills, social contact, and community-based participation (Kloseck et al., 1996).

The Comprehensive Evaluation in Recreational Therapy—Psych/Behavioral, Revised (CERT-Psych/R) (burlingame and Blaschko, 1997; Parker, Ellison, Kirby, and Short, 1975) is an updated measure originally designed for use in short-term, acute-care psychiatric settings. The CERT-Psych/R identifies and defines behaviors relevant to the therapeutic recreation process. General lifestyle behaviors, as well as performance in individual and group therapeutic recreation activities are included. The revised version has changed slightly and is now also being used to document changes in clients' lifestyle and social interaction behaviors resulting from longer term interventions (burlingame and Blaschko, 1997).

Though concern over the paucity of standardized instruments continues to exist (Stumbo, 1996, 1997), the use of informal, nonstandardized assessments does not necessarily result in imprecise or irrelevant findings (Wilcox and Bellamy, 1987). In fact, when used in isolation, the results of formal assessments may provide a limited view of clients' capabilities. To be useful, the findings of formal assessments must be studied in concert with information obtained from additional instruments through a variety of techniques (O'Morrow and Reynolds, 1989). Assessment information may also be obtained by reviewing health and social histories; medical and psychiatric records; academic, developmental, and adaptive tests results; and basic demographic data including age, sex, racial or ethnic background, education, and occupation (Horvat and Kalakian, 1996).

Portfolio Assessment

The use of client portfolios is an alternative method for collecting assessment information and for monitoring progress over time (Gredler, 1996). The portfolio showcases clients' efforts, progress, and achievement. The portfolio reflects growth and also indicates the diversity of clients' accomplishments. In addition, portfolios provide an ongoing opportunity for self-evaluation (DeGraaf and Jordan, 1996). Materials in clients' portfolios used in an adolescent unit of a psychiatric hospital may include an admission questionnaire, patient self-evaluation, autobiography, and drug chart (indicating drug use, effects, and consequences).

Essential Characteristics of Assessment Procedures

Assessments may be *criterion referenced;* that is, they evaluate clients based on some expectation perceived to be necessary for functioning in a leisure environment. Clients are compared to predetermined performance or behavior criteria (Horvat and Kaladian, 1996). These assessments are functional-environmental in nature when they measure the interaction between clients and their environments (burlingame and Blaschko, 1997). An example of a criterion is "adults with mental retardation will be able to manage all activities of daily living in order to participate in the residential camp." Using this criterion, a functional-environmental assessment might measure a client's ability to use public transportation (burlingame and Blaschko, 1997).

Assessments may also be *norm referenced*; that is, they compare clients' performances to a larger (reference) group. For instance, adults with mild mental retardation are typically or "normally" able to manage all activities of daily living. Norm-referenced assessments are frequently used to determine a client's eligibility for services; however, these assessments have limited value for determining a client's actual skill level (burlingame and Blaschko, 1997).

Therapeutic recreation specialists must determine the purpose of the assessment prior to selecting the instrument and procedure. Specialists then identify which procedure(s)—interview, observation, interest survey, test, record review—can provide information that will enable them to make appropriate program planning decisions with clients. There is no one approach that can be used with all individuals. Assessment procedures must be compatible with clients' skills and should capitalize on their strengths rather than penalize their limitations. Considering clients' developmental and functional levels, along with specific characteristics such as health status and disabling conditions, enables therapeutic recreation specialists to determine the suitability of a potential assessment procedure.

Therapeutic recreation specialists must also establish the practicality of the assessment procedure (Horvat and Kalakian, 1996). Even the most comprehensive, sophisticated assessment procedure will not provide accurate information unless therapeutic recreation specialists are qualified to administer, score, and interpret the instrument, and have adequate time. The feasibility and practical usability of assessment procedures should be considered in relation to the client, agency, staff, and situation.

Fine and Fine (1996) state that the most important characteristic of assessment procedures may be the therapeutic recreation specialist's judgment. Interpreting the findings of an assessment procedure is both a difficult and crucial aspect of the assessment process. Ultimately, it is the responsibility of therapeutic recreation specialists to determine if the obtained assessment results accurately depict a client's strengths, potentials, and limitations. All elements of the assessment process should be taken into account when interpreting the assessment.

Therapeutic recreation specialists must be alert to the possibility that standardized procedures may be culturally biased (Pope and Vasquez, 1991). They should also not underestimate the significance of their interactions with clients, particularly those of diverse cultural, ethnic, or lifestyle backgrounds, on the viability of the assessment process (Pope and Vasquez, 1991).

No matter which assessment approach is used, therapeutic recreation specialists should ascertain how well the instrument and/or procedure measures what is intended to be measured (validity) as well as the accuracy or consistency of the findings (reliability). Measurements that are valid actually measure those areas therapeutic recreation specialists wish to measure; they are considered to be "right" measures (Martin and Bateson, 1986). Measures that are reliable generate repeatable and consistent results, free from random errors; they are considered to be "good" measures (Martin and Bateson, 1986).

Summary

Assessment is the first step in establishing the relationship between the therapeutic recreation intervention and the achievement of desirable client outcomes. Assessments create opportunities for clients to experience leisure in a personally meaningful and appropriate manner. Therapeutic recreation specialists recognize the varying levels of clients' abilities, knowledge, skills, and interests as well as the range of factors that make up the environment in which these clients live. Specialists should gather this information through a well-planned, systematic examination involving a variety of assessment techniques.

Assessment leads to the development of general statements about what clients can and hope to gain through participation in therapeutic recreation interventions. The importance of the match between assessment results and the design of therapeutic recreation interventions is highlighted in chapter two, *Therapeutic Recreation Program Planning*. That chapter describes how clients' expectations are translated into long-term and short-term goals, outcome measures, and intervention strategies.

Bibliography

Austin, D. R., and Crawford, M. E. (1996). *Therapeutic recreation: An introduction* (2nd ed.). Needham Heights, MA: Allyn & Bacon.

Buettner, L., and Martin, S. L. (1995). *Therapeutic recreation in the nursing home*. State College, PA: Venture Publishing, Inc.

burlingame, j., and Blaschko, T. M. (1997). *Assessment tools for recreational therapy: Red book #1* (2nd ed.). Ravensdale, WA: Idyll Arbor.

Carter, M. J., Van Andel, G. E., and Robb, G. M. (1995). *Therapeutic recreation: A practical approach* (2nd ed.). Prospect Heights, IL: Waveland.

Crawford, M. E., and Mendell, R. (1987). *Therapeutic recreation and adapted physical activities for mentally retarded individuals*. Englewood Cliffs, NJ: Prentice Hall.

Dattilo, J., and Kleiber, D. A. (1993). Psychological perspectives for therapeutic recreation research: The psychology of enjoyment. In M. J. Malkin and C. Z. Howe (Eds.), *Research in therapeutic recreation: Concepts and methods* (pp. 57–76). State College, PA: Venture Publishing, Inc.

Dattilo, J., Kleiber, D., and Williams, R. (1998). Self-determination and enjoyment enhancement: A psychologically based service delivery model for therapeutic recreation. *Therapeutic Recreation Journal, 32*(4), 258–271.

Dattilo, J., and Murphy, W. D. (1987). *Behavior modification in therapeutic recreation.* State College, PA: Venture Publishing, Inc.

DeGraff, D. G., and Jordan, D. J. (1996). The use of a portfolio system as a pedagogical tool. *Schole: A Journal of Leisure Studies and Recreation Education, 11*, 37–44.

Ferguson, D. D. (1992). Problem identification and protocol usage in therapeutic recreation. In G. L. Hitzhusen, L. T. Jackson, and M. A. Birdsong (Eds.), *Global therapeutic recreation II: Selected papers from the 2nd international symposium on therapeutic recreation* (pp. 1–11). Columbia, MO: University of Missouri.

Ferguson, D. D. (1997). Protocols in therapeutic recreation: Dancing on the bubble. In D. M. Compton (Ed.), *Issues in therapeutic recreation: Toward the new millennium* (2nd ed.) (pp. 403–417). Champaign, IL: Sagamore.

Fine, A. H. (1996). Assessment: A need for further attention. In A. H. Fine and N. M. Fine (Eds.), *Therapeutic recreation for exceptional children: Let me in, I want to play* (2nd ed.) (pp. 181–241). Springfield, IL: Charles C. Thomas.

Fine, A. H., and Fine, N. M. (Eds.) (1996). *Therapeutic recreation for exceptional children: Let me in, I want to play* (2nd ed.). Springfield, IL: Charles C. Thomas.

Gredler, M. E. (1996). *Program evaluation.* Englewood Cliffs, NJ: Prentice Hall.

Gerteis, M., Edgman-Levitan, S. E., Daley, J., and Delbanco, T. L. (Eds.). (1993). *Through the patient's eyes: Understanding and promoting patient-centered care.* San Francisco, CA: Jossey-Bass.

Hamilton, B., Granger, C., Sherwin, F., Zielezny, M., and Tashman, J. (1987). A uniform national data system for medical rehabilitation. In M. Fuhrer (Ed.), *Rehabilitation outcomes: Analysis and measurement* (pp. 137–147). Baltimore, MD: Brookes.

Haun, P. (1966). *Recreation: A medical viewpoint.* New York, NY: Teachers College Press.

Horvat, M., and Kalakian, L. (1996). *Assessment in adapted physical education and therapeutic recreation* (2nd ed.). Madison, WI: Brown & Benchmark.

Iso-Ahola, S. E. (1980). *The social psychology of leisure and recreation.* Dubuque, IA: Wm. C. Brown.

Kelly, J. R. (1987). *Freedom to be: A new sociology of leisure.* New York, NY: MacMillan.

Kelly, J. R. (1996). *Leisure* (3rd ed.). Needham Heights, MA: Allyn & Bacon.

Kloseck, M., Crilly, R. G., Ellis, G. D., and Lammers, E. (1996). Leisure competence measure: Development and reliability testing of a scale to measure functional outcomes in therapeutic recreation. *Therapeutic Recreation Journal, 30*(1), 13–26.

Knight, L., and Johnson, A. (1991). Therapeutic recreation protocols: Client problem centered approach. In B. Riley (Ed.), *Quality management: Applications for therapeutic recreation* (pp. 137–147). State College, PA: Venture Publishing, Inc.

Landrum, P. K., Schmidt, N. D., and McLean, A. (Eds.). (1995). *Outcome-oriented rehabilitation: Principles, strategies, and tools for effective program management.* Gaithersburg, MD: Aspen.

Lavay, B. W., French, R., and Henderson, H. L. (1997). *Positive behavior management strategies for physical educators.* Champaign, IL: Human Kinetics.

Martin, P., and Bateson, P. (1986). *Measuring behavior: An introductory guide.* New York, NY: Cambridge University.

Martini, E. B., Weeks, M. A., and Wirth, P. (1996). *Long-term care for activity and social service professionals* (2nd ed). Ravensdale, WA: Idyll Arbor.

Mobily, K. E. (1996). Therapeutic recreation philosophy revisited: A question of what leisure is good for. In S. Sylvester (Ed.), *Philosophy of therapeutic recreation: Ideas and issues* (Volume II) (pp. 57–70). Arlington, VA: National Recreation and Park Association.

O'Morrow, G. S., and Reynolds, R. P. (1989). *Therapeutic recreation: A helping profession* (3rd ed.). Englewood Cliffs, NJ: Prentice Hall.

Parker, R. A., Ellison, C. H., Kirby, T. F., and Short, M. J. (1975). The comprehensive evaluation in recreation therapy scale: A tool for patient evaluation. *Therapeutic Recreation Journal, 9*(4), 43-52.

Peterson, C. A., and Stumbo, N. J. (2000). *Therapeutic recreation program design: Principles and procedures* (3rd ed.). Englewood Cliffs, NJ: Prentice Hall.

Pope, K. S., and Vasquez, M. J., T. (1991). *Ethics in psychotherapy and counseling: A practical guide for psychologists*. San Francisco, CA: Jossey-Bass.

Ragheb, M. G. (1996). The search for meaning in leisure pursuits: Review, conceptualization and a need for a psychometric development. *Leisure Studies, 15*, 245–258.

Richter, K. J., and Kaschalk, S. M. (1996). The future of therapeutic recreation: An existential outcome. In C. Sylvester (Ed.), *Philosophy of therapeutic recreation: Ideas and issues volume II* (pp. 86–91). Arlington, VA: National Recreation and Park Association.

Schleien, S. J., Ray, M. T., and Green, F. P. (1997). *Community recreation and people with disabilities*. Baltimore, MD: Brookes.

Schleien, S. J., Meyer, L. H., Heyne, L. A., and Brandt, B. B. (1995). *Lifelong leisure skills and lifestyles for persons with developmental disabilities*. Baltimore, MD: Brookes.

Stumbo, N. J. (1997). Issues and concerns in therapeutic recreation assessment. In D. M. Compton (Ed.), *Issues in therapeutic recreation: Toward the new millennium* (2nd ed.) (pp. 347– 371). Champaign, IL: Sagamore.

Stumbo, N. J. (1996). A proposed accountability model for therapeutic recreation services. *Therapeutic Recreation Journal, 30*(4), 246–259.

Sylvester, C. (1992). Therapeutic recreation and the right to leisure. *Therapeutic Recreation Journal, 26*(2), 9–20.

Wilcox, B., and Bellamy, G. T. (1987). *A comprehensive guide to the activities catalog.* Baltimore, MD: Brookes.

Witt, P. A., and Ellis, G. (1987). *The leisure diagnostic battery: Users manual and sample forms.* State College, PA: Venture Publishing, Inc.

Dementia is a deterioration of the brain's functioning that affects memory loss. This memory loss is severe enough to interfere with work, social skills, problem-solving skills, and other abilities related to abstract thinking. Senile dementia of the Alzheimer's type (AD) is the most common form of dementia. People 65 and under are diagnosed with presenile dementia, while individuals diagnosed at or after age 65 are diagnosed with dementia or senile dementia. An estimated 15% of the U.S. population aged 65 and over, or 4.4 million people, have been diagnosed with senile dementia. AD has been linked with the aging process. There are three stages of AD. The first stage is mild, and lasts between two and four years from the appearance of the first symptoms. The second, or moderate stage, lasts from two to ten years, while the third, or severe stage, lasts from one to three years. Each stage has symptoms that are distinct and progressive, but frequently overlap (Alzheimer's Association, 1994).

CASE 1 - ALFRED MARTIN

Alfred Martin, an 84-year-old, married, White male with a diagnosis of Alzheimer's disease (AD), non-insulin dependent diabetes, hypertension, and congestive heart failure, was referred for assessment to the certified therapeutic recreation specialist (CTRS) by clinical staff. According to his medical history, Mr. Martin was admitted to a rural long-term care (LTC) facility after a long battle with depression. Mr. Martin is 6 feet, 1 inch tall and weighs 174 pounds. Mr. Martin is unique in the fact that he lived in the same area all his life. He did not serve in the armed services.

According to his wife, Mr. Martin worked for an automobile dealer for 41 years as a car salesman, bookkeeper, and a mechanic. His wife claims he was a workaholic with no hobbies. After he retired, he worked hard maintaining his rental houses and a vegetable garden. Fifteen years ago, Mr. Martin had a heart attack and received a pacemaker. Thereafter, he could no longer work.

Because of his increased confusion, memory loss, and paranoia, he had been first admitted to a rural mental health facility and was subsequently admitted to the rural LTC facility. Mr. Martin has been living in the special care unit (SCU) and attending therapeutic recreation programs for residents with AD for the past three years.

Mr. Martin is in the second stage (moderate) of AD. His symptoms, or impairments, include losses of recent and past memory, concentration, orientation, judgment, and functioning and self-care. He wanders the halls with gait disturbances (apraxia) and then sits staring or sleeping for long periods. Occasionally, Mr. Martin needs help getting up, and he is unsteady on his feet. He does ambulate on his own with supervision. However, the staff is encouraged to hold on to him in some manner even if he is physically aggressive, since he could fall due to his unsteadiness. He occasionally is incontinent and has communication deficits (anomia aphasia).

Mr. Martin's treatment goal is to maintain his current physical condition. Although Mr. Martin is compliant, he occasionally refuses to do things that the CTRS and other staff ask him to do. He isolates himself, and when prodded, becomes aggressive, hitting and kicking the staff. His chart denotes a fall precaution (strong probability of falling) and he is taking Haldol for his aggression.

Once Mr. Martin is engaged in an activity that he likes, he can and frequently does stay engaged for an hour or more with few verbal prompts, depending on how his day is going. Last week, Mr. Martin was taken off his psychotropic medication (Haldol) so that he could have a tooth pulled, and since then he has not participated in therapeutic recreation or cooperated with the staff. When the staff attempts to guide Mr. Martin into positive activity, he refuses and becomes physically aggressive. The therapeutic recreation staff feel that if Mr. Martin continues to be isolated and sedentary, he will decline at a faster rate.

The activity room is equipped with a variety of books, games, puzzles, and crafts. There are three enclosed patios (four walls with two doors for access, but no roof), each containing two raised flower beds. Various amateur groups are scheduled regularly to perform at the LTC, but community outings are discouraged.

Discussion Questions

1. What type of information will you need in order to recommend a therapeutic recreation program plan for Mr. Martin? Discuss specific sources of assessment information, methods of obtaining the information, and uses of the information.
2. What assessment tool will you use to obtain relevant information? Why? (Be specific.)
3. What therapeutic recreation program components will you recommend? Justify your answer. How will you include Mr. Martin and his family in the development of his plan?
4. What are the possible side effects of Haldol? What are the implications for therapeutic recreation?
5. Discuss the various environments in which Mr. Martin may be comfortable. Might these change over time? How and why?
6. Do any special considerations need to be kept in mind relative to Mr. Martin's diabetes, hypertension, and congestive heart failure? If so, what?

In-Class Exercises

1. Make a list of the functional characteristics of Mr. Martin's diagnoses.
2. List the viable assets of Mr. Martin. Also list his deficits.
3. Prioritize and list the primary problems that need to be addressed by the CTRS.
4. Invite a CTRS working in a LTC facility to share examples of assessments conducted with individuals with AD.

Field Experience

Visit a CTRS who works with individuals diagnosed with dementia. Discuss various assessment tools used. If possible, obtain copies of the instrument(s) used by the CTRS. Discuss the facility's policies for aggressive residents and the various recreation activities available. Report your findings and share written information.

Selected References for Case Study

Alzheimer's Association. (1994, December). *Alzheimer's disease: Statistics. Alzheimer's Disease and Related Disorders Association, Inc.* (Issue Brief No. INQ230Z). Chicago, IL: Author.

American Diabetes Association. [On-line]. Available: http://www.diabetes.org

Austin, D. R. (1997). *Therapeutic recreation: Processes and techniques* (3rd ed.). Champaign, IL: Sagamore.

Bridges, B. J. (1995). *Therapeutic caregiving: A practical guide for caregivers of persons with Alzheimer's and other dementia causing diseases.* Mill Creek, WA: PJB Publishing.

Buettner, L., and Martin, S. L. (1995). *Therapeutic recreation in the nursing home.* State College, PA: Venture Publishing, Inc.

Dailey, S. (Ed.). (1998). *Alzheimer's notebook* (3rd ed.). Columbia, MO: University of Missouri.

Grote, K., Hasl, M., Krider, R., and Mortensen, D. M. (1995). *Behavioral health protocols for recreational therapy.* Ravensdale, WA: Idyll Arbor.

Hawkins, B. A., May, M. E., and Rogers, N. B. (1996). *Therapeutic activity intervention with the elderly: Foundations and practices.* State College, PA: Venture Publishing, Inc.

Martini, E. B., Weeks, M. A., and Wirth, P. (1996). *Long-term care for activity and social service professionals* (2nd ed.). Ravensdale, WA: Idyll Arbor.

National Alzheimer's Association. [On-line]. Available: http://www.alz.org

Nissenboim, S., and Vroman, C. (1998). *The positive interactions program of activities for people with Alzheimer's disease.* Baltimore, MD: Health Professions.

Parker, S. D., and Will, C. (1993). *Activities for the elderly: A guide for working with residents with significant physical and cognitive disabilities* (Vol. 2). Ravensdale, WA: Idyll Arbor.

Tedrick, T., and Green, E. R. (1995). *Activity experiences and programming within long-term care.* State College, PA: Venture Publishing, Inc.

Audiovisual Resources

American Association of Diabetes Educators. (1996). *What is diabetes? (*Non-insulin dependent*).* [videotape]. Available from Milner-Fenwick, Inc., 2125 Greenspring Drive, Timonium, MD 21093.

Creative interventions with the Alzheimer's patient. [videotape]. Available from Geriatric Resources, Inc., 931 S. Semoran Blvd., #200, Winter Park, FL 32792.

Don Lennox Productions. (1997). *Lost in the mind: The mystery of Alzheimer's disease.* [videotape]. Available from Lennox Productions, 2627 Connecticut Ave., Suite 300, Washington, DC 20008.

Rosemond, C. (1996). *Exercise and diabetes.* [videotape]. Available from Health Sciences Consortium Distribution Department, 201 Silver Cedar Court, Chapel Hill, NC 27514-1517.

CASE 2 - RUTH AVERY

Ruth Avery is a 75-year-old widowed, African American female with a diagnosis of hypertension and Alzheimer's Disease (AD). She was referred for assessment to the CTRS by clinical staff. According to her family, Mrs. Avery was a food service manager in a large river city, loved to listen to music, and was an exceptional dancer. After retirement, she became confused and began to report delusional thoughts about family members. She was admitted to a psychiatric facility where she was diagnosed with AD. Her family physician placed her on Cognex, a drug in the Tacrine family that is used for memory maintenance. She was discharged from the psychiatric facility and referred to a long-term care (LTC) facility.

Upon admission to a rural LTC facility, the CTRS completed the Brief Cognitive Rating Scale (Reisberg, 1983) to assess the level of functional deterioration. The results of Mrs. Avery's tests showed moderately severe deterioration, indicating loss of concentration and impairment of recent and past memory, orientation, functioning, and self-care. These results were consistent with observed behavior. For example, during the assessment period, Mrs. Avery was observed making fun of peers functioning at a lower level, criticizing their faults, while not being aware of her own. Routinely, Mrs. Avery called staff her "brothers and sisters" or "uncles and aunts." She reported that someone had come to her room in the night and poured gasoline all over her. Mrs. Avery also often indicated that her brother just arrived from a nearby city and would be here to visit at any time. At times, Mrs. Avery would verbalize aggression toward a peer and then strike the person, especially if her "father" had told her too.

Mrs. Avery spent most of her time sitting passively with minimal social interaction and physical activity. She could complete activities of daily living on her own with verbal prompts and physical guidance. However, nursing staff at the LTC facility fed Mrs. Avery her meals.

After initial assessments were completed, it was recommended that Mrs. Avery live on the special care unit (SCU) and participate in therapeutic recreation activities. The SCU maintains a census of 40 individuals diagnosed with AD, multi-infarct dementia, and/or other related dementia. Therapeutic recreation is provided by a CTRS specializing in working with people with dementia.

Discussion Questions

1. What type of information (i.e., physical, cognitive, affective, social, and spiritual) will you need to gather to recommend a therapeutic recreation

program plan for Mrs. Avery? What therapeutic recreation program components will you recommend?

2. Besides the Brief Cognitive Rating Scale, what are some potential objective and subjective sources for the assessment data in question one? Describe and justify the methods you will use to collect the data.

In-Class Exercises

1. Develop a master list of Mrs. Avery's adaptive and maladaptive behaviors. Identify barriers to her independence in leisure functioning.
2. Identify interests and skills that a CTRS could use to assist with developing and implementing individual therapeutic recreation program plans.
3. Explore various ways to search for information about drugs on the Internet. Look up the drug Cognex and determine its implications for developing the therapeutic recreation plan.

Selected References for Case Study

Beck, C. K., and Shue, V. M. (1994). Interventions for treating disruptive behavior in demented elderly people. *Nursing Clinics of North America, 29*(1), 143–155.

Bourgeois, M. S. (1993). Effects of memory aids on the dyadic conversations of individuals with dementia. *Journal of Applied Behavior Analysis, 26*(1), 77–87.

Buettner, L., and Martin, S. L. (1995). *Therapeutic recreation in the nursing home*. State College, PA: Venture Publishing, Inc.

Buss, D. D. (1994). The legacy of Dr. Alzheimer. *Contemporary Long-Term Care, 17*(2), 42–46.

Creighton, C. (1992). The origin and evolution of activity analysis. *American Journal of Occupational Therapy, 46*(1), 45–48.

Gastel, B. (1994). *Working with your older patient: A clinician's handbook*. Bethesda, MD: National Institute on Aging, National Institutes of Health.

Gaudet, G., and Dattilo, J. (1994). Reacquisition of a recreation skill by adults with cognitive impairments: Implications to self-determination. *Therapeutic Recreation Journal, 28*(3), 118–132.

Hawkins, B. A., May, M. E., and Rogers, N. B. (1996). *Therapeutic activity intervention with the elderly: Foundations and practices*. State College, PA: Venture Publishing, Inc.

Lundervold, D. A., and Lewin, L. M. (1992). *Behavioral analysis and therapy in nursing homes*. Springfield, IL: Charles C. Thomas.

Mace, N. L., and Rabins, P. V. (1991). *The thirty-six-hour day* (2nd ed.). Baltimore, MD: The Johns Hopkins University.

Martini, E. B., Weeks, M. A., and Wirth, P. (1996). *Long-term care for activity and social service professionals* (2nd ed.). Ravensdale, WA: Idyll Arbor.

Nissenboim, S., and Vroman, C. (1998). *The positive interactions program of activities for people with Alzheimer's disease*. Baltimore, MD: Health Professions.

O'Neill, R. E., Horner, R. H., Albin, R. W., Storey, K., and Sprague, J. R. (1990). *Functional analysis of problem behavior: A practical assessment guide*. Pacific Grove, CA: Brooks/Cole.

Reisberg, B. (1983). Clinical presentation, diagnosis, and symptomatology of age-associated cognitive decline and Alzheimer's disease. In B. Reisberg (Ed.), *Alzheimer's disease: The standard reference* (pp. 173-187). New York, NY: The Free Press.

Tedrick, T., and Green, E. R. (1995). *Activity experiences and programming within long-term care*. State College, PA: Venture Publishing, Inc.

Zgola, J. M. (1987). *Doing things: A guide to programming activities for persons with Alzheimer's disease and related disorders.* Baltimore, MD: The Johns Hopkins University.

Audiovisual Resources

The George Glenner Alzheimer's Family Centers, Inc. (1989). *Sharing the caring II: A therapeutic activity training program for Alzheimer's patients.* [videotape]. Available from Alzheimer's Family Center, San Diego, CA.

CASE 3 - MILDRED SUMMERS

Mildred Summers, a retired school teacher, is a 90-year-old White widow living alone in her own home in a suburban area within five miles of her 65-year-old daughter, who is her primary caregiver. For Mrs. Summers, the one-story house is not physically accessible from the outside, nor is the bathroom accessible. The house is equipped with smoke and burglar alarms, and Mrs. Summers wears an emergency call button that is connected to the local rescue squad station. Her neighbors are aware of her health needs and frequently look in on her and/or call her daughter if necessary. She has been receiving home healthcare for nearly two years and is part of the Alzheimer's support network.

Mrs. Summers has led a very active life despite intermittent colitis and daily arthritis medication. Since the death of her granddaughter, who had Down syndrome, noticeable changes have occurred in her eating, memory, reality orientation, and functional activity skills. Mrs. Summers underwent surgery for cervical and breast cancer at age 37 and 44, respectively, with a hysterectomy at age 62. At age 85, a scan revealed some dementia-like changes in the brain. After the death of her granddaughter, when Mrs. Summers was 88, she would sometimes tell her daughter that she heard and saw other deceased family members; she even prepared to invite them for meals. Irregular heart beats required that she be placed on various heart medications such as Lanoxin, a cardiac digitalis. Several other medications were prescribed for her ulcers (Cytotec and Pepcid) and arthritis (Clinoril). Esophageal strictures caused swallowing difficulties. These were managed with repeated dilations (esophagoscopes) and medications such as Reglan. Her daughter organized her medications in a daily organizer containing a one week's supply; frequent prompting was necessary to encourage her to comply with her medication regimen.

Mrs. Summers preferred to continue driving her car, yet she indicated to friends that she was concerned about her ability. As a consequence, family members discouraged her from driving, and eventually were able to convince her not to use the vehicle.

Mrs. Summers had provided some evening and weekend care in her home for her granddaughter for nearly 32 years. One of her two bedrooms was considered to be her granddaughter's room. Soon after the death of her granddaughter, Mrs. Summers' daughter contracted home healthcare aides and companions to come into Mrs. Summers' home because her personal care, housekeeping, reality awareness, and nutrition were rapidly declining. The amount of time spent by the aides/companions per week varied from two hours once per week to three or more hours three days per week. If the daughter was on vacation, daily calls to Mrs. Summers were made by the home healthcare agency and more frequent visits were planned. When Mrs. Summers became aggravated, visitation time was decreased and aides or companions were switched.

Home health aides, or companions, joined in the completion of household tasks such as washing windows and painting and outside yard and garden work. Knitting, watching sports, planting flowers, attending to Mrs. Summers' dog's needs, listening to music, chair caning, reading religious materials, going for a ride in the country, and visiting the local ice cream parlor were favorite activities shared with the home healthcare personnel and neighbors. Social workers from the Alzheimer's support network provided personal care needs when Mrs. Summers began to experience loss of bowel and bladder control, so that she could continue her neighborhood walks, tricycle rides, and weekend rides and visits to her daughter's house.

Mrs. Summers enjoyed contributing to the city's therapeutic recreation program prior to and following the death of her granddaughter. She volunteered for special events, provided transportation, refreshments and decorations, and taught crafts and handarts to children with various disabilities. Her home served as a collecting point for items to be used in programs. She preferred not to socialize with other aging persons whose main conversations focused on ill health.

Discussion Questions

Home healthcare agencies in Mrs. Summers' metropolitan area provide a range of services that allow older adults to remain safely at home with assistance in daily living including medical, cooking, personal hygiene, transportation, companionship, rehabilitation, and aggressive support after surgery. The intent is to access community and medical resources to promote as much independence, safety, and lifestyle satisfaction as possible. Following assessment, a coordinated care plan is generated. The assessment generally includes examination of prior medical records, a complete physical, family involvement, and multidisciplinary evaluations. Indicators for referral to home healthcare include: impairment in activities of daily living, especially after age 70, cognitive impairment, living alone, absent or limited support system, repetitive emergency room visits, history of frequent falls, caregiver and/or family stress, and inability to fulfill healthcare needs.

1. What role might a CTRS assume in the coordinated healthcare plan with Mrs. Summers?
2. Based on the home healthcare assessment areas, what needs might suggest therapeutic recreation intervention?
3. Of the indicators for referral, which seem relevant to Mrs. Summers?
4. How could the CTRS interface with the social worker, daughter, and home healthcare aides/companions in developing a care plan?

5. Assess the caregiver's needs. The needs of caregivers will become more important as more older adults begin caring for their aged parents.

Role-Playing

Role-play a "hearing" regarding who should pay for care of the frail elderly (e.g., home care, respite services). One student assumes the role of a taxpayer who insists that these individuals are not going to get better anyway, so their spouses and family should take care of them. One student assumes the role of the wife of a man with dementia who states, "I'm afraid to leave him alone." One student is an adult day center worker who believes, "They need the stimulation, and the caregiver needs time out." A fourth student is the hearing chairperson. All students can question the witnesses.

Field Experiences

1. Visit with home healthcare agencies and workers to learn about the types of training and preparation offered and the standards regulating home healthcare.
2. Visit with a physician and social workers to study medicare, medicaid, and private insurance regulations and reimbursement requirements. In addition, you may wish to visit the web site of the Health Care Financing Administration for information on insurance regulations and reimbursement requirements.
3. Visit with a community CTRS to ascertain the types of outreach and home health activities provided and the procedures for accessing these opportunities.

Selected References for Case Study

The ALZHEIMER Page. [On-line]. Available: http://www. biostat.wustl.edu/ALZHEIMER

Austin, D. R. (1999). *Therapeutic recreation processes and techniques* (4th ed.). Champaign, IL: Sagamore.

Beattie, M. (1987). *Codependent no more.* New York, NY: Harper and Row.

Caregiver's Resource Homepage. [On-line]. Available: http://www.caregiver911.com

Carter, M. J., Browne, S., LeConey, S. P., and Nagle, C. J. (1991). *Designing therapeutic recreation programs in the community.* Reston, VA: American Alliance for Health, Physical Education, Recreation, and Dance.

Carter, M. J., Van Andel, G. E., and Robb, G. M. (1995). *Therapeutic recreation a practical approach* (2nd ed.). Prospect Heights, IL: Waveland.

Dychtwald, K., and Flower, J. (1990). *Age wave: The challenges and opportunities of an aging America.* New York, NY: Bantam Books.

Foret, C. M., and Keller, M. J. (1993). A society growing older: Its implications for leisure. *Leisure Today/JOPERD, 64*(4), 29–59.

Hagan, L. P., Green, F., and Starling, S. (1997/98). Addressing stress in caregivers of older adults through leisure education. *Annual in Therapeutic Recreation, 7,* 42–51.

Hawkins, B. A., May, M. E., and Rogers, N. B. (1996). *Therapeutic activity intervention with the elderly: Foundations and practices.* State College, PA: Venture Publishing, Inc.

Health Care Financing Administration. [On-line]. Available: http://www.hcfa.gov

Lewis, C. B. (1990). *Aging: The health care challenge* (2nd ed.). Philadelphia, PA: F. A. Davis.

Nissenboim, S., and Vroman, C. (1998). *The positive interactions program of activities for people with Alzheimer's disease.* Baltimore, MD: Health Professions.

Searle, M. S., Mahon, M. J., Iso-Ahola, S. E., Sdrolias, H. A., and van Dyck, J. (1995). Enhancing a sense of independence and psychological well-being among the elderly: A field experiment. *Journal of Leisure Research, 27*(2), 107–124.

Teague, M. L., and MacNeil, R. D. (1992). *Aging and leisure: Vitality in later life* (2nd ed.). Dubuque, IA: Brown & Benchmark.

Wilhite, B. (1992). In-home alternatives for community recreation participation by older adults. *Leisure Today/JOPERD, 63*(8), 44–46, 55–56.

CASE 4 - SUSIE

Susie is a nine-year-old White female with Down syndrome, Trisomy 21/normal mosaicism. Susie lives with her mother, father, and 13-year-old brother in a small rural community (population less than 4,000). The community offers only summer sports programs in a city park. Children with disabilities are transported to integrated school programs in other nearby rural communities. Both parents commute to a metropolitan area 15 to 30 miles one-way per day to work. The 13-year-old sibling has assumed childcare responsibilities before and after school, during school vacations, and in the summer. Susie has received medical and social services support since birth, yet she is limited in her access to services due to the demands of her parents' careers, residence in a rural area, and absence of local resources.

Chromosomal defects attributable to Trisomy 21 also caused congenital heart disease in Susie's case, as well as ventricular septal disease (VSD), and atrial septal disease (ASD), which resulted in openings in the septum that separate the ventricles and atria. Two days after birth, Susie had heart surgery to implant a shunt; a month later she underwent surgery to remove an intestinal blockage and at nine months, eye surgery to correct her strabismus. Corrective lenses have been worn since age two. At age five, Susie again underwent heart surgery to repair the openings (VSD and ASD closures) in her heart walls. With each heart surgery, postoperative medications, Lasix and Lanoxin, were prescribed for periods of six weeks to three months. Stair climbing was contraindicated, and Susie has been observed closely to prevent falls that could traumatize the chest area. She is checked routinely by her cardiologist.

Social service and home care specialists began intervention at nine months and continued for three years until Susie entered preschool. Weekly interventions included movement and range of motion exercises, sensory stimulation, play skills, and family assistance in self-care. An initial focus in preschool was to develop communication through facilitated communication techniques with family involvement. Cognitive test results noted high to moderate intelligence; social tests suggested Susie's interaction skills are within expectations for her age group. She entered public school at age five in another rural community, where she was integrated in physical education and music classes and received academic support from education specialists. Her parents and family members indicated that Susie exhibits brief periods of attention and tends to be physically active. Speech therapists continue to assist Susie in developing clear, understandable vocalizations to accompany her use of signs. Family members use a behavior management program that involves a gradual reduction of signs as Susie's language becomes more comprehensible.

Susie appears to have definitive likes and dislikes. If she has a preference, she points to herself and says "me." She tends to be animated and demands attention when playing with family members. Susie's parents have used similar discipline techniques with both children; yet, there is a noticeable difference in Susie's response to each parent. Her father's presence tends to command immediate response. Her interests include music, dancing, puzzles, coloring, beanbag animals, looking at pictures in books, and games such as Memory and Bingo. She and her brother spend time with computer games and TV watching. During the summer, her parents are able to transport her to horseback riding lessons for children with disabilities. Through school, she participates in spring Special Olympics. As reported by her mother "she has needs and feelings just like any other child. She is a joy to have around. It is very hard to be in a bad mood around her. She won't let you. She won't let you get in a hurry. You have to slow down, and when you do, you realize what's important."

Discussion Questions

1. Keeping in mind her need for assisted communication, what instruments and techniques are available to assess Susie's leisure needs and assets?
2. What activities might be designed for Susie and her brother to participate in during the summer to promote social skills? Attempt to identify activities that would be of interest to both Susie and her brother.
3. Assuming summer school is not an option for Susie due to limited parental transportation to distant rural schools, what interventions could a CTRS plan during the school year to prepare Susie and her brother for recreation participation in the summer?

In-Class Exercises

Using the Internet, search for information concerning Susie's disability. Create a list of her abilities. Identify where Susie may need assistance or accommodation.

Role-Playing

Role-play an assessment interview with the parents, Susie, and the sibling in which each becomes aware of their own and other family members' leisure needs and assets.

Field Experiences

1. Invite an early intervention specialist to class to discuss his or her services to preschool age children with disabilities and family members during in-home visits. Compare early intervention goals with those of a CTRS using experiential interventions such as play therapy, sensory stimulation, and movement exploration.

2. Invite into class family members who have relatives with disabilities. Discuss the impact of a disability on family life and leisure patterns of the various family members. If possible, visit someone's home and observe the adaptations made in family life.

3. Visit a school where various degrees of inclusion are in evidence. Project the advantages for the school children and compare these benefits to the adjustments families make to access such opportunities.

Selected References for Case Study

Bedini, L. A., and Bilbro, C. W. (1991). Caregivers, the hidden victims: Easing caregiver's burden through recreation and leisure services. *Annual in Therapeutic Recreation, 2*, 49–54.

Bedini, L. A., Bullock, C. C., and Driscoll, L. B. (1993). The effects of leisure education on factors contributing to the successful transition of students with mental retardation from school to adult life. *Therapeutic Recreation Journal, 27*(2), 70–82.

Bullock, C. C., and Morris, L. H. (1991). Responding to current needs: A community reintegration program. *Leisure Today/JOPERD, 62*(4), 28–30.

Carter, M. J., Browne, S., LeConey, S. P., and Nagle, C. J. (1991). *Designing therapeutic recreation programs in the community*. Reston, VA: American Alliance for Health, Physical Education, Recreation, and Dance.

Carter, M. J., and Foret, C. M. (1994). Building transition bridges for the disabled. *Parks and Recreation, 29*(4), 78–83.

Dattilo, J., and Jekubovich-Fenton, N. (1995). Leisure services trends for people with mental retardation. *Parks and Recreation, 30*(5), 46–52.

Dattilo, J., and Light, J. (1993). Setting the stage for leisure: Encouraging reciprocal communication for people using augmentative and alternative communication systems through facilitator instruction. *Therapeutic Recreation Journal, 27*(3), 156–171.

Keller, M. J. (1992). The role of leisure education with family caregivers. *Leisure Today/JOPERD, 63*(8), 47–49, 56.

Kelly, J. R., and Kelly, J. (1994). Multiple dimensions of meaning in the domains of work, family, and leisure. *Journal of Leisure Research, 26*(3), 250–274.

Kurcinka, M. S. (1991). *Raising your spirited child*. New York, NY: Harper Perennial.

Mactavish, J., and Schleien, S. (1998). Playing together growing together: Parents' perspectives on the benefits of family recreation in families that include children with a developmental disability. *Therapeutic Recreation Journal, 32*(3), 207–230.

Monroe, J. E. (1987). Family leisure programming. *Therapeutic Recreation Journal, 21*(3), 44–51.

National Down Syndrome Society. [On-line]. Available: http://www.ndss.org/

Sable, J., Powell, L., and Aldrich, L. (1994). Transdisciplinary principles in the provision of therapeutic recreation services in inclusionary school settings. *Annual in Therapeutic Recreation, 4*, 69–81.

Sneegas, J. J. (1989). Social skills: An integral component of leisure participation and therapeutic recreation services. *Therapeutic Recreation Journal, 23*(2), 30–40.

Stumbo, N. J. (1995). Social skills instruction through commercially available resources. *Therapeutic Recreation Journal, 29*(1), 30–55.

CASE 5 - STAN

Stan, a 25-year-old single, African American male, is a patient in the rehabilitation unit of a general hospital. He has an above-knee amputation on his right side which resulted from trauma sustained in a motorcycle accident. A CTRS has been consulted to provide additional strategies for pain management. Stan reports pain in the stump and "phantom" limb. The pain is at times described as burning, tingling, or throbbing. Stan reports that his pain ranges from two to six (annoying to dreadful) on the pain scale provided. He states that the pain is worse upon awakening, when sitting, and when holding his stump vertically for more than five minutes. He has pain-free periods, but then the pain returns abruptly. Pain worsens when he stays in one position for more than five minutes. Stan takes nonsteroidal anti-inflammatory drugs in prescription strength four times daily for pain. Stan receives physical therapy and resistance training on his left leg and upper body and occupational therapy for assistance with activities of daily living. Stan reports that pain disrupts his sleeping and eating.

Stan is becoming increasingly isolated. He states that prior to the accident and amputation he dealt with stress by keeping busy and socializing. Stan has had limited contact with his family at the hospital and no contact with friends or co-workers. Stan reports that prior to his accident he worked 50 hours or more every week as a mechanic and spent his leisure time riding his motorcycle, playing basketball, and dating. Stan hopes to be free of right-side lower extremity pain upon discharge. He hopes to return to work within three months at a desk job.

Discussion Questions

1. What functional domains would you consider top priority for therapeutic recreation intervention and why?
2. If preliminary adjustment to physical challenges is the treatment team's projected outcome, what potential interdisciplinary goals could be established?

3. Describe a community reentry plan that would be appropriate for Stan.
4. Are group interventions appropriate for Stan? If so, what group interventions would you recommend and why? If not, why not?
5. If Stan leaves the hospital, remains in pain, and is unable to return to work, what problems could arise?

In-Class Exercises

Collect a variety of published pain assessment scales. Select the one most appropriate for this case, in your opinion, and describe how it would be used in outcome-oriented treatment planning.

Field Experiences

1. Attend a meeting of a support group in your community for persons with amputations.
2. Visit a prosthetist. Ask questions related to recreational activities and adaptive devices.
3. Visit a facility where a CTRS conducts a pain management group. Discuss what types of interventions are used and why.

Selected References for Case Study

American Pain Society. [On-line]. Available: http://www.ampainsoc.org

Carr, D., and Jacox, A. (1992). Acute Pain Management. *Abstracts: A Joint Commission on Accreditation of Healthcare Organizations Newsletter, 4*(2), 15–22.

Carter, M. J., Van Andel, G. E., and Robb, G. M. (1995). *Therapeutic recreation: A practical approach* (2nd ed.). Prospect Heights, IL: Waveland.

Catalano, E. M., and Hardin, K. N. (1996). *The chronic pain control workbook* (2nd ed.). New York, NY: MJF Books.

Hanson, R., and Gerver, K. (1990). *Coping with chronic pain: A guide to patient self-management*. New York, NY: Guilford Press.

National Foundation for the Treatment of Pain. [On-line]. Available: http://www.paincare.org

Peebles, J., McWilliams, L., Norris, L. H., and Park, K. (1999). Population-specific norms and reliability of the Leisure Diagnostic Battery in a sample of patients with chronic pain. *Therapeutic Recreation Journal, 33*(2), 135–141.

Sherrill, C. (1998). *Adapted physical activity, recreation and sport: Crossdisciplinary and lifespan* (5th ed.). Boston, MA: WCB McGraw-Hill.

Audiovisual Resources

Adaptive Equipment. [videotape]. Available from Indiana University, Department of Recreation and Park Administration, HPER Building, Room 133, Bloomington, IN 47405-4711.

CASE 6 - PATRICIA BARRON

You are a CTRS employed by a company that provides residential services to deinstitutionalized adults. The following is your annual assessment of one of the residents:

Patricia Barron is a 59-year-old White female diagnosed as having severe mental retardation, a seizure disorder, and spastic hemiplegia involving her left extremities. She uses a wheelchair for mobility. She has lived in an intermediate care facility/mental retardation (ICF/MR) group home with four other individuals for two years. Prior to moving to the ICF/MR facility, she had resided at a large state institution since the age of three years. Her current medications are Hydrochlorothiazide, 25 mg. q. am; Phenobarbital, 30 mg. q. am, 45 mg. q. pm; Zantac (Ranitidine), 150 mg. q. pm; and Dilantin, 300 mg. h.s.

Patricia's gross motor abilities are restricted. She displays voluntary movement of her right lower extremity, but it remains weak. She has good range of motion and dexterity in her right upper extremity and is able to use her left arm and hand as a brace when executing certain movements. She tends to sit slumped in her chair, but is able to propel herself independently. She generally enjoys group exercises, making an effort to extend her arms and right leg as far as possible. She enjoys playing catch with a Nerf ball. She also likes to listen to the radio and sing along. She keeps excellent time to music, usually by beating her hand on her chest and arm.

Patricia's fine motor abilities with her right hand are adequate for participation in leisure activities. Her left hand is not functional, other than as a brace for holding or steadying objects. Patricia likes to participate in certain fine-motor activities at home, but does not request to do them. She is able to hold a pencil or crayon and likes to color and paint. She remains in the scribble stage of development. She also likes to put puzzles together, sort beads, and work on craft projects. Her level of concentration is high during such activities, and she will remain on task for a long period of time to completion.

Patricia's cognitive abilities, as they relate to independent leisure functioning, are limited. Her communication abilities have previously been found to be at the two-year age equivalency. In the past, she has spoken very little, except when angered. Over the last year her verbalizations have increased, and she now makes occasional spontaneous comments in short sentences about things that are going on around her. She has recently begun to answer questions.

Patricia does not read, write, nor understand money concepts. She is familiar with her daily routine, responding well to structure, but is unaware of time concepts. She does not identify colors or shapes. She is unable to follow games with complex rules, but can take turns and share supplies with others. Unless structured for her, she tends to engage in activities by copying others.

Patricia displays various moods that can be discerned from her expressions, body language, and gestures. She is sometimes very happy, and has a contagious grin. At other times she is grumpy—angry—but is usually not able to express the reasons behind her feelings. She does not want to be bothered when she is in her grumpy moods. She may sometimes verbalize her anger with very sharp words that can be startling to others who are accustomed to her quiet demeanor.

Patricia has a best friend in the home, with whom she enjoys leisure activities. This friend also uses a wheelchair, and Patricia is dependent on having her friend sit close to her during various activities.

Patricia has certain preferences for leisure activities. She will indicate what she wants to do, which often is to be taken outside during nice weather. When she hears group home staff discussing certain activities, she expresses her desire to do them. She enjoys almost all outings, especially attending spectator sports, going to parks, and going out to eat. In the community, she requires supervision and hands-on assistance for all activities.

Over the last quarter, Patricia has been improving in her ability to carry out activities in the house independently. She has learned to locate supplies, such as drawing paper and crayons, and take them to the table independently.

Discussion Questions

1. From your assessment, list Patricia's strengths, needs, and leisure interests.
2. List the side effects of each of Patricia's current medications.
3. Consider the fact that Patricia has lived in an institution with minimal stimulation for almost her entire life. In what other specific areas could you expect to observe some improvement?
4. Identify Patricia's two greatest needs and select activities or interventions that you feel will best address the needs. Explain fully why you selected the activities.

Field Experiences

1. Visit a group home (an ICF/MR group home, if possible) and discuss with staff the potential and the challenges for creating and implementing leisure activities with the various group home residents.

2. Volunteer for one hour on six occasions with an adult with characteristics similar to Ms. Barron; experience various leisure activities together. Keep a journal of your experiences during each visit. Reflect on what it would be like to be a CTRS providing leisure experiences to individuals who have multiple disabilities. Be prepared to discuss your experiences and reflections in class.

Selected References for Case Study

American Association on Mental Retardation. [On-line]. Available: http://www.aamr.org

Bullock, C. C., and Mahon, M. J. (1997). *Introduction to recreation services for people with disabilities: A person-centered approach.* Champaign, IL: Sagamore.

Peniston, L. C. (1998). *Developing recreation skills in persons with learning disabilities.* Champaign, IL: Sagamore.

Schleien, S. J., and Fahnestock, M. K. (1996). Severe multiple disabilities. In D. R. Austin and M. E. Crawford (Eds.), *Therapeutic recreation: An introduction* (2nd ed.) (pp. 153–183). Needham Heights, MA: Allyn & Bacon.

Schleien, S. J., Meyer, L. H., Heyne, L. A., and Brandt, B. B. (1995). *Lifelong leisure skills and lifestyles for persons with developmental disabilities.* Baltimore, MD: Brookes.

Schleien, S. J., Ray, M. T., and Green, F. P. (1997). *Community recreation and people with disabilities: Strategies for inclusion.* Baltimore, MD: Brookes.

CASE 7 - ANNA

Anna is a 34-year-old, married, Hispanic female with advanced breast cancer that has metasticized to the bones of her right arm and ribs. She has been treated with surgery, radiation therapy, and chemotherapy. Anna reports constant pain in her chest and right arm. Her pain is described as weighty, throbbing, and squeezing. On a pain scale, Anna reports pain ranging from four to eight (uncomfortable to horrible). Anna receives Percoset, Darvon, and Methadone for pain on a schedule that allows her to receive some kind of medication for pain every hour. Anna participates in no physical activity; even sitting is painful. Anna reports that she copes by looking forward to the next scheduled dose of medication. Anna's husband is a daily visitor and is most often observed reading at his wife's bedside. Prior to her illness, Anna enjoyed square dancing, playing cards, and singing in the community choir. Anna has been receiving disability pay for eight months. She had been employed as a secretary, and her husband is a salesman. Anna's pain control goal is to be able to sleep without pain for at least six hours uninterrupted. Marital life prior to her illness was stressful, according to Anna, because she was caring for an aged parent (now in a skilled nursing home), and because she and her husband did not communicate effectively.

Discussion Questions

1. List as many symptoms associated with the patient's experience with metastatic breast cancer as you can identify. (*Note*: You may use the Internet to help you search for information.)
2. Identify the patient's previous leisure skills.
3. What are the patient's strengths, and what are her areas of concern?
4. What measurable outcomes for this client would guide your programmatic decision making?
5. How might cultural issues or cultural barriers affect diagnosis and assessment as well as treatment efforts? What are possible implications for Anna's cultural belief in fatalism, the involvement of family

in decision making, and the value of self-reliance or noninterference?

6. Would you involve Anna's husband in the development of her treatment plan? If so, why and how?

Role-Playing

Role-play a conversation between the patient and her husband in which they plan an afternoon leisure activity together. Assess the communication of the role-played couple and make suggestions for improvement.

Field Experiences

1. Contact your local American Cancer Society to ask about programs for support and recreation for individuals with cancer and their family. Go to the American Cancer Society Web Page and look for information regarding recreation with persons with cancer. Report your findings to class.
2. Volunteer at your local "Race for the Cure" event.
3. Invite a local oncologist to your class to discuss cancer treatments and their side effects.
4. Invite a CTRS who works with pain management to class to discuss the role therapeutic recreation could play in helping Anna manage pain.

Selected References for Case Study

American Cancer Institute. (n.d.). *Questions and answers about pain control: A guide for people with cancer and their families.* Betheseda, MD: Author.

American Cancer Society. [On-line]. Available: http://www.cancer.org

American Pain Society. [On-line]. Available: http://www.ampainsoc.org

Berrian, R. (1992). *Interdisciplinary team approach for the treatment and management of individuals with acute and chronic pain.* Paper presented at the American Therapeutic Recreation Association Conference, Spokane, WA.

Carr, D., and Jacox, A. (1992). Acute pain management. *Abstracts: A Joint Commission on Accreditation of Healthcare Organizations newsletter,* 4(2), 15–22.

Cassel, E. (1983). *The nature of suffering.* New York, NY: Guildford.

Foley, D., and Payne, A. (1989). *Current theory of pain.* Philadelphia, PA: 3 C Decker.

Hanson, R., and Gerver, K. (1990). *Coping with chronic pain: A guide to patient self-management.* New York, NY: Guilford.

National Foundation for the Treatment of Pain. [On-line]. Available: http://www.paincare.org/

Rhoades, M. (1992). *Recreation therapy and the treatment for individuals suffering from pain disorders.* Paper presented at the American Therapeutic Recreation Association Conference, Spokane, WA.

U.S. Department of Health and Human Services, Public Health Service, Agency for Health Care Policy and Research. (1992). *Clinical practice guidelines for acute pain management: Operative, medical procedures or trauma.* Washington, DC: Author.

U.S. Department of Health and Human Services, Public Health Service, Agency for Health Care Policy and Research. (1994). *Management of cancer pain.* Washington, DC: Author.

CASE 8 - LAWRENCE PAYNE

Lawrence Payne is a 28-year-old White male who sustained a severe brain injury in a motor vehicle accident. He has spasticity on the right side, ataxia on the left side, and dysarthria. He uses a wheelchair but is able to stand with maximum assist of one.

Lawrence lives semi-independently in a supervised apartment in a medium-sized community; he doesn't work. His parents are divorced, and his mother lives in the same community as Lawrence. He has an older brother and sister who are both married and living out-of-town.

Lawrence has problems with impulsivity, low frustration tolerance, and appropriate social behavior. He becomes angry quickly when people have problems understanding him, and his anger escalates into abusive behavior. He has been hospitalized twice for alcohol abuse.

Despite the above problems, Lawrence can be charming, witty, and sensitive to others' needs. He has become socially isolated and extremely lonely since his discharge from outpatient therapy.

While it has been a few years since he was discharged, Lawrence does come back to the hospital approximately once per year for intensive outpatient services. During this time, he has 10 therapeutic recreation sessions over a four-week period.

Discussion Questions

1. What are the viable assets this client possesses? What are his deficits? Be sure to validate assets and deficits with demonstrated behaviors.
2. What are the primary problems that need to be addressed by the CTRS?
3. How would you prioritize these problems?
4. Given a four-week period, what would your discharge goals be?
5. How could community recreation services support Lawrence?

In-Class Exercises

Divide into four groups. Each group should learn as much as possible about one of the domains of functioning (e.g., physical, cognitive, social, and affective) related to severe brain injury. Each group should prepare a resource list and share it with other members of the class.

Field Experiences

Visit a CTRS who works in a physical medicine and rehabilitation environment with adults with brain injuries. Ask if you can participate (with patient's and family's permission) in a treatment session. Ask if you can review the patient's chart prior to the session. After the session, discuss your observations with the CTRS.

Selected References for Case Study

American Therapeutic Recreation Association. (1993). *Standards for the practice of therapeutic recreation and self-assessment guide.* Hattiesburg, MS: Author.

Brain Injury Association, Inc. [On-line]. Available: http://www. biausa.org/

Kwan, W., and Sulzberger, A. (1994). Issues and realities in brain injury, leisure and the rehabilitation process: Input from key stakeholders. *Leisurability, 21*(2), 26–33.

Lahey, M. (1996). Cognitive rehabilitation. In D. R. Austin and M. E. Crawford (Eds.), *Therapeutic recreation: An introduction* (2nd ed.) (pp. 213–226). Boston, MA: Allyn & Bacon.

Lloyd, L. F., Malkin, M. J., and Poppen, R. (1997). Development of a leisure planning training package for persons with traumatic brain injury. In G. L. Hitzhusen and L. Thomas (Eds.), *Expanding horizons in therapeutic recreation XVII* (pp. 167–179). Columbia, MO: University of Missouri.

Stumbo, N., and Bloom, C. (1990). The implications of traumatic brain injury for therapeutic recreation services in rehabilitation settings. *Therapeutic Recreation Journal, 24*(3), 64–80.

Sherrill, C. (1998). *Adapted physical activity, recreation and sport: Crossdisciplinary and lifespan* (5th ed.). Boston, MA: WCB McGraw-Hill.

Traumatic Brain Injury FAQs. [On-line]. Available: http://www.geneseo. edu/~bga99/tbi_page2.html

CASE 9 - BERNIE

Bernie is a nine-year-old White male with spina bifida. He is preparing to attend Camp Rolling Thunder, a camp for children with spina bifida, for the first time; he will be in camp for three weeks. Bernie's parents found out about Camp Rolling Thunder through the Spina Bifida Association in their area. They were impressed by what the other parents shared about the increases in independence in their children while at camp. The camp facility offers a variety of activities for the campers including canoeing, fishing, swimming, archery, target shooting, challenge course, arts and crafts, group sports, small animal farm, evening activities, and individual projects.

At age nine, Bernie is obese. Bernie's spinal opening occurred in the L1 region of his back. He uses a wheelchair for mobility. Bernie uses diapers to control his incontinence. He has a shunt in his head to maintain drainage for hydrocephalus. Bernie's family consists of his mom, dad, and sister (one year older than he). He has several pets, including two dogs, a cat and a hamster. Bernie attends regular school during the school year.

The CTRS met with Bernie prior to his attending camp. Bernie was very curious about camp and a little nervous about going. He asked many questions about what he would be doing at camp and what the other campers were like. He seemed reassured when the CTRS explained that all the campers also had spina bifida. Aside from visits to the clinic, this would be the first time Bernie would be around others with spina bifida.

Upon arriving at camp, Bernie was greeted by the CTRS and introduced to his counselors. The cabin Bernie was placed in consisted of four other boys and three counselors. Bernie frequently stayed close to his counselors, both physically and emotionally, during the first half of camp. On several occasions he reported being teased by his cabin mates about snoring too loud and being overweight. Bernie was willing to try new activities, but frequently waited for a counselor to reassure him about the safety of an activity.

Discussion Questions

1. How would you assess Bernie's interests and needs? Discuss specific sources of assessment information, methods of obtaining the information, and uses of the information.
2. Will you involve Bernie's family in the assessment process? How? When?
3. The CTRS discovered that Bernie was interested in playing baseball, collecting baseball cards, hockey, Nintendo, and swimming. Bernie appeared to be a friendly, intelligent, and emotionally sensitive young man. On occasion, he would stare out into the distance and roll his head while speaking. Bernie's parents explained that he required help in dressing with everything except his shirt, help with activities of daily living, especially toileting/diapering, and some assistance with transfers. Discuss how you will use this information to develop goals and objectives for Bernie during the three-week camping program.
4. How will you periodically reassess Bernie's progress throughout his three weeks at camp?

In-Class Exercises

Therapeutic recreation services occur in a variety of settings. In a round-table discussion, discuss the differences, if any, between practicing therapeutic recreation services in the outdoors versus other settings (e.g., rehabilitation hospital, long-term care setting, psychiatric facility). Discuss how the outdoors can be used to benefit clients. How does therapeutic recreation in the outdoors impact the development of young people in general?

Field Experiences

Visit a facility that primarily serves individuals with disabilities in a camp setting. Discuss with program staff, counselors, a CTRS, and administrators their various roles. Inquire if you can volunteer with campers for a weekend or a short period of time for hands-on or observation experience. Consider spending a summer working at a camp for persons with disabilities.

Selected References for Case Study

Adams, R. C., and McCubbin, J. A. (1991). *Games, sports and exercise for the physically disabled* (4th ed.). Philadelphia, PA: Lea and Febiger.

Austin, D. R. (1999). *Therapeutic recreation: Processes and techniques* (4th ed.). Champaign, IL: Sagamore.

Blum, R. W. (1983). The adolescent with spina bifida. *Clinical Pediatrics, 22*(5), 331–335.

Duncan, C. C., and Ogle, E. M. (1995). Spina bifida. In B. Goldberg (Ed.), *Sports and exercise for children with chronic health conditions* (pp. 79–87). Champaign, IL: Human Kinetics.

Hicks, J. (1995). *Marc's story.* [On-line]. Available: http://www. waisman.wisc.edu/~rowley/sb-kids/st-marc.htm

Paciorek, M. J., and Jones, J. A. (1994). *Sports and recreation for the disabled* (2nd ed.). Carmel, IN: Cooper.

Peterson, C. A., and Stumbo, N. J. (2000). *Therapeutic recreation program design: Principles and procedures* (3rd ed.). Needham Heights, MA: Allyn & Bacon.

Spina Bifida Association of America. [On-line]. Available: http://www.spaa.org.

Audiovisual Resources

Stimac, D. J. (Executive Producer). (1993). *Living with spina bifida.* [videotape]. Available from the Spina Bifida Association of Dallas, 705 W. Avenue B., Suite 300, Garland, TX 75040.

CASE 10 - DAN WINDER

Dan Winder, a 38-year-old African American male, is diagnosed as having mild mental retardation and paranoid schizophrenia. He takes thioridazine (Submellaril) 75 mg. q. pm. He has resided in an intermediate care facility/mental retardation (ICF/MR) apartment for approximately one-and-a-half years. He has one roommate.

Dan's gross motor abilities are within normal limits. He tends to be sedentary, but expresses an interest in various sports. He understands the importance of physical activity, but, due to his persistent fears, he is often reluctant to actually carry out any of his expressed interests. Physical activities in which he engages include taking walks and riding his bike one time a week.

Dan's fine motor abilities are good. He is able to write in cursive, and perform a number of fine-motor tasks, such as cutting with scissors, and copying geometric figures. He does not pursue any fine-motor activities as hobbies. He does, however, prepare his own meals daily.

Dan's cognitive abilities, apart from his emotional problems, enable him to pursue complex leisure activities with a high degree of independence. He is able to read, spell, and perform math problems at the second-grade level. He can express his needs and desires both orally and in writing. He is able to tell time and use a calendar to make future plans. He can plan and shop for meals. He displays good phone skills and likes to talk on the phone. He keeps abreast of some current events.

In the area of leisure functioning, Dan's developmental level, according to the General Recreation Screening Tool (burlingame, 1997), is generally within the seven- to ten-year age equivalency. His language abilities are good. His strengths are in problem solving and in object use and understanding.

Over the last six months, Dan has had some emotional difficulties that have superceded his functioning in other areas. Starting in January, he developed extreme paranoia. He would not leave the apartment nor bathe, and he often would not get out of bed. He spoke of fears regarding others who might harm him. His behavior gradually improved, and, in the spring, he began to resume his daily routine.

In general, Dan is friendly with familiar persons, but prefers to be alone. He dislikes fast-paced situations or events, preferring quiet, calm activities that are a part of his routine. He is rebellious toward authority, especially when chores are involved.

Dan is articulate and highly expressive of his opinions when engaged in conversation. He is able to talk abstractly about his goals, which center on gaining greater independence in life. He continues to be somewhat paranoid about interacting with others in the community, but is able to go to work daily.

Dan has the ability to be highly independent in the community, which affords him much freedom during his leisure. He is able to travel by the subway and bus and can manage his money with some assistance. He displays appropriate social skills when in the community and can shop independently.

Dan spends much of his leisure time "sitting and resting," either while listening to music or while watching TV. He also enjoys sitting outside. His philosophy is that after a hard day at work, he should be able to rest. He has needed encouragement, in general, to carry out certain leisure activities. From January to April, he engaged in very few recreational activities. Now that he is emotionally stable, he is more willing to plan some activities although his level of actual participation continues to be of concern.

Leisure activities that Dan enjoyed prior to January included going to movies, attending sporting events, and going out to eat. He planned his leisure activities using a calendar, and filled out his own data sheet, which required him to record his planned activities.

Dan's previous goal was to demonstrate his ability to engage in an independent leisure lifestyle by planning a schedule of leisure activities one time every two weeks, which will include four physical activities and four social community leisure activities; in addition, he hoped to carry out all of the activities for three consecutive months. He was able to plan and carry out five activities in November and December of the previous year. He was unable to plan or carry out any leisure activities after that time until May of this year. He planned activities in May and June, but did not carry them out.

Discussion Questions

1. What are Dan's strengths and needs? Make a list and discuss.
2. What are potential sources of objective and subjective assessment information in this case?
3. What types of assessment methods (e.g., instruments, approaches, sources) could you use to obtain information relative to Dan's goals?
4. If Dan's previous annual goal was too difficult for him, how would you make it simpler?
5. From this assessment, in what areas might you develop goals?
6. Dan expresses his feelings well during interdisciplinary meetings. He makes it very clear that he does not want people telling him what to do. How will you address this in developing the goals?

Field Experiences

Visit the local mental health or mental retardation facility and discuss with staff the various levels of community living arrangements and support services offered by the agency to help persons with mental health and/or mental retardation concerns. Discuss the role therapeutic recreation could play in meeting the needs of clients.

Selected References for Case Study

burlingame, j. (1997). General recreation screening tool. In j. burlingame and T. M. Blaschko (Eds.), *Assessment tools for recreation therapy, red book #1* (2nd ed.) (pp. 145–154). Ravensdale, WA: Idyll Arbor.

Gimmestad, K. (1995). A comprehensive therapeutic recreation intervention: A woman with schizophrenia. *Therapeutic Recreation Journal, 29*(1), 56–62.

Kinney, J. S., and Kinney, W. B. (1996). Psychiatry and mental health. In D. R. Austin and M. E. Crawford (Eds.), *Therapeutic recreation: An introduction* (2nd ed). (pp. 57–77). Boston, MA: Allyn & Bacon.

Malley, S. M. (1995). Two years of progress: Therapeutic recreation with a person with mental retardation and mental illness. *Therapeutic Recreation Journal, 29*(4), 307–315.

National Alliance for Research on Schizophrenia and Depression. [On-line]. Available: http://www.mhsource.com/narsad.html

Pestle, K., Card, J., and Menditto, A. (1998). Therapeutic recreation in a social-learning program: Effect over time on appropriate behaviors of residents with schizophrenia. *Therapeutic Recreation Journal, 32*(1), 28–41.

Schleien, S. J., Ray, M. T., and Green, F. P. (1997). *Community recreation and people with disabilities: Strategies for inclusion.* Baltimore, MD: Brookes.

CASE 11 - WALTER BYRD

Walter Byrd, a 72-year-old male with a diagnosis of right cerebral vascular accident (CVA) with left hemiparesis, was referred for assessment for therapeutic recreation services by the rehabilitation center's medical director. This is Mr. Byrd's second CVA.

Mr. Byrd is married and has three children, one of whom lives in the area. For the last 10 years, Mr. Byrd and his wife have worked at a marina camp site. Their duties have been to check in the patrons, collect fees for the camp site, and perform daily inspections of the grounds. Before the first CVA, Mr. Byrd and his wife performed the inspections using a golf cart, but the subsequent visuospatial neglect prohibits him from driving. Since that time, he and his wife have taken daily walks to perform their duties.

Mr. Byrd's left hemiparesis has resulted in limited use of his left arm and leg, causing difficulty in coordination and standing balance. Additionally, Mr. Byrd has poor endurance. During the initial assessment, Mr. Byrd's heart rate increased to 130 beats per minute in eight minutes of a standing activity. When objects were placed to the left of his field of vision, he could not visually track objects left of center.

There are also cognitive issues. Mr. Byrd displays slight aphasia when attempting to express himself. His attention span is poor, requiring four redirection cues in a 30-minute session. When asked for the date and location, he did not answer correctly and became noticeably agitated. When he was asked how his standing balance was, he impulsively jumped out of his wheelchair and nearly fell. After this, his affect decreased, which led to little motivation for the remainder of the session.

It was determined that Mr. Byrd and his wife participated together in many leisure activities. They enjoy taking walks at the marina and socializing with friends and patrons there. They also enjoy listening to music, reading, and gardening. Mr. Byrd stated that his favorite thing to do was to go fishing.

Discussion Questions

1. What are the functional characteristics of a right-side CVA?
2. Is Mr. Byrd a candidate for therapeutic recreation services? Explain your answer. Thinking of possible

therapeutic recreation service components, which components are most appropriate for Mr. Byrd? Again, justify your answer.

3. What are the viable assets of Mr. Byrd? What are his deficits?

4. What are the primary problems that need to be addressed by the CTRS? How would you prioritize these problems?

5. How would you further assess Mr. Byrd's interests and needs? Discuss specific sources of assessment information, methods of obtaining the information, and uses of the information.

6. What role, if any, might Mrs. Byrd play in the assessment of Mr. Byrd's strengths and weaknesses as they relate to leisure functioning?

Selected References for Case Study

Auerbach, J., and Benezra, A. (1998). Therapeutic recreation and the rehabilitation of the stroke patient. *Loss, Grief, and Care, 8*(1/2), 123–127.

burlingame, J., and Blaschko, T. M. (1997). *Assessment tools for recreation therapy* (2nd ed.). Ravensdale, WA: Idyll Arbor.

burlingame, J., and Skalko, T. K. (1997). *Idyll Arbor's glossary for therapists*. Ravensdale, WA: Idyll Arbor.

Carmi, S., and Mashiah, T. (1996). Painting as language for a stroke patient. *Art Therapy: Journal of the American Art Therapy Association, 13*(4), 265–269.

Hawkins, B. A., May, M. E., and Rogers, N. B. (1996). *Therapeutic activity intervention with the elderly: Foundations and practices*. State College, PA: Venture Publishing, Inc.

Martini, E. B., Weeks, M. A., and Wirth, P. (1996). *Long-term care for activity and social service professionals* (2nd ed.). Ravensdale, WA: Idyll Arbor.

National Stroke Foundation. [On-line]. Available: http://www. stroke.org

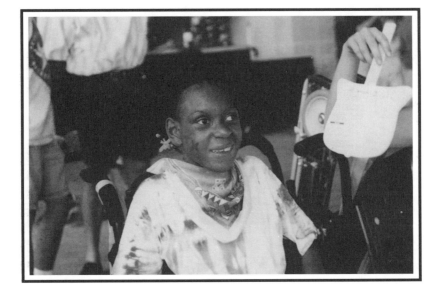

Chapter Two
Individual Therapeutic Recreation Program Planning

The practice of therapeutic recreation is influenced strongly by beliefs about its nature and purpose (Carter, Van Andel, and Robb, 1995; Gruver, 1993/94). Therefore, a review of various models of practice is an important underpinning for the discussion of individual therapeutic recreation program planning.

Individual program planning in therapeutic recreation indicates that there is a need for intervention and service delivery, based on assessment information, with the intention of altering clients' personal and/or leisure functioning. Early leaders in therapeutic recreation, such as Ball (1970), Avedon (1974), Frye and Peters (1972), and Gunn and Peterson (1978) were among the first to conceptualize the desired outcome or result of the intervention along a hierarchial continuum of care, where fulfilling higher order client needs presupposes the fulfillment of needs at lower levels. Clients' needs and issues determine the level of care, a specific site or setting for care (ranging from most restrictive to least restrictive), as well as possible therapeutic recreation service components (e.g., assessment, treatment or rehabilitation, leisure education, recreation participation, advocacy for leisure). Different outcomes are indicated at each point of the continuum, and clients may enter the continuum at any point appropriate for their needs. The interaction that occurs along the continuum is sometimes directed toward resolving existing problems. At other times, the goal is to enhance nonproblematic functioning and encourage further personal development (Peterson and Gunn, 1984).

Ball (1970) provided an interpretation of this hierarchial movement along a continuum in her depiction of a sequence of steps through which clients progress until they reach a "true recreative experience." In her model, clients first move through a functionally deficient level in which they participate in recreation just for the sake of "reality participation." Clients then acquire attitudes, skills, and knowledge regarding recreation participation and gradually begin to exercise personal recreation participation choices.

Frye and Peters (1972) and Avedon (1974) furthered the continuum concept by describing the relationship between the control imposed by therapeutic recreation specialists and the freedom experienced by clients. Frye and Peters acknowledged that a client's disability might initially limit his or her participation in a truly recreative experience. The various dimensions of the continuum thus imply a differentiation between short- and long-term goals. Immediately obtainable goals may require more authority to be exerted by the therapeutic recreation specialist while long-term goals represent an expanding area of freedom for clients (Frye and Peters, 1972). Avedon (1974) described eight leadership roles assumed by the therapeutic recreation specialist based upon "the patient or client's relative level of maturity—that is, how much internal control over his or her own behavior a patient or client manifests, and how much external control is needed in order to function effectively in social situations" (p. 157). Avedon described these eight styles as controller, director, instigator, stimulator, educator, adviser, observer, and enabler.

In response to calls for a deeper exploration and understanding of therapeutic recreation (see Gruver, 1993/94; Howe-Murphy and Halberg, 1987; Mobily, 1985, 1996; Russoniello, 1997; Shank, 1987; Sylvester, 1996; Voelkl, Carruthers, and Hawkins, 1997), newer models of therapeutic recreation are increasingly integrative and holistic, and they promote the idea that both general well-being and specific treatment goals may be addressed (see Carter et al., 1995; Coyle, 1998; Kraus and Shank, 1992; Shank, Kinney, and Coyle, 1993; Van Andel, 1998). This view stresses the importance of recreation and leisure "both as treatment and as a human experience" (Shank et al., 1993, p. 323). Therapeutic recreation specialists are thus responsible for helping clients to improve interdependent functioning, including leisure functioning, and eliminating or minimizing barriers that prevent or limit the attainment of this goal. At the same time, therapeutic recreation specialists help to improve general health and well-being (quality of life) through facilitating engagement in self-motivated and self-determined, enjoyable (leisure) activities (Dattilo, Kleiber, and Williams, 1998; Howe-Murphy and Charboneau, 1987; Mobily, 1996; Shank et al., 1993; Sylvester, 1987, 1996; Wilhite, Keller, and Caldwell, 1999).

These newer models of therapeutic recreation have placed greater emphasis on definitions of health that pertain not only to the absence of disease, but also to the enhancement of physical and psychosocial well-being (Coyle, Kinney, Riley, and Shank, 1991). Authors Austin and Crawford have helped to advance concepts of health enhancement by suggesting that therapeutic recreation may also be viewed as preventive (Austin, 1999, 1998; Austin and Crawford, 1996). Still, prevention and health promotion have received minimal attention to date (Austin, 1999, 1998) and have been concerned primarily with reducing secondary disability and associated higher healthcare cost (Coyle et al., 1991; Shank, Coyle, Boyd, and Kinney, 1996). While some believe that therapeutic recreation services are ideally suited to addressing health enhancement needs, research in the therapeutic recreation field has not yet supported this notion (Gerber, 1994/95). Moreover, guidelines as to how to extend therapeutic recreation beyond acute care and rehabilitation to include health maintenance and preventive education are lacking.

As Widmer and Ellis (1997) pointed out, it is possible to achieve functional independence that involves an inappropriate leisure lifestyle. "For example, a client might want to get drunk or high in an effort to find pleasure" (Widmer and Ellis, 1997, p. 184). In the long run, this behavior may lead to the abuse of substances and a related myriad of personal, familial, and societal problems at a tremendous cost to all. Through their interpretation of Aristotelian ethics, Widmer and Ellis (1997, 1998) suggested that the "good life" should be facilitated through a focus on leisure pursuits that promote intellectual, creative, and moral attainment, as well as meaningful relationships. This view is similar to that expressed by Kelly (1996) discussed in chapter one. From a health enhancement perspective, the ultimate goal of this approach is to facilitate clients' engagement in leisure choices that promote health, prevent disabling or dysfunctional conditions, and/or prevent secondary consequences to those persons who already experience a chronic or disabling condition. In addition, clients must be prepared to alter these choices or find substitutes, when necessitated, by changing personal and environmental characteristics.

Drawing from and building on the ideas of Widmer and Ellis (1997; 1998) and Kelly (1996), among others (e.g., Atchley, 1989; Austin, 1996, 1998; Baltes and Baltes, 1990; Bateson, 1990; Brill,

1990; Carter et al., 1995; Howe-Murphy and Charboneau, 1987; Stumbo and Peterson, 1998), Wilhite, Keller, and Caldwell (1999) proposed the *Optimizing Lifelong Health and Well-Being Through Therapeutic Recreation* (OLH-TR) model of therapeutic recreation practice. This model is based on the belief that engagement in a healthy lifestyle, which includes experiencing leisure, reduces the probability of pathology and/or secondary consequences across the life course. In this model, health includes a flexibility that enables clients to make continuous accommodations to internal and external changes. The major activities driving the model, adapted from Baltes and Baltes (1990), involve selection, compensation, optimization, and evaluation (see Figure 2.1).

When we think of "life as a work in progress" as coined by Bateson (1990), we realize that clients receiving therapeutic recreation services will need to reinvent themselves again and again in response to changing situations, health status, and environments. Lifelong learning and adaptation rely on maximizing or optimizing assets and resources. Selection, optimization, compensation, and

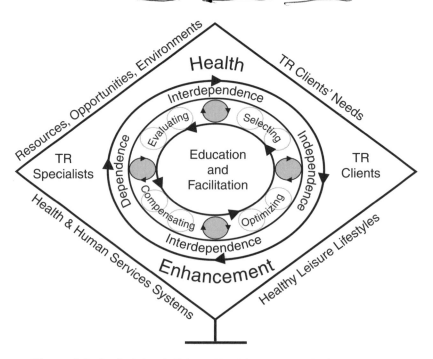

Figure 2.1 Optimizing Lifelong Health and Well-Being Through Therapeutic Recreation Model.

evaluation efforts are the primary activities involved in achieving and maintaining leisure pursuits across the life course that may enhance an optimal level of personal health and well-being. *Selecting* involves focusing clients' energies and resources on domains of functioning that are of a high priority. High priority domains are those that match environmental demands with individual capacity, skills, and motivations, and support efforts to achieve, maintain, and/ or regain a leisure lifestyle that optimizes health. *Optimizing* focuses on actively engaging in behaviors and activities that maximize general personal and environmental resources (including financial resources) and make it possible for clients to pursue their chosen leisure pursuits. *Compensating* includes psychological, social, and technological compensatory efforts which are adopted when certain behavioral abilities are lost, or are reduced below the minimum level required for desired functioning. *Evaluating* addresses aspects of inputs (resources/costs) and outputs (outcomes). Personal meaning and well-being are evaluated in light of evolving changes/transitions and their consequences.

In the OLH-TR model, a holistic view of health is taken, and the therapeutic recreation specialist's primary concern is to provide educational opportunities and to design and/or facilitate supports and opportunities that will promote the total well-being of clients over the life course, not just at a particular moment in time or in a particular service setting. The education focus of the therapeutic recreation intervention is on opportunities for acquiring awareness, knowledge, and understanding of various leisure options for minimizing health risks and promoting health (again, refer to Figure 2.1). The facilitation focus is on experiences for clients to apply the learning, to enable leisure to occur, and to advocate on clients' behalf. These two foci are oriented toward and intertwined with a variety of health enhancement outcomes including prevention, health promotion, habilitation, rehabilitation, and palliative care.

This model values the interrelatedness of all aspects of clients—cognitive, physical, social, affective, spiritual—and the relationship between clients and their environments. Additionally, it stresses that desired changes or outcomes should be both functional and fulfilling as Sylvester (1994/95) and others have suggested. The model also takes into account those individuals who will not "get better" or return to a "productive" life. This includes individuals with dementia, terminal illness, chronic and severe mental illness, or progressive disease. Therapeutic recreation practice is defined according to clients' needs for achieving and maintaining maximum functioning and optimal health and well-being in relation to leisure and life, and the fact that these needs and the resources available to meet them, change repeatedly over time.

This capacity for adjustment and readjustment is the essence of healthy interdependence (Brill, 1990). Blum (1992) described optimal development as "movement from dependence *through* independence *to* interdependence" (p. 367). Each individual possesses a range of capacity for interdependence; adaptation to demands across the life course require the ability to move back and forth from dependence to independence—the give and take of life. As Brill (1990) pointed out, too much of either, extreme dependence or independence, tends to be negative. Therefore, in the OLH-TR model, clients do not move from a position of dependence to one of independence and remain there (a linear concept present in some continuum models). Therapeutic recreation specialists help clients achieve self-determination (i.e., autonomy, control) through a balance of dependence and independence. Clients who achieve this balance will be able to take responsibility for their behavior, make choices in light of self and others' needs, and develop mutually supportive relationships (Gilligan, 1982).

This balance is illustrated in Figure 2.1 by depicting the elements of the model as ball bearings. The actions taken by clients (i.e., selecting, optimizing, compensating, and evaluating) turn clockwise which enable the outside of the mechanism (the outer circle of the figure representing the achievement of interdependence) to turn clockwise. The inside of the mechanism (the inner circle of the figure representing the therapeutic recreation specialists' actions of educating and facilitating) revolves in the opposite direction portraying the creation and maintenance of balance or interdependence as clients and therapeutic recreation specialists work together (for more details concerning the OLH-TR model see Wilhite et al., 1999).

Even though differences in the OLH-TR model and other newer therapeutic recreation models exist, several commonalities important to individual program planning exist. All therapeutic recreation models are based on the need and potential for people to change. All are client-centered and emphasize the achievement of prioritized needs or outcomes. While differences exist about whether leisure represents an endpoint or a progression toward an endpoint, or both, a primary goal of therapeutic recreation intervention is to support and extend clients' personal freedom and capacity for self-determination so that they might embrace health and truly experience leisure and its benefits.

When applied to practice, these principles guide the development of individual therapeutic recreation program planning. In the following discussion, six program planning steps will be highlighted:

Principles of program planning

1. determining direction,
2. identifying content and process,
3. analyzing activities,
4. selecting activities,
5. modifying activities,
6. selecting appropriate interventions,
7. considering service delivery options, and
8. developing a written plan.

Determining Direction

When therapeutic recreation specialists attempt to discover what is preventing maximum interdependent functioning in all life domains (including leisure) and causing diminishing quality of life, they must consider the question of where to begin. "Problems" related to clients' current functioning levels can be discovered through reviewing assessment data and formulating a list of strengths, areas of need, and interests. This process should also include clients' and their families' perceptions of problems, their expectations of participation, and their desired overall outcomes. By analyzing this list, therapeutic recreation specialists can determine which areas need to be addressed first and how clients' strengths and interests might be used to ameliorate problems. Possessing a particular leisure skill or interest and having the support of family/friends are examples of client strengths (Carter et al., 1995). Crawford and Mendell (1987) advise specialists to target first those deficiencies that are prerequisites to other desired skills and outcomes. Other problems may be more effectively addressed at a later stage of treatment or participation (Landrum, Schmidt, and McLean, 1995). In addition, the resolution of some problems will require assistance from other members of an interdisciplinary team or from various community representatives (O'Morrow and Reynolds, 1989). At times, two different disciplines may decide to co-treat a client to achieve desired outcomes. Those problems that are expected to have little impact on the ultimate result or desired outcomes sought may not require significant attention (Landrum et al., 1995).

First, the ultimate result or global outcome of all treatments/ interventions is identified. This outcome is referred to as the discharge goal in some settings (Carter et al., 1995). Keeping this end goal in mind, next, desired client outcomes and behaviors are developed and stated as observable short-term and long-term goals for which clients will strive and toward which therapeutic recreation specialists will direct their programmatic efforts. According to Peterson and Gunn (1984), there are no universal definitions distinguishing short-term and long-term goals. The length of time implied by the terms will vary according to individuals' level of care and setting. Frye and Peters (1972) stated that the various dimensions of the therapeutic recreation continuum imply a discrimination between short-term and long-term goals. Thus, the therapeutic recreation specialist might think of short-term goals, for example, identifying accessible leisure programs, demonstrating community integration skills, and ambulating independently, as the acquisition of behaviors and skills, or steps needed in order to accomplish the intent of the long-term goals. Wilcox and Bellamy (1987) pointed out that activities directed toward accomplishing short-term goals should be combined with efforts directed toward accomplishing long-term goals. For example, if a client's long-term goal is to develop social interaction skills, she can participate in a nonverbal small group activity even before she has demonstrated the ability to respond verbally to leader or participant initiated questions.

The use of critical or clinical pathways is one method for achieving outcomes in an efficient and integrated manner. The critical pathway highlights those tasks that must be accomplished within a given time frame in order for the overall or global (discharge) outcome to be realized with optimum efficiency (burlingame and Skalko, 1997; Landrum et al., 1995; Rath and Page, 1996). Critical pathways are being established for many "high-volume and high-cost diagnoses and procedures for which inefficient variations in care extend or decrease quality of patient care" (Rickerson and burlingame, 1998, p. 212). Examples of these diagnoses include acquired brain injury, cerebral vascular accident, hip and knee replacement, bipolar disorder, and chemical dependency. Using this method, therapeutic recreation specialists designate those short-term goals that must be achieved within a specific time frame so that the overall outcome may be achieved within the designated length of stay.

In their most useful form, short-term goals are restated as measurable objectives—specific behaviors that are to be demonstrated within a specified period of time, under a certain set of conditions, and judged by a predetermined standard or criterion. They are often referred to as behavioral objectives, performance measures, or outcome statements. These objectives: (1) identify what the client will be doing to demonstrate the intent of the objective (the behavior); (2) explain the situation under which the behavior will occur, such as "on request..." "without assistance..." "when given a choice of..." (the conditions); and (3) describe the criteria by which the client's progress will be evaluated, such as accuracy, amount of time, and form. Objectives are often stated in behavioral domains including cognitive, physical, social, affective, and spiritual (Carter et al., 1995; Melcher, 1999; Smith, Austin, and Kennedy, 1996). They may also be written as outcomes to be achieved in one or more therapeutic recreation service functions such as habilitation, treatment, education, recreation participation, or facilitation. Habilitation or treatment objectives should address deficiencies that could limit functioning and leisure involvement. Education and recreation participation objectives should focus on acquiring the knowledge and skills required for preserving immediate and long-term health and promoting well-being in relation to leisure and life. Objectives in these service components are also directed toward achieving an appropriate level of functioning within clients' communities. Facilitation of leisure objectives should pertain to creating opportunities for clients to use general and recreation-related skills while engaging in activities and experiences of choice.

Identifying Content and Process

Once therapeutic recreation specialists have determined with clients their goals, activities and approaches must be selected. Activity *content* refers to the specific activity or combination of activities and media (e.g., table games, sports, crafts, leisure education program, music, drama, dance) that will be used to address individual objectives.

In essence, content is what will be done. As described in the OLH-TR model (Wilhite et al., 1999), selected content should focus on domains of functioning that are high priority, (i.e., which support clients' efforts to achieve desired outcomes). Therapeutic recreation specialists select and sequence content so that identified outcomes will result (Carter et al., 1995). *Process* refers to the specific leadership interaction and intervention techniques that will be used, as well as the activity structure or format. In other words, process is "how" the content will be presented to clients.

Activities and approaches are selected that contribute to clients' objectives and reflect preferences and other personal and/or environmental characteristics. These activities and approaches should reflect best practices based on clinical experience and judgment, and research on outcomes of interventions (Rickerson and burlingame, 1998). Peterson and Stumbo (2000) state that content and process should also produce the desired result (effectiveness) with the least expenditure of time, energy, or resources (efficiency).

Analyzing Activities

As the individual program planning process unfolds, therapeutic recreation specialists must analyze potential activities to determine what activity characteristics contribute to the accomplishment of clients' objectives and help to optimize personal and environmental resources. Activity analysis reveals why an experience is likely to result in the desired benefits for particular clients and how it will enable clients to pursue their chosen life and leisure pursuits (Austin, 1999; Wilhite et al., 1999). Although activity analysis is conducted independent of clients (i.e., without a specific individual or need in mind), it identifies what abilities are necessary for successful participation.

To engage in activities requires action in at least three behavioral areas—cognitive, affective, and physical—and may also involve social and spiritual areas. When analyzing the cognitive aspects of activities, therapeutic recreation specialists should consider required academic skills, such as reading, math, and spelling, as well as such things as the type and amount of memory required, and degree of concentration and/or strategy involved.

Analysis of affective aspects should take into account the various emotional responses likely to be stimulated by the activity (Peterson and Stumbo, 2000). Does the activity have the potential to relieve stress, allow the participant to communicate feelings, or promote creativity? Are characteristics of the activity fun, stimulating, or exciting? Does frustration commonly arise from engaging in the activity?

When analyzing the physical aspects of activities, therapeutic recreation specialists might determine the type of manipulative movement involved, the degree of mobility or the level of exertion and endurance required. Various types of sensory demands (e.g., sight, hearing, touch) inherent in the activity should be specified.

Examples of the social aspects of an activity that therapeutic recreation specialists might analyze include the degree of cooperation or competition and opportunities for interaction with individuals without disabilities and of the opposite sex. Determining the amount of communication required (i.e., vocal and nonvocal) and the general types of interactions that occur (e.g., contact with the environment, leaders, or others) will also help therapeutic recreation specialists understand social skills needed by clients to successfully participate in activities.

"Spiritual is defined as the animating or vital principle which gives life to physical organisms" (Brill, 1990, p. 21). Spiritual aspects of activities do not pertain just to a specific religion, although organized religion may provide a medium for expressing spirituality (Brill, 1990). These aspects of activities include the opportunity to care for others, to experience spiritual value in the aesthetic sense— beauty, awe, and grandeur—and to gain peace of mind. As activities are analyzed in the spiritual area, concepts of helplessness, control, perceived freedom, generativity, and reciprocity should be considered.

Selecting Activities

Once potential activities have been identified, the appropriateness of each selection must be determined. As previously discussed, this decision is influenced by the activity's potential contribution to clients' goals and objectives (desired changes), interests and abilities, and characteristics of their living environments. Clients' choices and preferences, however, are vital to the pursuit of enjoyable and meaningful participation, and therefore must be given top priority when selecting activities (Dattilo, 1994; Dattilo and Kleiber, 1993; Schleien, Meyer, Heyne, and Brandt, 1995; Wilhite et al., 1999).

Limitations of clients or their environment should not be the primary reason for rejection of an activity. To the contrary, recognizing limitations should include determining the need for, interest in, and ability to compensate for lost or diminished functional abilities and develop necessary participation skills. Personal skills and capabilities needed for participation in the activity of choice may be acquired through leisure education or skill development programs. Environments in which clients live, work, or recreate may be capable of supporting efforts to acquire and utilize recreation participation skills. If these conditions do not exist, the feasibility of personal and environmental compensatory efforts or adaptations can be explored and determined before making activity selections.

Some clients may not readily indicate their personal preferences and interests. In such situations, it may be necessary to encourage participation in a wide variety of activities that contribute to clients' goals and objectives so that, over time, therapeutic recreation specialists may rank individual preferences from most to least favorite activities. Opportunities for making choices and for cultivating choice-making abilities must be systematically provided and taught to some individuals, particularly those who have significant disabilities (Dattilo and Rusch, 1985; Schleien, Ray, and Green, 1997).

Schleien and colleagues (1995) provided additional insight regarding selection of activities. According to these authors, it is helpful when activity selections are also valued and supported by people with whom clients come into contact. The activity's appeal and adaptability to people without disabilities, family members, and other caregivers should be considered.

In addition, Schleien and colleagues (1995) suggested that therapeutic recreation specialists and clients should consider how participation skills can extend beyond a specific, highly structured recreation activity and setting to an environment more closely approximating naturally occurring leisure opportunities. "For an activity to be functional, a person must be able to perform under a range of conditions" (Wilcox and Bellamy, 1987, p. 64). Therefore, emphasis should be placed on developing a variety of transferable competencies and establishing opportunities for clients to practice newly acquired skills in a number of different settings. For example, participating in a painting class in a special recreation program could expand in a variety of ways, such as painting as a hobby, or painting a set for a community theater.

Modifying Activities

To facilitate clients' participation in activities, therapeutic recreation specialists and clients may have to make modifications that involve individual, programmatic, or environmental changes that will reduce, eliminate, or compensate for barriers. Therapeutic recreation specialists and clients should work together to develop activity adaptations and modifications. For example, therapeutic recreation specialists may simply ask:

- How can you best do this?
- What would allow you to perform this more easily?
  or
- How does this feel?

These adaptations should be individualized and designed to highlight clients' abilities rather than disabilities.

Activities can be modified in several ways (Dattilo, 1994, 1999; Howe-Murphy and Charboneau, 1987; Project LIFE, 1988; Schleien et al., 1995; Schleien et al., 1997). The *materials* or *equipment* might be modified. In addition to homemade equipment and devices, commercially marketed items are available.

Technological adaptations have increased access to participation in recreation activities for many individuals (Broach, Dattilo, and Deavours, 2000; Crouse and Deavours, 1993). For example, the introduction of microswitch technology has enabled individuals with severe or multiple disabilities to demonstrate more choice and control in leisure environments. Microswitches provide increased access to electronic equipment, battery-operated toys, computers, musical instruments, communication devices, card shufflers, and even popcorn poppers (Crouse and Deavours, 1993; York and Rainforth, 1995). "Activation mode options for microswitches vary greatly from simple touch pressure to eye blinking, to sound or breath" (York and Rainforth, 1995, p. 128). Additionally, technological innovations including lightweight wheelchairs, all-terrain wheelchairs, monoskis, and handcycles have increased access to participation in a variety of recreation activities (Smith, 1995).

The activity could also be modified by changing *procedures and/ or rules*. Clients may sit or walk rather than stand or run. Additional trials (e.g., strikes, throws, or misses) may be permitted and extra players may be added. Playing dimensions (e.g., size of court, height of net or basket) may be altered as well. Clients can also be challenged to design their own procedures and rules, thus creating new activities.

Therapeutic recreation specialists can change the way *activities are introduced and presented*. For example, they can use simple rather than complex words, suggest physical prompts, offer guidance, demonstrate the task, and emphasize more than one sense (touch, sight, hearing, etc.). *Lead-up activities* can be used to prepare clients for full participation in an original activity (Schleien et al., 1997). For example, kickball, Wiffle ball, and/or the use of a batting tee can be lead-up activities to prepare clients for participation in softball. Participating with a leisure partner/advocate can lead to participating with a friend or independent access (Rynders and Fahnestock, 1997).

The *environment* in which an activity takes place may a require modification. For example, accessible parking, ram drinking fountains, and toilets may be needed, as well as lifts, grab bars, nonslip and nonabrasive floor surfaces, level play areas, adequate lighting, and reduced background noise.

Selecting Specific Interventions

Intervention techniques may be used to bring about desired client outcomes. Peterson and Stumbo (2000) pointed out that the intervention strategy should be chosen in light of clients' characteristics, objectives, program content, and therapeutic recreation specialists' abilities to use the techniques. It is common practice to use interventions with a group of clients based on disability characteristics that imply similar needs (Stumbo, 1996). No one approach will be appropriate for all clients, however. Therapeutic recreation specialists should strive, therefore, to develop proficiency in a variety of techniques. Several of many intervention techniques are discussed.

Behavior management is based on learning theory and involves the systematic use of various strategies and techniques to alter observable and measurable client behaviors. Clients' behaviors may be considered a problem, and thus targeted for change, if they occur too often, not often enough, or inappropriately (e.g., in the wrong place or at the wrong time). Accordingly, therapeutic recreation specialists may wish to decrease, increase, or change certain behaviors. When clients' behaviors are considered appropriate, maintaining these behaviors should be emphasized.

A variety of behavioral techniques may increase desired behaviors. For example, a behavioral or contingency contract is a written agreement between a therapeutic recreation specialist wishing to change a behavior and the client whose behavior is to be changed. The contract specifies the required behavior and the consequence(s) contingent on the performance of the required behavior. Token economy, another example of a behavioral technique, is a reinforcement system in which tokens are earned when previously defined behaviors are performed. The tokens have no specific value, but may be exchanged for rewards such as objects, activities, and privileges. Additional techniques, such as task analysis and skill sequencing, verbal cuing, and physical prompting are briefly discussed in other chapters of the text.

Sensory stimulation utilizes various activities to improve one's perception and interpretation of stimuli, thus maintaining sensoristasis: "the level of sensory information necessary for alertness and normal brain functioning" (Buettner and Martin, 1995). Sensory stimulation is directed toward all five senses, and includes kinesthetic awareness, tactile stimulation, smelling, listening, tasting, and visual activities (Davis and White, 1995). Sensory stimulation has been used extensively with clients who have severe or profound mental retardation, clients who have brain injuries, and clients with dementia (Wilhite, Keller, Gaudet, and Buettner, 1999).

Remotivation, resocialization, and *reality orientation* are intervention techniques often used with a variety of clients such as older adults who are disoriented, individuals who have brain injuries, and people who are in transition to community settings. Remotivation and resocialization approaches promote renewal of interests and establishment of relationships through group interaction. Remotivation group sessions follow a structured five-phase process centered around a chosen theme (Dennis, 1994). Resocialization group sessions are less structured than remotivation groups and encourage awareness of self and others. In reality orientation, clients are continually oriented to basic personal and current information including time, place, names, events of the day, and things in the environment. To be most successful, reality orientation is highly structured and continually presented through environmental management, teaching/training, and consistent involvement of family and staff members (Bowlby, 1993; Wilson, 1994).

Therapeutic recreation specialists are increasingly using *relaxation* and *visualization techniques* to reduce stress. One of the most popular techniques is progressive muscle relaxation (Jacobson, 1974), in which the individual alternately relaxes and tenses each major muscle group, thereby achieving a feeling of deep relaxation. Other relaxation techniques may include deep abdominal breathing, meditation, hatha yoga, t'ai chi ch'uan, biofeedback, and imagery (Allsop and Dattilo, 2000; Catalano and Hardin, 1996; Davis, Eschelman, and McKay, 1995; Malley and Dattilo, 2000). Often, these various techniques are used in combination.

Interactions with others can be a source of considerable stress. *Assertiveness training* is an attempt to reduce stress by teaching more effective coping techniques. It is believed that the assertive person is more relaxed in interpersonal situations. Assertiveness training has been found to be an effective approach for dealing with depression, anger, resentment, and interpersonal anxiety (Davis et al., 1995).

Evidence supports the idea that contact with animals may enhance the quality of life of humans (Dattilo, Born, and Cory, 2000). Psychological, physical, social, and behavioral benefits have been achieved for older adults, people with physical disabilities, people at risk for cardiovascular disease or those who have experienced heart attacks, and adolescents with few familial resources who engage in animal-assisted therapy (Wilson and Turner, 1998). *Animal-assisted therapy* is a goal-directed intervention in which an animal meeting specific criteria is used in an integral aspect of treatment (Delta Society, 1996). For example, Bernard (1995) reported using animals to assist with upper extremity exercise for clients who had experienced strokes or head injuries in order to increase strength, endurance, respiratory status, and independence in activities of daily living. Burch (1995) used animals as a contingent reinforcer to decrease tantrums in young children with behavioral problems. Animal-assisted activities provide opportunities for motivational, informational, and/or recreational benefits to enhance quality of life (Delta Society, 1996). Therapeutic recreation specialists may deliver animal-assisted activities and therapy, or they may recruit, train, and monitor their own group of volunteers and schedule their and the animals' interactions with the clients (Boldt and

Dellmann-Jenkins, 1992). In either case, volunteers and animals must be properly trained and screened (Delta Society, 1996).

Aquatic therapy uses swimming and exercise activity in the water to achieve treatment as well as education and recreation participation goals (Austin, 1999; Beaudouin and Keller, 1994; Broach and Dattilo, 1996, 2000). A variety of physiological and psychosocial benefits of aquatic therapy have been asserted, including increased strength, endurance, range of motion, decreased pain and depression, and enhanced mood and body image (Austin, 1999; Beaudouin and Keller, 1994; Broach and Dattilo, 1996, 2000; Broach, Groff, and Dattilo, 1997). Structured methods such as Bad Ragaz, Watsu, or Halliwick (Boyle, 1981; Campion, 1990) may be used, as well as simple stretching, toning, flexibility, and endurance exercises (Beaudouin and Keller, 1994; Broach and Dattilo, 1996, 2000). An added advantage of aquatic therapy is that it helps clients develop interest and skills in a lifelong recreation/leisure activity, thus facilitating continued participation (Broach and Dattilo, 1996; Broach et al., 1997). Austin (1999) pointed out that due to the popularity and success of aquatic therapy, "turf battles" concerning who should provide it have increased. Aquatic therapy workshops and training programs abound and are usually marketed to physical therapists, occupational therapists, therapeutic recreation specialists, and others. It is likely that a variety of professionals will continue to provide aquatic therapy (Austin, 1999).

Activities included in *adventure therapy* may range from extended wilderness experiences, initiative games, low and high ropes courses, and long-term residential camping to single "high adventure" activities such as rock climbing, caving, snow skiing, and kayaking. Important characteristics of these various adventure therapy activities are based in experiential learning principles, including active engagement, immersion in new, unfamiliar, and unique situations, eustress (the healthy use of stress or challenge which leads to a valuable climate for changing dysfunctional behaviors), and team or group development (Anderson, Schleien, McAvoy, Lais, and Seligman, 1997; Gass, 1993a; Groff and Dattilo, 2000; Kimball and Bacon, 1993; Witman and Preskenis, 1996). As in the therapeutic recreation process, clients are viewed as agents for their own change and assume increasing responsibility for these desired changes as the experience progresses (Austin, 1999).

In addition to commonly held beliefs about the therapeutic potential of wilderness and the importance of challenge, a key to the success of adventure therapy programs is the use of metaphors to frame the adventure therapy experience as well as to facilitate transfer of learning. Generally, activities are "framed" around specific behavioral and psychological issues with a focus on changing dysfunctional behaviors and facilitating growth and positive development (Gillis and Simpson, 1992). Adventure therapy experiences become metaphors for challenges in clients' daily lives and home environments. For example, a long hike with heavy packs may create a metaphor for interdependence and healthy social functioning (Kimball and Bacon, 1993). Being blindfolded and participating in the *maze* activity (a maze of ropes connected in and around a group of trees at the waist level of participants) may serve as a metaphor for the obstacles that a person may encounter when trying to attain a chemical-free lifestyle (Gass, 1993b). The well-known *spider's web* initiative (a rope tied and crisscrossed between two fixed poles or trees allowing enough usable space for each participant to make it through one of the openings created by the crossed ropes) can serve as a metaphor for following rules and confronting broken rules (Mathias, 1995). Whitewater river rafting may help individuals who are newly disabled focus on potentialities and adopt an "If I can do this, I can do anything!" attitude toward their rehabilitation and reintegration in daily life.

Sports and fitness opportunities for and including people with disabilities have increased tremendously (Dattilo, Loy, and Keeney, 2000; Wilhite, Adams Mushett, and Calloway, 1996). Wankel and Berger (1991) identified four main benefits of sport and physical activity: personal enjoyment, personal growth (including physical and psychological well-being), social harmony (including socialization and community integration), and social change (including educational attainment and social status). These authors pointed out, however, that the realization of these outcomes is contingent upon participation in an appropriate program, structured and directed by goals relevant to these desired benefits.

Historically, the physical, psychological, and sociocultural benefits of sports and fitness activities resulted in their inclusion in therapeutic recreation programs (Wilhite et al., 1996). More recently, the original "rehabilitation through sport" purpose has given way to sport, fitness, and competition for their own sake (DePauw and Gavron, 1995). Therapeutic recreation specialists continue to be expected to play an integral part in the development of sports and fitness opportunities by introducing clients to sports and physical activity and providing leisure education and recreation participation opportunities. Therapeutic recreation specialists may also assist in developing adaptive equipment and techniques; organizing education, training, and competition opportunities; developing sports technical rules; training officials and classifiers; and managing/ coaching (Wilhite et al., 1996).

As community recreation and parks programs downsize, therapeutic recreation specialists, both in institutional and community-based settings, are challenged further to ensure that opportunities exist for people with disabilities to develop both fitness and sports skills and participate in recreational as well as elite sports. Additionally, therapeutic recreation specialists are discovering a key role in the promotion of access to all types of recreation and leisure experiences for persons with disabilities.

Developing a Written Plan

The written individual therapeutic recreation program plan, a "visible manifestation of the intervention process" (Howe-Murphy and Charboneau, 1987, p. 215), is a way of assuring and documenting that quality appropriate services are being delivered (Carter et al., 1995; Kraus and Shank, 1992; Stumbo, 1996). Documentation, the recordkeeping process associated with individual program planning, is essential for noting client progress, maintaining appropriate intervention techniques, and accounting for outcome achievement.

In comprehensive individual program plans, the services of different disciplines, including therapeutic recreation, are integrated, and a designated staff member is responsible for monitoring the plan and serving as primary advocate for a client. These care plans may be referred to as Individualized Treatment Plans (ITPs), Individualized Habilitation Plans (IHPs), or Individualized Service Plans (ISPs) depending on the setting. Generally individualized program plans are developed by an interdisciplinary team involving staff who evaluate and deliver services to clients. Involvement of clients and their families is considered essential to this process. These plans are reviewed regularly by team members to ensure appropriate integrated coordinated services are continued.

In some facilities, critical or clinical pathways are being used in place of care plans (burlingame and Skalko, 1997; Landrum et al., 1995; Rickerson and burlingame, 1998). Although approaches may vary, critical pathways used in this manner typically include not only the plan of care (i.e., pathway events and tasks), but also documentation information, expected outcomes, and variances (Askins and Groff, 1997; burlingame and Skalko, 1997; Rath and Page, 1996). Variances are deviations from the clients' pathway that can alter the length of stay, resource utilization, or expected outcomes (Rath and Page, 1996). Rath and Page reported that variances may be caused by factors related to clients or families, staff involved in caregiving, deviations in the specific care setting, and deviations in clients' home or community setting. Variances require that an explanation be provided along with a plan for returning to the expected pathway events and tasks (Rickerson and burlingame, 1998). "Evaluating variances provides the framework for continuous quality improvement" (Rickerson and burlingame, 1998, p. 215).

In addition to the comprehensive individual program plan developed by an interdisciplinary team, personnel in each service area, such as therapeutic recreation, may develop and maintain a separate, detailed individual program plan (Kraus and Shank, 1992). The individual therapeutic recreation program plan includes the outcomes or goals established with a client (including those relating to discharge), measurable objectives that relate to the goals, activity content and leadership methods that will be utilized to achieve selected goals, anticipated time frame for accomplishment of goals, and time intervals at which outcomes will be reviewed.

The individual therapeutic recreation program plan can be written in a format known as SOAP. Utilizing the SOAP format, a written plan would include:

- **S**ubjective assessment information,
- **O**bjective assessment information,
- **A**ssessment from the specialist of the client's problems, and
- **P**lan for ameliorating the problems.

Some therapeutic recreation specialists add a fifth component to this format:

- **E**valuation

to create the acronym SOAPE. In the evaluation component, therapeutic recreation specialists identify information sources necessary to determine goal attainment and reporting strategies. Other formats that may be used include PIE and DAP. Using PIE, written plans include:

- **P**roblems,
- **I**ntervention, and
- **E**valuation of the intervention's effectiveness (Rath and Page, 1996).

Therapeutic recreation professionals in some settings use the DAP approach to developing plans. DAP includes:

- **D**escription of the problems,
- **A**ssessment or conclusion concerning the problems, and a
- **P**lan for ameliorating the problems.

Summary

This chapter has focused on procedures relating to therapeutic recreation individual program planning phases. Once desired client changes are identified and short-term and long-term goals relating to these changes are formulated, then a written plan for accomplishing expected outcomes is designed. This individual plan includes the selection of specific activities (content) and leadership approaches (process) that will be used to accomplish objectives. The delineation of short- and long-term goals constitutes the basis for documenting and evaluating individual progress toward and eventual accomplishment of ultimate or overall goals.

The individual assessment and planning phases discussed in chapters one and two have provided the basis for implementing the individualized therapeutic recreation program. Program implementation is discussed in chapter three, *Implementing Individual Therapeutic Recreation Program Plans.*

Bibliography

Allsop, J. A., and Dattilo, J. (2000). Therapeutic use of t'ai chi ch'uan. In J. Dattilo (Ed.), *Facilitation techniques in therapeutic recreation* (pp. 245–272). State College, PA: Venture Publishing, Inc.

Anderson, L., Schleien, S. J., McAvoy, L., Lais, G., and Seligmann, D. (1997). Creating positive change through an integrated outdoor adventure program. *Therapeutic Recreation Journal, 31*(4), 214–229.

Askins, J., and Groff, D. (1997, October). *Clinical paths: The future of rehabilitation documentation.* Session presented at the annual meeting of the National Recreation and Park Association, Salt Lake City, UT.

Atchley, R. (1989). A continuity theory of normal aging. *The Gerontologist, 29,* 183–190.

Austin, D. R. (1996). Introduction and overview. In D. R. Austin and M. E. Crawford (Eds.), *Therapeutic recreation: An introduction* (2nd ed.) (pp. 1–21). Needham Heights, MA: Allyn & Bacon.

Austin, D. R. (1998). The health protection/health promotion model. *Therapeutic Recreation Journal 32*(2), 109–117.

Austin, D. R. (1999). *Therapeutic recreation: Process and techniques* (4th ed.). Champaign, IL: Sagamore.

Austin, D. R., and Crawford, M. E. (Eds.). (1996). *Therapeutic recreation: An introduction* (2nd ed.). Needham Heights, MA: Allyn & Bacon.

Avedon, E. M. (1974). *Therapeutic recreation service: An applied behavioral science approach.* Englewood Cliffs, NJ: Prentice-Hall.

Ball, E. L. (1970). The meaning of therapeutic recreation. *Therapeutic Recreation Journal, 4*(1), 17–18.

Baltes, P. B., and Baltes, M. M. (1990). Selective optimization with compensation. In P. B. Baltes and M. M. Baltes (Eds.), *Successful aging: Perspectives from the behavioral sciences* (pp. 1-34). New York, NY: Cambridge University.

Bateson, M. C. (1990). *Composing a life.* New York, NY: Plume.

Beaudouin, N. M., and Keller, M. J. (1994). Aquatic-solutions: A continuum of services for individuals with physical disabilities in the community. *Therapeutic Recreation Journal, 28*(4), 193–202.

Bernard, S. (1995). *Animal-assisted therapy: A guide for health-care professionals and volunteers.* Whitehouse, TX: Therapet L. L. C.

Blum, W. (1992). Chronic illness and disability in adolescence. *Journal of Adolescent Health, 13*, 364–368.

Boldt, M. A., and Dellmann-Jenkins, M. (1992). The impact of companion animals in later life and considerations for practice. *Journal of Applied Gerontology, 11*, 228–239.

Bowlby, C. (1993). *Therapeutic activities with persons disabled by Alzheimer's disease and related disorders*. Gaithersburg, MD: Aspen.

Boyle, A. (1981). The Bad Ragaz ring method. *Physiotherapy, 67*, 265–268.

Brill, N. (1990). *Working with people: The helping process* (4th ed.). White Plains, NY: Longman.

Broach, E., and Dattilo, J. (1996). Aquatic therapy: A viable therapeutic recreation intervention. *Therapeutic Recreation Journal, 30*(3), 213–229.

Broach, E., and Dattilo, J. (2000). Aquatic therapy. In J. Dattilo (Ed.), *Facilitation techniques in therapeutic recreation* (pp. 65–98). State College, PA: Venture Publishing, Inc.

Broach, E., Dattilo, J., and Deavours, M. (2000). Assistive technology. In J. Dattilo (Ed.), *Facilitation techniques in therapeutic recreation* (pp. 99–132). State College, PA: Venture Publishing, Inc.

Broach, E., Groff, D., and Dattilo, J. (1997). Effects of an aquatic therapy swimming program on adults with spinal cord injuries. *Therapeutic Recreation Journal, 31*(3), 160–173.

Buettner, L., and Martin, S. L. (1995). *Therapeutic recreation in the nursing home*. State College, PA: Venture Publishing, Inc.

Burch, M. R. (1995). The role of pets in therapeutic programmes: Animal-assisted therapy. In I. Robinson (Ed.), *The Waltham book of human-animal interaction: Benefits and responsibilities of pet ownership* (pp. 57–60). Oxford, UK: Pergamon/Kidlington.

burlingame, j., and Skalko, T. K. (1997). *Idyll Arbor's glossary for therapists*. Ravensdale, WA: Idyll Arbor.

Campion, M. R. (1990). *Adult hydrotherapy*. Oxford, UK: Heinemann Medical Books.

Carter, M. J., Van Andel, G. E., and Robb, G. M. (1995). *Therapeutic recreation: A practical approach* (2nd ed.). Prospect Heights, IL: Waveland Press.

Catalano, E. M., and Hardin, K. (1996). *The chronic pain control workbook* (2nd ed.). New York, NY: MJF Books.

Coyle, C. P. (1998). Integrating service delivery and outcomes: A practice model for the future? *Therapeutic Recreation Journal, 32*(3), 194–201.

Coyle, C. P., Kinney, W. B., Riley, B., and Shank, J. W. (1991). *Benefits of therapeutic recreation: A consensus view*. Ravensdale, WA: Idyll Arbor.

Crawford, M. E., and Mendell, R. (1987). *Therapeutic recreation and adapted physical activities for mentally retarded individuals.* Englewood Cliffs, NJ: Prentice Hall.

Crouse, J., and Deavours, M. N. (1993). Switch technology in therapeutic recreation programming. *Palasetra, 9*(4), 41–44.

Dattilo, J. (1994). *Inclusive leisure services: Responding to the rights of people with disabilities*. State College, PA: Venture Publishing, Inc.

Dattilo, J. (1999). *Leisure education program planning: A systematic approach* (2nd ed.). State College, PA: Venture Publishing, Inc.

Dattilo, J., Born, E., and Cory, L. (2000). Therapeutic use of animals. In J. Dattilo (Ed.), *Facilitation techniques in therapeutic recreation* (pp. 327–354). State College, PA: Venture Publishing, Inc.

Dattilo, J., and Kleiber, D. A. (1993). Psychological perspectives for therapeutic recreation research: The psychology of enjoyment. In M. J. Malkin and C. Z. Howe (Eds.), *Research in therapeutic recreation: Concepts and methods* (pp. 57–76). State College, PA: Venture Publishing, Inc.

Dattilo, J., Kleiber, D., and Williams, R. (1998). Self-determination and enjoyment enhancement: A psychologically-based service delivery model for therapeutic recreation. *Therapeutic Recreation Journal, 32*(4), 258–271.

Dattilo, J., Loy, D., and Keeney, R. (2000). Therapeutic use of sports. In J. Dattilo (Ed.), *Facilitation techniques in therapeutic recreation* (pp. 439–476). State College, PA: Venture Publishing, Inc.

Dattilo, J., and Rusch, F. (1985). Effects of choice on behavior. Leisure participation for persons with severe handicaps. *Journal of the Association for Persons with Severe Handicaps, 11*, 194–199.

Davis, A. E., and White, J. J. (1995). Innovative sensory input for the comatose brain-injured patient. *Critical Care Nursing Clinics of North America, 7*(2), 351–361.

Davis, M., Eshelman, E., and McKay, M. (1995). *The relaxation and stress reduction workbook* (4th ed.). Oakland, CA: New Harbinger.

Delta Society (1996). *Standards of practice for animal-assisted activities and animal-assisted therapy* (2nd ed.). Renton, WA: Author.

Dennis, H. (1994). Remotivation groups. In I. Burnside and M. G. Schmidt (Eds.), *Working with older adults: Group process and techniques* (pp. 153–162). Boston, MA: Jones and Bartlett.

DePauw, K. P., and Gavron, S. J. (1995). *Disability and sport.* Champaign, IL: Human Kinetics.

Frye, V., and Peters, M. (1972). *Therapeutic recreation: Its theory, philosophy, and practice.* Harrisburg, PA: Stackpole Books.

Gass, M. A. (1993a). Foundations of adventure therapy. In M. A. Gass (Ed.), *Adventure therapy: Therapeutic applications of adventure programming* (pp. 3–10). Dubuque, IA: Kendall/Hunt.

Gass, M. A. (1993b). Enhancing metaphor development in adventure therapy programs. In M. A. Gass (Ed.), *Adventure therapy: Therapeutic applications of adventure programming* (pp. 245– 258). Dubuque, IA: Kendall/Hunt.

Gerber, L. (1994/95). Keynote address for the first annual ATRA research institute. *Annual in Therapeutic Recreation, 5*, 1–4.

Gilligan, C. (1982). *In a different voice*. Boston, MA: Harvard University.

Gillis, H. L., and Simpson, C. (1992). Project Choices: Adventure-based residential drug treatment for court referred youth. *Journal of Addictions and Offender Counseling, 12*, 12–27.

Groff, D., and Dattilo, J. (2000). Adventure therapy. In J. Dattilo (Ed.), *Facilitation techniques in therapeutic recreation* (pp. 13–40). State College, PA: Venture Publishing, Inc.

Gruver, B. M. (1993/94). Theories and models: An heuristic analysis of therapeutic recreation practice. *Annual in Therapeutic Recreation, 4*, 1–10.

Gunn, S. L., and Peterson, C. A. (1978). *Therapeutic recreation program design: Principles and procedures*. Englewood Cliffs, NJ: Prentice Hall.

Howe-Murphy, R., and Charboneau, B. G. (1987). *Therapeutic recreation intervention: An ecological perspective*. Englewood Cliffs, NJ: Prentice Hall.

Howe-Murphy, R., and Halberg, K. (1987). Evolution of a philosophy in therapeutic recreation: An essential and continual quest. *Therapeutic Recreation Journal, 21*(2), 79–80.

Jacobson, E. (1974). *Progressive relaxation*. Chicago, IL: The University of Chicago Press, Midway Reprint.

Kelly, J. R. (1996). *Leisure* (3rd ed.). Needham Heights, MA: Allyn & Bacon.

Kimball, R. O., and Bacon, S. B. (1993). The wilderness challenge model. In M. A. Gass (Ed.), *Adventure therapy: Therapeutic applications of adventure programming* (pp. 11–41). Dubuque, IA: Kendall/Hunt.

Kraus, R., and Shank, J. (1992). *Therapeutic recreation service: Principles and practices* (4th ed.). Dubuque, IA: Wm. C. Brown.

Landrum, P. K., Schmidt, N. D., and McLean, A. (1995). *Outcome-oriented rehabilitation: Principles, strategies, and tools for effective program management.* Gaithersburg, MD: Aspen.

Malley, S., and Dattilo, J. (2000). Stress management. In J. Dattilo (Ed.), *Facilitation techniques in therapeutic recreation* (pp. 215–244). State College, PA: Venture Publishing, Inc.

Mathias, N. B. (1995). The spider's web as a metaphor for rules and confronting broken rules. In M. A. Gass (Ed.), *Book of metaphors, volume II* (pp. 182–183). Dubuque, IA: Kendall/Hunt.

Melcher, S. (1999). *Introduction to writing goals and objectives: A manual for recreation therapy students and entry-level professionals.* State College, PA: Venture Publishing, Inc.

Mobily, K. (1985). A philosophical analysis of therapeutic recreation: What does it mean to say, "We can be therapeutic?" Part I. *Therapeutic Recreation Journal, 19*(1), 14–26.

Mobily, K. (1996). Therapeutic recreation philosophy revisited: A question of what leisure is good for. In C. Sylvester (Ed.), *Philosophy of therapeutic recreation: Ideas and issues, volume II* (pp. 57–70). Arlington, VA: National Recreation and Park Association.

O'Morrow, G. S., and Reynolds, R. P. (1989). *Therapeutic recreation: A helping profession* (3rd ed.). Englewood Cliffs, NJ: Prentice Hall.

Peterson, C. A., and Stumbo, N. J. (2000). *Therapeutic recreation program design: Principles and procedures* (3rd ed.). Englewood Cliffs, NJ: Prentice Hall.

Project LIFE. (1988). *LIFE forms, the LIFE training guide.* Chapel Hill, NC: Project LIFE, Curriculum in Leisure Studies and Recreation Administration, University of North Carolina at Chapel Hill.

Rath, K. V., and Page, G. (1996). *Understanding financing and reimbursement issues*. Arlington, VA: National Recreation and Park Association.

Rickerson, N., and burlingame, j. (1998). Healthcare delivery systems. In F. Brasile, T. K. Skalko, and j. burlingame (Eds.), *Perspectives in recreational therapy: Issues of a dynamic profession* (pp. 205–220). Ravensdale, WA: Idyll Arbor.

Russoniello, C. (1997). Behavioral medicine: A model for therapeutic recreation. In D. M. Compton (Ed.), *Issues in therapeutic recreation: Toward the new millennium* (pp. 461–487). Champaign, IL: Sagamore.

Rynders, J. E., and Fahnestock, M. K. (1997). Intervention strategies for inclusive recreation. In S. J. Schleien, M. T. Ray, and F. P. Green, *Community recreation and people with disabilities: Strategies for inclusion* (pp. 101–128). Baltimore, MD: Brookes.

Schleien, S. J., Meyer, L. H., Heyne, L. A., and Brandt, B. B. (1995). *Lifelong leisure skills and lifestyles for persons with developmental disabilities*. Baltimore, MD: Brookes.

Schleien, S. J., Ray, M. T., and Green, F. P. (1997). *Community recreation and people with disabilities: Strategies for inclusion*. Baltimore, MD: Brookes.

Shank, J. W., Coyle, C. P., Boyd, R., and Kinney, W. B. (1996). A classification scheme for therapeutic recreation research grounded in the rehabilitative sciences. *Therapeutic Recreation Journal, 30*(3), 179–196.

Shank, J. W., Kinney, W. B., and Coyle, C. P. (1993). Efficacy studies in therapeutic recreation research: The need, the state of the art, and future implications. In M. J. Malkin and C. Z. Howe (Eds.), *Research in therapeutic recreation: Concepts and methods* (pp. 301–335). State College, PA: Venture Publishing, Inc.

Shank, P. A. (1987). Therapeutic recreation philosophy: A state of cacophony. In C. Sylvester, J. L. Hemingway, R. Howe-Murphy,

K. Mobily, and P. A. Shank (Eds.), *Philosophy of therapeutic recreation: Ideas and issues* (pp. 27–40). Alexandria, VA: National Recreation and Park Association.

Smith, R. W. (1995). Trends in therapeutic recreation. *Parks and Recreation, 30*(5), 66–71.

Smith, R. W., Austin, D. R., and Kennedy, D. W. (1996). *Special recreation: Opportunities for persons with disabilities* (3rd ed.). Dubuque, IA: Wm. C. Brown.

Stumbo, N. J. (1996). A proposed accountability model for therapeutic recreation services. *Therapeutic Recreation Journal, 30*(4), 246–259.

Stumbo, N. J., and Peterson, C. A. (1998). The leisurability model. *Therapeutic Recreation Journal, 32*(2), 82–96.

Sylvester, C. (1987). Therapeutic recreation and the end of leisure. In C. Sylvester, J. L. Hemingway, R. Howe-Murphy, K. Mobily, and P. A. Shank (Eds.), *Philosophy of therapeutic recreation: Ideas and issues* (pp. 76–89). Alexandria, VA: National Recreation and Park Association.

Sylvester, C. (1994/95). Critical theory, therapeutic recreation, and health care reform: An instructive example of critical thinking. *Annual in Therapeutic Recreation, 5,* 94-109.

Sylvester, C. (1996). Instrumental rationality and therapeutic recreation: Revisiting the issue of means and ends. In C. Sylvester (Ed.), *Philosophy of therapeutic recreation: Ideas and issues, volume II* (pp. 92–105). Arlington, VA: National Recreation and Park Association.

Van Andel, G. E. (1998). TR service delivery and TR outcome models. *Therapeutic Recreation Journal, 32*(3), 180–193.

Voelkl, J., Carruthers, C., and Hawkins, B. A. (1997). Special series on therapeutic recreation practice models: Guest editors' introductory comments. *Therapeutic Recreation Journal, 31*(4), 210–212.

Wankel, L. M., and Berger, B. G. (1991). Personal and social benefits of sport and physical activity. In B. L. Driver, P. J. Brown, and G. L. Peterson (Eds.), *Benefits of leisure* (pp. 121–144). State College, PA: Venture Publishing, Inc.

Widmer, M., and Ellis, G. D. (1997). Facilitating the good life through therapeutic recreation. In D. M. Compton (Ed.), *Issues in therapeutic recreation: Toward the new millennium* (2nd ed.) (pp. 173–191). Champaign, IL: Sagamore.

Widmer, M. A., and Ellis, G. D. (1998). The Aristotelian good life model: Integration of values into therapeutic recreation services delivery. *Therapeutic Recreation Journal, 32*(4), 290–302.

Wilcox, B., and Bellamy, G. T. (1987). *The activities catalog: An alternative curriculum for youth and adults with severe disabilities.* Baltimore, MD: Brookes.

Wilhite, B., Adams Mushett, C., and Calloway, J. (1996). Sport and disability across the lifespan: Introduction to the special issue. *Therapeutic Recreation Journal, 30*(2), 106–113.

Wilhite, B., Keller, M. J., and Caldwell, L. (1999). Optimizing lifelong health and well-being: A health enhancing model of therapeutic recreation. *Therapeutic Recreation Journal, 33*(2), 98–108.

Wilhite, B., Keller, M. J., Gaudet, G., and Buettner, L. (1999). The efficacy of sensory stimulation with older adults with dementia-related cognitive impairments. *Annual in Therapeutic Recreation, 8,* 43–55.

Wilson, E. M. (1994). Reality orientation groups. In I. Burnside and M. G. Schmidt (Eds.), *Working with older adults: Group process and techniques* (pp. 139–152). Boston, MA: Jones and Bartlett.

Wilson, C. C., and Turner, D. C. (Eds.). (1998). *Companion animals in human health.* Thousand Oaks, CA: Sage.

Witman, J., and Preskenis, K. (1996). Adventure programming with an individual who has multiple personality disorder: A case history. *Therapeutic Recreation Journal, 30*(4), 289–296.

York, J., and Rainforth, B. (1995). Enhancing leisure participation by individuals with significant intellectual and physical disabilities. In S. J. Schleien, L. H. Meyer, L. A. Heyne, and B. B. Brandt, *Lifelong leisure skills and lifestyles for persons with developmental disabilities* (pp. 113–131). Baltimore, MD: Brookes.

CASE 1 - CRAWFORD CORRECTIONAL INSTITUTE

A large, well-established correctional facility can be viewed as a reflection of current "free world" communities in microcosm. All of the structural mainstays of the community can be found within its program format. The formal correctional community structure arises from the following areas: business in the form of correction industries and daily operation services provided by inmate work details, medical and dental services including an infirmary with a full medical staff, religious services provided by chaplaincy and volunteers, counseling and mental health services including a panel of psychiatrists and psychologists, education and trades provided by the education department, and recreational activities provided by the recreation department.

Crawford Correctional Institute (CCI) is a maximum security prison. It houses approximately 1,000 male inmates. The majority of these inmates are serving their second or third term of incarceration. The median age for this population is 35 years, but there are significant groups of 20–25 year olds and inmates over the age of 45. The average academic level completed is the sixth grade, and the average reading level ranges from the fourth to the eighth grade.

Approximately 250–280 of the inmates are housed in forensic or mental health living units. One of the units contains 25 beds allocated to crisis intervention. These beds can be operated on a 24 hour per day, lockdown status.

One hundred to 150 of the 280 inmates function in the low to moderate levels in activities of daily living. At any given time, 20–30 of these inmates are placed on unit restriction due to their mental health status. These inmates must have recreation services delivered in their unit's day room or small yard for at least one hour per day.

Diagnoses common to this population include schizophrenia, polysubstance abuse, bipolar disorder, post status brain injury from trauma and/or substance abuse, post traumatic stress disorder, mental retardation, antisocial personality disorder, and borderline personality disorder.

A review of individual case histories and formal therapeutic recreation assessments indicated the following data. Psychosocial deficits common to this population include increased impulsivity, decreased frustration tolerance, decreased interpersonal skills, social withdrawal, decreased activity levels, a limited recreational skills repertoire, unclear or inappropriate leisure values, decreased problem-solving and decision-making skills, and increased stress levels with decreased stress management skills.

A small portion of this population has physical disabilities such as decreased mobility and visual impairment. Also included in this group are persons experiencing extended infirmary stays due to temporary or chronic illness.

The recreation department is composed of a director, two activity therapists, and three recreation supervisors. The director is responsible for personnel management and administrative management of the department.

The activity therapists are responsible for assessing inmates, documenting progress, and participating in treatment team meetings. They are also responsible for planning and implementing programs for the general population as well as mental health inmates. Activity therapists also provide adapted recreation services for inmates in the infirmary on the basis of physician referral.

The recreation supervisors are responsible for implementing programs for general population inmates. They also manage the inmate work detail which performs maintenance on the recreation department's physical resources.

The department currently manages and maintains many areas within the prison. These areas include a large athletic field with a two-lane track, a gymnasium with a full basketball court, billiard room, music room (with band instruments), arts and crafts room, classroom with TV/VCR and stereo, game room, and a large greenhouse with adjacent garden area.

The facility maintains a library for inmate and staff use. It offers a wide selection of books including a full legal library. The library also maintains a selection of audio-visual and teaching resources.

Funds for the maintenance and provision of recreational resources are derived from a combination of sources. The largest portion of the recreation operations budget is generated from inmate contributions. For example, profits made from inmate purchases at the inmate store and inmate phone calls made through a private carrier system are used to support recreation. The department also receives a small quarterly allotment of state monies for the purchase of administrative resources and for staff continuing education.

The recreation department regularly offers seasonal intramural sports such as softball, volleyball, basketball, and flag football. The department also offers quarterly educational classes. Themes for these classes include stress and anger management, team-building activities, a therapeutic process group with a focus on music, therapeutic horticulture group, a therapeutic humor group, art, and drama. The department sponsors music groups that cover gospel, rap, rhythm and blues, and country and western. Special events are typically offered around yearly holidays.

Higher functioning mental health inmates are integrated in regular recreation programming as often as possible. Adapted classes and group activities are offered to the lower functioning inmates as stepping stones for future integration into general population programming.

Discussion Questions

1. How do you feel about the treatment of convicted felons? How does the public view this population and your involvement with it?

2. Society often views correctional facilities as inmate country clubs with many recreational resources. Hence, legislators have responded with the "get tough on crime" approach. This philosophy often calls for the removal of recreation services from these facilities. Should correctional facilities continue to provide general recreation and therapeutic recreation services to inmates? If so, why? What behavioral statistics can be used as a basis for your argument?

3. Imagine you are a new CTRS at CCI. There has not been a CTRS working in the institution for approximately two years. The CTRS carries an average caseload of 250 inmates.

   a. What steps would you take to establish a therapeutic recreation program?

   b. What general outcomes would be appropriate for these inmates: general population inmates, inmates with mental health needs, and inmates with physical disabilities? Why?

   c. What special considerations, if any, should be taken when programming for this population?

   d. What types of programming would be most effective with large caseloads?

   e. How would you recruit volunteers to work with this population?

4. Recent federal and state mandates have required prisons to remove weightlifting equipment, a major form of inmate recreation. How would you diffuse the tension created by this situation? What activities would you offer as a substitute? Complete a task analysis of weightlifting and the substitute activity you suggested and compare and contrast the two activities and their inherent characteristics.

5. Consider the age range and ethnic and racial backgrounds of inmates at CCI. Discuss how this may impact program design and activity selection.

In-Class Exercises

Hold a debate as to why and why not public resources should be spent on recreation services and equipment in correctional facilities. Possibly, ask several local elected officials to comment on the debate and share their conclusions after it.

Field Experiences

1. CTRSs can be found working in state and federal correctional facilities. Contact a CTRS at a facility near you and schedule an on-site visit. Please note: In some cases paperwork must be submitted prior to your visit. Remember to allow time for it to be processed. Check with the CTRS for appropriate clothing for your visit and ask what personal articles may be carried inside the institution. During the visit, interview one or two inmates regarding their recreation needs and activities while incarcerated.

2. If you are unable to schedule a visit to a correctional facility, invite a CTRS who has worked with this population to speak in class.

3. If you are interested in working with this population, contact your state or federal personnel agency. Remember that the qualifying process for employment candidacy for these agencies can take an extended period of time.

Selected References for Case Study

American Correctional Association. [Online]. Available: http://www.corrections.com/aca

Austin, D. R., and Crawford, M. E. (Eds.). (1996). *Therapeutic recreation: An introduction.* Englewood Cliffs, NJ: Prentice Hall.

Bell, R., and Cooney, M. (1993). Sporting chances. *Nursing Times, 89*(43), 62–63.

Dallao, M. (1996). Changing the rules of recidivism through recreation. *Corrections Today, 58*(1), 80, 101.

Little, S. (1995). Research on recreation in correctional settings. *Parks and Recreation, 30*(2), 20, 22, 24–27.

Mayfield, S. (1992). Quality assurance and continuous quality improvement: Tools for assessing "quality" in therapeutic recreation settings. In R. M. Winslow, and K. J. Halberg (Eds.), *The management of therapeutic recreation services* (pp. 137–162). Arlington, VA: National Recreation and Park Association.

McCall, G. E. (1996). Corrections and social deviance. In D. R. Austin and M. E. Crawford (Eds.), *Therapeutic recreation: An introduction* (pp. 78–94). Englewood Cliffs, NJ: Prentice Hall.

Munson, W. (1991). Juvenile delinquency as a societal problem and social disability: The therapeutic recreator's role as ecological change agent. *Therapeutic Recreation Journal, 25*(3), 19–28.

Nikkel, R. E. (1994). Areas of skill training for persons with mental illness and substance use disorders: Building skill for successful community living. *Community Mental Health Journal, 30*(1), 61–72.

Peterson, C. A., and Stumbo, N. J. (1999). *Therapeutic recreation program design: Principles and procedures* (3rd ed.). Needham Heights, MA: Allyn & Bacon.

Strength Tech. [On-line]. Available: http://www.strengthtech.com

Stumbo, N., and Bloom, C. (1990). The implications of traumatic brain injury for therapeutic recreation services in rehabilitation settings. *Therapeutic Recreation Journal, 24*(3), 64–79.

Tofig, D. (1997, August 4). Jail: Rough road—or easy street? Amenities important, prison officials say. *The Hartford Courant,* p. A1. [On-line]. Available: http://www.strengthtech.com/correct/issues/mediais/hartford.htm

Wankel, L., and Berger, B. (1990). The psychological and social benefits of sport and physical activity. *Journal of Leisure Research,* 22(2), 167–182.

Audiovisual Resources

Individual Program Planning. [videotape]. Available from Indiana University, Department of Recreation and Park Administration, HPER Building, Room 133, Bloomington, IN 47405-4711.

CASE 2 - ANTHONY CALDWELL

Anthony Caldwell is a 37-year-old, single, African American male referred to a psychiatric forensic facility from the department of corrections. Anthony's criminal offense was first degree murder, and he is serving a life sentence. He was transferred to the forensic facility because he was hostile, uncooperative, and displayed poor judgment and a lack of impulse control. Anthony also reported that he believed that his victim "set him up by pretending to be dead." Since admission, Anthony has been generally cooperative; however, he often projects hostility. He responds to social contact with brief responses.

Anthony reports that he completed the 11th grade. He has difficulty reading and completing single mathematical computations equivalent to the second grade level. His ability to express himself is functional but remains a barrier. Reports indicate that he attended special education classes, and his diagnosis also indicates that he is functioning in the mild mental retardation range. This condition has been exacerbated by chronic substance abuse. Anthony reports that he was employed in 1979 as a gardener for a local university and also for a housing complex.

Anthony has an extensive history of violence toward women. During his stay at the department of corrections, he received disciplinary actions for attempting to trip an officer and for being involved in a physical altercation with another inmate.

Anthony's history of polysubstance abuse dates back to age nine, when he inhaled paint and glue, and this later evolved into using amphetamines, Valium, cocaine, marijuana, PCP, and alcohol. In the past, he attended both Alcoholics Anonymous and Narcotics Anonymous support groups, but denies that he has problems with drugs or alcohol.

During therapeutic recreation groups, Anthony presented difficulties in both interpersonal and task skills. His interactions were disorganized, and he had difficulty following directions. He expressed emotions inappropriately and at unusual times. When asked to participate in activities requiring him to complete a simple task, he required continual prompting to do so, or did not participate at all. Anthony responded well to verbal reinforcement in the past. Currently, he requires supervision to ensure his own safety and to attain his basic needs.

Discussion Questions

1. Given that Anthony's next dispositional setting will again be the department of corrections, identify the specific skills he will need to learn and the general behavioral domains they represent to help him achieve optimal functioning in that setting.
2. In order to ensure that Anthony is achieving basic functional skills, what measurable outcomes would you develop?
3. What compensatory strategies might Anthony require in order to optimize his involvement in recreation and leisure experiences?
4. How would you help Anthony recognize and take responsibility for the contributing factors that necessitated his admission? Keep in mind that Anthony responds well to positive reinforcement.
5. Do notions of prevention and health promotion apply in Anthony's situation? Explain your answer.

In-Class Exercises

List and prioritize Anthony's strengths, areas of need, and interests. Identify which professional(s) or discipline(s) are most appropriate to address each area of need. Are areas of co-treatment apparent? Discuss how you can use Anthony's strengths and interests to help address his needs.

Role-Playing

One student assumes the role of Anthony and another of the CTRS. Demonstrate the approach you will use to involve a fearful, suspicious, and paranoid individual in the process of determining relevant goals and developing an individual program plan.

Field Experiences

Invite a CTRS or another professional from a forensic mental health facility to class. Ask him or her to consider the issues of safe environments, prison stressors, and returning individuals back to previous environments. What are some of the ethical dilemmas? What are the ethical responsibilities of the CTRS in a psychiatric forensic facility?

Selected References for Case Study

American Correctional Association. [On-line]. Available: http://www.corrections.com/aca

Bacrach, L. L. (1992). Psychosocial rehabilitation and psychiatry in the care of long-term patients. *American Journal of Psychiatry, 149*(11), 1455–1463.

James, M., and Townsley, R. (1989). Activity therapy services and chemical dependency rehabilitation. *Journal of Alcohol and Drug Education, 34*(3), 48–53.

Krupa, T., Eastabrook, S., Blake, P., and Goering P. (1992). Lessons learned: Introducing psychiatric rehabilitation in a multidisciplinary hospital. *Psychosocial Rehabilitation Journal, 15*(3), 29–36.

Liberman, R. P., Kopelowicq, S., and Young, A. (1994) Biobehavioral treatment and rehabilitation of schizophrenia. *Behavior Therapy, 25,* 89–108.

Liberman, R. P., Wallace, C. J., Blackwell, B., Eckman, T. A., Vacrro, J. V., and Kuehnel, T. G. (1993). Innovations in skills training for the seriously mentally ill: The UCLA social and independent living skills modules. *Innovations and Research, 2*(2), 43–58.

Linhorst, D. M. (1995). Implementing psychosocial rehabilitation in long-term inpatient psychiatric facilities. *The Journal of Mental Health Administration, 22*(1), 58–67.

McFarlane, N., Keogh Hoss, M. A., Jacobson, J. M., and James, A. (1998). *Finding the path: Ethics in action.* Hattiesburg, MS: American Therapeutic Recreation Association.

CASE 3 - TO LOOK AT HER YOU'D NEVER KNOW

If you were to look at Caroline, you would see a 30- to 40-something, intelligent, well-educated White female, who works in a high-stress, but highly paid and regarded profession. She appears to be confident and successful. To look at her, you'd never know that less than twelve months ago, she was preliminarily diagnosed by her primary care physician (PCP) as anxious and probably depressed, and then referred to a psychiatrist. This is her story.

After keeping her thoughts to herself for two to three weeks, Caroline finally confided in her husband. She told him that she felt so overwhelmed and out of control that the only way out seemed to be to kill herself and that she was afraid that she might do so. Caroline knew that her husband, as a strong Catholic, was totally opposed to suicide. So she knowingly reached out to him as a lifeline. He was alarmed but supportive, and immediately encouraged Caroline to see her PCP.

While continuing with her work and home life and awaiting her first appointment with the psychiatrist, Caroline was given a complete physical examination to rule out an organic or physical etiology. Then she saw her PCP for about 45 minutes, once a week for a month of monitoring, counseling, and support. Her PCP also gave her a referral for crisis counseling through a 24-hour mental health emergency unit in case it was needed.

Caroline began taking prescription antianxiety medication and stomach acid reducers (Zoloft, Aventyl, and Buspar). She continued to jog, but much less frequently. She totally dropped her other main recreation activities— avidly collecting music and reading mysteries.

After four weeks passed, it was time for Caroline's first appointment with the psychiatrist, Dr. Kincaid. Dr. Kincaid used both psychotherapy and psychotropic medications with her patients. At their biweekly sessions, some of Dr. Kincaid's questions and topics of conversation were the same as the PCP's. However, others were different and Caroline surmised that it was the different questions (and her responses to them) that led Dr. Kincaid to a primary diagnosis of major depressive disorder with associated anxiety. Although she knew better, Caroline felt that depression was caused more by weakness or needy behavior than anxiety.

Particularly revealing was Dr. Kincaid's detailed probing of Caroline's family history. Among Caroline's great-grandparents, there were instances of physical and verbal abuse, alcoholism, and excessive worrying. Among her grandparents, there were cases of alcoholism, worrying, and suicide. In her parents, there were again instances of alcoholism, panic attacks, and depression. Among her siblings and their spouses, the study revealed antisocial behavior, alcoholism, and unwed pregnancies. The family stories were sketchy and only mentioned by some members of the current generation of siblings and some parents. Sometimes the stories would be recollected, recounted, and laughed off as indicative of being the "Black Irish." At other times, the stories were recounted in the hushed tones associated with those who had the stigma of insanity in the family.

In addition to the suicidal ideations, Caroline's continuing symptoms included anhedonia, difficulty sustaining concentration, dramatic weight loss, fatigue, feelings of failure and inadequacy, and feeling stressed, overwhelmed and out of control. She also had gastrointestinal problems that did not respond to medication, insomnia, loss of self-confidence, social withdrawal, and what she described as painful feelings of electricity or electrical charges going through her upper body and limbs, especially in the early hours of the morning. Caroline called this time the "night morning," and stated that she hated being awake at 3:00 a.m. or 4:00 a.m. when it's still dark. Further, she dreaded the arrival of late fall when the days would be even shorter.

Caroline's work as a trial lawyer and senior partner definitely had stress and deadlines associated with it. Leaving work was not an option; the income from both Caroline and her husband was necessary in order to be comfortable, since they had recently received sole custody of his two teenaged children from a previous marriage. There was stress associated with role change, ambiguity about being a stepparent, and some adolescent-stepparent conflict even though she knew that it was natural and to be expected.

During the months that Caroline was seeing Dr. Kincaid, no one at her law practice knew how ill she was. She chose to tell her partners and associates that she was just stressed out, much like they all were, and having some stomach problems as a result of that. Eventually, she cut back a little by delegating, prioritizing, and narrowing her focus, as suggested by her psychiatrist. However, even with antidepressant and antianxiety medications, Caroline continued to feel depressed and anxious.

Caroline was additionally referred by Dr. Kincaid to group therapy at the Glacier Ridge Outpatient Mental Health Center (GROMHC). The five women in the group were of very similar ages, backgrounds, and diagnoses. This group was cofacilitated by a psychiatric nurse practitioner and a CTRS named Adrian.

The nurse practitioner and Adrian recognized that depression is one of the most common and treatable mental illnesses. They noted that at GROMHC they were seeing depression with anxiety among more and more women in their middle years who were homemakers, career women, or both. Adrian reminded herself that she wanted to talk to Dr. Kincaid about hormones and menopause, thinking that perhaps they were related to what was occurring with the outpatients who had been in their groups lately.

Meanwhile, the nurse practitioner and Adrian collaborated on their written subjective assessment information, objective assessment data, psychiatric and therapeutic recreation assessments about Caroline's problems, plan for addressing the problems, and plan to evaluate the outcomes of the treatment.

Depression affects people's feelings, thoughts, behavior, and physical condition. Therefore, Adrian knew that in the program plan she would need to address all of the behavioral domains: cognitive, physical, social, affective, and spiritual. Adrian wanted to enable Caroline to begin to make some lifestyle changes that could lead her to return to doing things that she enjoyed.

Discussion Questions

1. Review the descriptions of depression and anxiety in the *Diagnostic and Statistical Manual of Mental Disorders* (4th ed.). Based on the information available and her symptoms, discuss the appropriateness of Caroline's diagnosis.

2. Now that you know more about mood disorders, what might be some tentative explanations for Caroline's "electrical charges" symptom? (Hint: Check into paresthesia and panic disorder.)

3. Given Caroline's family history, medications, and participation in psychotherapy, to what extent should her spouse and stepchildren be included in her treatment?

4. Adrian alluded to an interest in hormones or menopause as related to the specific symptoms of depres-

sion and anxiety experienced by Caro'
cohorts. Might this be a useful avenu
if so, how should Adrian proceed?

In-Class Exercises

1. As Adrian, your job is to develop an individual
therapeutic recreation program plan for Caroline.
Begin this process by writing up and presenting the
following:
   a. Identification of the problems in each of the
   patient's behavioral domains.
   b. Identification of her strengths and interests.
   c. Short-term and long-term goals based on the
   analysis of problems and strengths or interests.
   d. Specific content and a process to meet the goals
   or at least impact the problems and facilitate the
   strengths.

2. Caroline shared in group that she felt very stressed
out, didn't feel very much joy, and wanted to recover
her zest and previously optimistic attitude toward
life. With this in mind, what program areas would be
valuable components of Caroline's therapeutic
recreation treatment plan? Why?

3. Based on the information you have about Caroline,
what activities would be appropriate for her to
engage in to address the problems you identified?
Why? Prepare an activity analysis for one of the
selected activities for Caroline.

4. The use of psychotropic medications with persons
with mental illness has remained an area of contro-
versy since the late 1950s. In one of four small
groups, using references from the literature, prepare
and present a position statement on one of the
following positions:
   a. Psychotropic medications are useful for relief of
   symptoms or immediate problems in order to get
   the patient comfortable enough to begin to
   resolve the deeper problems whether or not the
   patient continues on the medication long term.

b. Psychotropic medications mask symptoms, have side effects that are the leading cause of noncompliance, and don't encourage behavioral change or enduring personal empowerment of the patient.

c. Psychotropic medications, when used appropriately, have been shown to positively effect brain chemistry, specifically among persons with mood disorders.

d. Some other position on the use of psychotropic medications.

Be sure to have a literature-based rationale or justification for your position.

Field Experiences

1. Invite a member or speaker from a local mental health consumer organization to address the group about mental illness, neurobiological disorders, and/or depression.

2. Visit and speak with a CTRS who works with persons with mental illnesses on an outpatient basis. If permitted by the agency and the clients, follow the CTRS to observe what a day in the life of a CTRS is like in this setting. If not permitted, then discuss how program planning is accomplished. Also investigate whether or not a team approach is followed, the characteristics and behaviors of persons with mood disorders that are important for the CTRS to know, and the types of treatment and interventions that are used to improve clients' leisure functioning and quality of life.

Selected References for Case Study

American Psychiatric Association. (1994). *Diagnostic and statistical manual of mental disorders* (4th ed.). Washington, DC: Author.

Bullock, C. C., and Mahon, M. J. (1997). *Introduction to recreation services for people with disabilities: A person-centered approach*. Champaign, IL: Sagamore.

Copeland, M. E. (1994). Coping with... Dealing with depression and manic depression for people with mood disorders and those who love and support them. *Innovations and Research, 3*(4), 51–58.

Depression Resources List. [On-line]. Available: http:// www.execpc.com/~corbeau

Francell, E. G. (1994). Medication: The foundation of recovery. *Innovations and Research, 3(4),* 31–40.

Hickman, C. M. (1994). Leisure counseling and depressed women. In D. M. Compton and S. E. Iso-Ahola (Eds.), *Leisure and mental health, volume 1* (pp. 204–214). Park City, UT: Family Development Resources.

Kinney, J. S., and Kinney, W. B. (1996). Psychiatry and mental health. In D. R. Austin and M. E. Crawford (Eds.), *Therapeutic recreation: An introduction* (pp. 57–77). Englewood Cliffs, NJ: Prentice Hall.

Negley, S. K. (1994). Recreation therapy in an outpatient intervention. *Therapeutic Recreation Journal, 28*(1), 35–40.

Patrick, G. D. (1994). A role for leisure in treatment of depression. In D. M. Compton and S. E. Iso-Ahola (Eds.), *Leisure and mental health, volume 1* (pp. 175–190). Park City, UT: Family Development Resources.

Spaniol, L., and Koehler, M. (Eds.). (1994). *The experience of recovery.* Boston, MA: Center for Psychiatric Rehabilitation.

Audiovisual Resources

Freedom from Fear. (1994). *Depression and women: Dispelling the myths.* [videotape]. Available from Freedom from Fear, 308 Seaview Avenue, Staten Island, NY 10305.

Seligman, M. E. P. (Speaker). (1994). *What you can change and what you can't: The complete guide to self-improvement* [audio recording]. New York, NY: Simon & Schuster.

CASE 4 -

HAROLD AND SARAH WILSON

Harold Wilson, a 79-year-old African-American male with Alzheimer's disease (AD), and Sarah Wilson, his 76-year-old wife, were referred for assessment by their daughter. Mr. Wilson was diagnosed with AD four years ago when he started showing signs of confusion. Since that time, Mr. Wilson has become increasingly dependent on his wife. He currently requires 24-hour care. The couple has been living in their one-story home for 42 years.

The Wilson's daughter contacted the local Area Agency on Aging due to concern about her mother's health. Mrs. Wilson provides round-the-clock care for Mr. Wilson without any assistance. She is reluctant to allow in-home service providers to come into her home due to concern about the quality of care they provide. She only lets a family member stay with Mr. Wilson once a week while she goes to the store. For the Wilsons, financial constraints also are an issue related to in-home services, since the couple has limited financial resources and cannot afford to pay for services.

A case manager from the local Area Agency on Aging recently interviewed Mrs. Wilson and concluded that she is depressed. During the interview, Mrs. Wilson indicated that caregiving had become tremendously burdensome. She cried several times during the interview and indicated, "I never expected it would be like this." Mr. Wilson no longer recognized Mrs. Wilson all the time and sometimes would ask her, "Where's my wife?" He also was uncooperative with Mrs. Wilson. It was a struggle to get him to eat, take his medicine, get out of bed in the morning, and take out his teeth.

Mr. Wilson sleeps quite a bit during the day. He does not want to get up in the morning and usually goes right back to bed after eating breakfast. About 6:00 p.m. every evening, he starts telling Mrs. Wilson he wishes to go to bed. Mrs. Wilson tries to keep him up until at least 9:00 p.m. If she can do that, he will sleep for about five hours. Then he usually wakes up about every half hour and shakes Mrs. Wilson to wake her. She has tried sleeping in another room, but the last time she tried, Mr. Wilson arose and emptied the contents of his closet onto the floor. As a consequence, she is now afraid to sleep in the other room.

Mrs. Wilson leaves the couple's house once a week to go shopping. During that time, her son-in-law stays with Mr. Wilson and her daughter accompanies her to the store. Mr. Wilson has not left the house for over a year except to go to the doctor. Mrs. Wilson found it too exhausting to make arrangements to take him out at other times. A year ago, she sold the couple's car at the request of her daughter. Mrs. Wilson still is a competent driver; however, her daughter was concerned that Mr. Wilson would find the keys and try to leave.

Mrs. Wilson's doctor is concerned about the lack of respite she has from caregiving. Her blood pressure is dangerously high, and the doctor is fearful of her having a stroke. When Mrs. Wilson is asked about taking some time for herself, she indicates that she feels guilty for going out when she knows Mr. Wilson cannot.

Mrs. Wilson is adamant about not placing her husband in a nursing home. Several years ago, she promised her husband that she would never institutionalize him as long as she is "on her own two feet." The burden of providing 24-hour care has reduced Mrs. Wilson's quality of life and contributed to a decline in her physical and mental health. Currently, Mrs. Wilson's life is totally consumed by the caregiving role. She clearly could benefit from respite and leisure; however, she is reluctant to take time away from her husband due to the guilt she experiences and her belief that requesting assistance is a poor reflection on her ability to be a good wife. The case manager believes Mrs. Wilson could benefit from the services of a CTRS.

Discussion Questions

1. Identify the complexities of this case as they relate to program planning. How might you plan to address these issues, concerns, and circumstances?

2. What components of therapeutic recreation service seem most appropriate for Mrs. Wilson? Explain your answer.
3. Are there any therapeutic recreation services that could benefit both Mr. and Mrs. Wilson together?
4. Consider maintaining health and well-being in all aspects of life for the Wilsons. What areas of concern would you identify as a CTRS?

In-Class Exercises

1. What overall outcome would be appropriate for Mrs. Wilson? In relation to this global outcome, make a list of relevant long-term and short-term goals for Mrs. Wilson.
2. Based on the goals you identified in the previous question, determine what intervention activities and approaches will be used. Incorporate formal and informal support services in your ideas.
3. Create a list of social services agencies in your community that could be of some support to the Wilsons and their daughter. Identify at least five agencies or organizations and discuss how their services could support the Wilsons.

Field Experiences

1. Contact your local Area Agency on Aging or other service providers to determine what types of in-home services are available for caregivers in your community.
2. Locate public and private resources that provide recreation and leisure services for older adults.

Selected References for Case Study

Aronson, J. (1992). Women's sense of responsibility for the care of old people: "But who else is going to do it?" *Gender and Society,* 6(1), 8–29.

Bollin, S., Voelkl, J. E., and Lapidos, C. (1998). The at-home independence program: A recreation program implemented by a volunteer. *Therapeutic Recreation Journal, 32*(1), 54–61.

Butin, D. N. (1991). Helping those with dementia to live at home: An educational series for caregivers. *Physical and Occupational Therapy in Geriatrics, 9*(3/4), 69–82.

Caregiver's Resource Homepage. [On-line]. Available: http://www.caregiver911.com

Couper, D. P. (1989). *Aging and our families: Leader's guide to caregiver programs.* New York, NY: Human Sciences.

Deem, R. (1989). *All work and no play? The sociology of women and leisure.* Milton Keynes: UK: Open University.

Hagan, L. P., Green, F., and Starling, S. (1997/98). Addressing stress in caregivers of older adults through leisure education. *Annual in Therapeutic Recreation, 7,* 42–51.

Hughes, S., and Keller, M. J. (1992). Leisure education: A coping strategy for family caregivers. *Journal of Gerontological Social Work, 19*(1), 115–128.

Keller, M. J. (Ed.). (1999). Caregiving—Leisure and aging. [Special issue]. *Activities, Adaptation, and Aging, 24*(2).

Keller, M. J., and Hughes, S. (1991). The role of leisure education with family caregivers of persons with Alzheimer's disease and related disorders. *Annual in Therapeutic Recreation, 11,* 1–7.

Melcher, S. (1999). *Introduction to writing goals and objectives: A manual for recreation therapy students and entry-level professionals.* State College, PA: Venture Publishing, Inc.

Robinson, K. M. (1988). Social skills training program for adult caregivers. *Advances in Nursing Science, 10*(2), 59–72.

Rogers, N. B. (1999). Family obligation, caregiving, and loss of leisure: The experiences of three caregivers. *Activities, Adaptation, and Aging, 24*(2), 35–49.

Sommers, T., and Shields, L. (1987). *Women who take care: The consequences of caregiving in today's society.* Gainesville, FL: Triad.

Voelkl, J. (1998). The shared activities of older adults with dementia and their caregivers. *Therapeutic Recreation Journal, 32*(3), 231–239.

Audiovisual Resources

Individual Program Planning. [videotape]. Available from Indiana University Department of Recreation and Park Administration, HPER Building, Room 133, Bloomington, IN 47405-4771.

CASE 5 - MILDRED SUMMERS

You were introduced to Mildred Summers, a 90-year-old retired school teacher who lives alone, in chapter one, case 3 (page 32). Mrs. Summers has a variety of functional needs and has been receiving home health-care for about two years. She is also served by the Alzheimer's support network.

The home healthcare agency working with Mrs. Summers provides a range of services that allow her to remain safely at home with assistance in daily living, including medical needs, cooking, personal hygiene, transportation, companionship, rehabilitation, and aggressive support after surgery. The intent of these services is to access community and medical resources to promote as much independence, safety, and lifestyle satisfaction as possible. Following assessment, a coordinated care plan is generated. The assessment generally includes examination of prior medical records, complete physical, family involvement, and multidisciplinary evaluations. Indicators of referral include activities of daily living impairment, especially after age 70; cognitive impairment; living alone; absent or limited support system; repetitive emergency room visits; history of frequent falls;

caregiver and/or family stress; and noncompliance with healthcare needs.

In-Class Exercises

1. Develop a therapeutic recreation program plan for Mrs. Summers that includes appropriate therapeutic recreation assessments, long-term and short-term goals in each behavioral domain, and activity content and interventions. Discuss how you will incorporate her daughter in the design of the plan.
2. Select one of the activities you identified for Mrs. Summers and complete an activity analysis. Consider any modifications to the activity that may be needed to make it more effective with Mrs. Summers.

Role-Playing

1. Role-play an interdisciplinary team meeting with the daughter, Mrs. Summers, a social worker, a home healthcare aide or companion, and a CTRS.
2. Role-play an in-home conversation with the daughter and Mrs. Summers in which the CTRS recommends that therapeutic recreation be incorporated into the overall plan of care.

Selected References for Case Study

Austin, D. R. (1999). *Therapeutic recreation processes and techniques* (4th ed.). Champaign, IL: Sagamore.

Beattie, M. (1987). *Codependent no more*. New York, NY: Harper & Row.

Bollin, S., Voelkl, J. E., and Lapidos, C. (1998). The at-home independence program: A recreation program implemented by a volunteer. *Therapeutic Recreation Journal, 32*(1), 54–61.

Carter, M. J., Browne, S., LeConey, S. P., and Nagle, C. J. (1991). *Designing therapeutic recreation programs in the community.*

Reston, VA: American Alliance for Health, Physical Education, Recreation, and Dance.

Carter, M. J., Van Andel, G. E., and Robb, G. M. (1995). *Therapeutic recreation a practical approach* (2nd ed.). Prospect Heights, IL: Waveland.

Dychtwald, K., and Flower, J. (1990). *Age wave: The challenges and opportunities of an aging America*. New York, NY: Bantam Books.

Foret, C. M., and Keller, M. J. (1993). A society growing older: Its implications for leisure. *Leisure Today/JOPERD, 64*(4), 29–59.

Hawkins, B. A., May, M. E., and Rogers, N. B. (1996). *Therapeutic activity intervention with the elderly: Foundations and practices*. State College, PA: Venture Publishing, Inc.

Lewis, C. B. (1990). *Aging: The healthcare challenge* (2nd ed.). Philadelphia, PA: F. A. Davis Company.

Nissenboim, S., and Vroman, C. (1998). *The positive interactions program of activities for people with Alzheimer's disease*. Baltimore, MD: Health Professions.

Peterson, C. A., and Stumbo, N. J. (2000). *Therapeutic recreation program design: Principles and procedures* (3rd. ed). Needham Heights, MA: Allyn & Bacon.

Searle, M. S., Mahon, M. J., Iso-Ahola, S. E., Sdrolias, H. A., and van Dyck, J. (1995). Enhancing a sense of independence and psychological well-being among the elderly: A field experiment. *Journal of Leisure Research, 27*(2), 107–124.

Teague, M. L., and MacNeil, R. D. (1992). *Aging and leisure: Vitality in later life* (2nd ed.). Dubuque, IA: W. C. Brown & Benchmark.

Wilhite, B. (1992). In-home alternatives for community recreation participation by older adults. *Leisure Today/JOPERD, 63*(8), 44–46, 55–56.

Audiovisual Resources

Individual Program Planning. [videotape]. Available from Indiana University, Department of Recreation and Park Administration, HPER Building, Room 133, Bloomington, IN 47405-4711.

CASE 6 - SUSIE

As described in chapter one, case 4 (page 37), Susie is a nine-year-old female with Down syndrome living with her family in a small rural community. Services in this community are severely limited with access to integrated services only through public transportation to another distant rural school system. Both of Susie's parents work outside the home. For Susie to participate in recreation activities, her parents must provide transportation, but they are limited by their work schedules. Susie's leisure companion is her 13-year-old brother who is "missing out" on vacation and summer recreation time with children his age so that he can be her primary caregiver.

Discussion Questions

1. How could a CTRS intervene to introduce family leisure education?
2. What would be desirable outcomes of family leisure education within the context of a rural environment with limited recreation resources?
3. Knowing that Susie's social skills, such as compliance, attending, responding to commands, and carrying out assigned tasks, regress in the summer without the structure of the school environment, describe the outcomes of a social skills training program conducted during the school year by a CTRS. What would be the intent of incorporating family members into this program? How could the program be continued in the summer?
4. What alternatives are feasible to assist the family with transportation issues, e.g., no rural bus lines other than the school routes during the school year? How does this barrier impact the leisure patterns of the family as a whole?

In-Class Exercises

1. Develop appropriate individual education plan (IEP) goals based on Susie's interests.
2. Develop a coordinated IEP in which the CTRS works with the special educator, adaptive physical educator, speech therapist, and family members in developing year-round interventions using an outreach or in-home delivery model.
3. Design a social skills training program for families with special children that could be maintained and delivered in the home with consultation from a CTRS.
4. Create two or three activities that Susie and her brother can engage in together that could be meaningful to both. Perform an analysis of the activities and discuss modifications that could enhance the meaning of the activities to both individuals. Consider the goals or purposes of the activities.
5. Invite a CTRS working in a public school setting to talk about his or her role and duties in this setting. If possible, have this CTRS critique the following role-play with the class.

Role-Playing

Play the roles of the speech therapist, adapted physical educator, special educator(s), and CTRS in an IEP meeting in which goals and intervention strategies are identified for Susie and her family during the summer.

Selected References for Case Study

Bedini, L. A., and Bilbro, C. W. (1991). Caregivers, the hidden victims: Easing caregiver's burden through recreation and leisure services. *Annual in Therapeutic Recreation, 2*, 49–54.

Bedini, L. A., Bullock, C. C., and Driscoll, L. B. (1993). The effects of leisure education on factors contributing to the successful transition of students with mental retardation from school to adult life. *Therapeutic Recreation Journal, 27*(2), 70–82.

Bullock, C. C., and Morris, L. H. (1991). Responding to current needs—A community reintegration program. *Leisure Today/ JOPERD, 62*(4), 28–30.

Carter, M. J., Browne, S., LeConey, S. P., and Nagle, C. J. (1991). *Designing therapeutic recreation programs in the community.* Reston, VA: American Alliance for Health, Physical Education, Recreation, and Dance.

Carter, M. J., and Foret, C. M. (1994). Building transition bridges for the disabled. *Parks and Recreation, 29*(4), 78–83.

Dattilo, J. (1999). *Leisure education program planning: A systematic approach* (2nd ed.). State College, PA: Venture Publishing, Inc.

Dattilo, J., and Jekubovich-Fenton, N. (1995). Leisure services trends for people with mental retardation. *Parks and Recreation, 30*(5), 46–52.

Dattilo, J., and Light, J. (1993). Setting the stage for leisure: Encouraging reciprocal communication for people using augmentative and alternative communication systems through facilitator instruction. *Therapeutic Recreation Journal, 27*(3), 156–171.

Keller, M. J. (1992). The role of leisure education with family caregivers. *Leisure Today/JOPERD, 63*(8), 47–49, 56.

Kelly, J. R., and Kelly, J. (1994). Multiple dimensions of meaning in the domains of work, family, and leisure. *Journal of Leisure Research, 26*(3), 250–274.

Kurcinka, M. S. (1991). *Raising your spirited child.* New York, NY: Harper Perennial.

Mactavish, J., and Schleien, S. (1998). Playing together growing together: Parents' perspectives on the benefits of family recreation in families that include children with a developmental disability. *Therapeutic Recreation Journal, 32*(3), 207–230.

Monroe, J. E. (1987). Family leisure programming. *Therapeutic Recreation Journal, 21*(3), 44–51.

National Down Syndrome Society. [On-line]. Available: http://www.ndss.org

Nelson, D., Capple, M., and Adkins, D. (1995). Strengthening familes through recreation. *Parks and Recreation, 30*(6), 44–47.

Sable, J., Powell, L., and Aldrich, L. (1993/94). Transdisciplinary principles in the provision of therapeutic recreation services in inclusionary school settings. *Annual in Therapeutic Recreation, 4,* 69–81.

Smith, D. (1997). Strengthening family values in the twenty-first century—Home-centered recreation. *Leisure Today/JOPERD, 68*(8), 39–41.

Sneegas, J. J. (1989). Social skills: An integral component of leisure participation and therapeutic recreation services. *Therapeutic Recreation Journal, 23*(2), 30–40.

Stumbo, N. J. (1995). Social skills instruction through commercially available resources. *Therapeutic Recreation Journal, 29*(1), 30–55.

CASE 7 - RUTH AVERY

Ruth Avery, a 75-year-old widowed, African American female with a diagnosis of hypertension and senile dementia of the Alzheimer's type (AD) was introduced in chapter one, case 2 (page 28). She was referred for assessment to the CTRS by clinical staff. Prior to admission to a rural long-term care facility (LTC), Mrs. Avery was a food service manager in a large river city, loved to listen to music, and was an exceptional dancer. After retirement she became confused and began to report delusional thoughts about family members, often placing roles on others. She was first admitted to a psychiatric facility where she was diagnosed with AD. Her family physician placed her on Cognex, a drug in the Tacrine family, which is used for memory maintenance. She was discharged from the psychiatric facility and referred to the LTC facility. Results of the Brief Cognitive Rating Scale were moderately severe, indicating loss of concentration, and impairment of recent and past memory, orientation, functioning and self-care.

Mrs. Avery is living on the special care unit of the LTC facility. Treatment goals include cognitive and physical stimulation intended to help her maintain or increase her independence.

Discussion Questions

1. On the basis of information about this case provided here and in chapter one, develop long-term and short-term goals for Mrs. Avery.
2. Mrs. Avery sometimes has delusional thoughts. She will also verbalize aggression toward peers, occasionally striking them. What techniques might be used by the CTRS to manage Mrs. Avery's behavior? What techniques might be used to motivate Mrs. Avery to participate in therapeutic activities?
3. Describe special environmental supports or characteristics that may be needed by persons who live in congregate settings and have AD.

In-Class Exercises

Select an activity that may be held on a special care unit of a LTC facility. Analyze the activity and modify it so that Mrs. Avery could participate as fully as possible. After you have completed the activity analysis, consider leadership approaches that could be used to help Mrs. Avery engage successfully in the activity.

Role-Playing

Interview one person who has worked in a LTC facility for at least 10 years and ask about the changes that have occurred. Prepare and present a short skit illustrating "then and now."

Selected References for Case Study

Beck, C. K., and Shue, V. M. (1994). Interventions for treating disruptive behavior in demented elderly people. *Nursing Clinics of North America, 29*(1), 143–155.

Bourgeois, M. S. (1993). Effects of memory aids on the dyadic conversations of individuals with dementia. *Journal of Applied Behavior Analysis, 26*(1), 77–87.

Bowlby, C. (1993). *Therapeutic activities with persons disabled by Alzheimer's disease and related disorders.* Gaithersburg, MD: Aspen.

Buss, D. D. (1994). The legacy of Dr. Alzheimer. *Contemporary Long-Term Care, 17*(2), 42–46.

Creighton, C. (1992). The origin and evolution of activity analysis. *American Journal of Occupational Therapy, 46*(1), 45–48.

Gastel, B. (1994). *Working with your older patient: A clinician's handbook.* Bethesda, MD: National Institute on Aging, National Institutes of Health.

Gaudet, G., and Dattilo, J. (1994). Reacquisition of a recreation skill by adults with cognitive impairments: Implications to self-determination. *Therapeutic Recreation Journal, 28*(3), 118–132.

Hawkins, B. A., May, M. E., and Rogers, N. B. (1996). *Therapeutic activity intervention with the elderly: Foundations and practices.* State College, PA: Venture Publishing, Inc.

Health Care Financing Administration. (1998). *Sharing innovations in quality.* [On-line]. Available: http://www.hcfa.gov/medicaid.htm

Lundervold, D. A., and Lewin, L. M. (1992). *Behavioral analysis and therapy in nursing homes.* Springfield, IL: Charles C. Thomas.

Mace, N. L., and Rabins, P. V. (1991). *The thirty-six-hour day* (2nd ed.). Baltimore, MD: The Johns Hopkins University.

Melcher, S. (1999). *Introduction to writing goals and objectives: A manual for recreation therapy students and entry-level professionals.* State College, PA: Venture Publishing, Inc.

National Alzheimer's Association. [On-line]. Available: http://www.alz.org

O'Neill, R. E., Horner, R. H., Albin, R. W., Storey, K., and Sprague, J. R. (1990). *Functional analysis of problem behavior: A practical assessment guide.* Pacific Grove, CA: Brooks/Cole.

Therapeutic Recreation Directory—Activity and Treatment Ideas. [On-line]. Available: http://www.recreationtherapy.com/tractv.htm

Audiovisual Resources

The George Glenner Alzheimer's Family Centers, Inc. (1989). *Sharing the Caring II: A therapeutic activity training program for Alzheimer's patients.* [videotape]. Available from Alzheimer's Family Center, San Diego, CA.

CASE 8 - STELLA BARNES

Shady Shores is a 13-bed, privately owned, transitional care facility for older adults. Most of its residents consist of frail older adults who have been discharged from area hospitals after being treated for bone fractures and/or joint replacements. These individuals are admitted to Shady Shores due to the lack of family and/or social support that might aid in home recovery. The goal of Shady Shores is to offer a wide array of services to those older adults with recent physical disabilities in order to make the return home more successful. The average patient stay is about two weeks, depending on the individual's rate of healing. Shady Shores is conveniently located near many recreational opportunities, such as a YMCA, a library, bowling alley, mall, and senior center. Shady Shores is currently staffed by a doctor, several nurses, two case managers, an occupational therapist, a physical therapist, a CTRS, and a dozen direct contact employees. There are at least three direct contact staff and one nurse available 24 hours a day. Transportation is available through both the center and public vehicles. A team meeting is held within three days of a resident's admission to discuss appropriate program planning.

Stella Barnes is a 77-year-old White female who has just been admitted to Shady Shores following a recent fall that resulted in a left hip replacement operation. Mrs. Barnes's family and social support is relatively nonexistent. Her daughter is a single mother who lives in another state, and all of her friends either live with family members or are physically incapable of assisting her with her current needs.

Mrs. Barnes had always been relatively active in social and recreational activities until approximately two years ago, when she began to experience excessive fatigue, significant joint pain, and trouble sleeping. Due to her intense joint pain and constant fatigue, Mrs. Barnes began to withdraw from recreational and social activities. She began to overindulge in food and gain weight. Mrs. Barnes is currently 40 pounds over her ideal weight and has trouble standing for extended periods of time. After many tests, medications, and specialists, Mrs. Barnes was finally diagnosed with fibromyalgia, a recurring form of arthritis.

During her assessment, she expressed an interest in community action groups, water activities, board games, cross-stitch, and visiting her two grandchildren. Mrs. Barnes had been attending a local deep water aerobics class two times a week in order to improve her joint strength and range of motion. She felt this class was very beneficial to help manage her fibromyalgia. Prior to her fall, Mrs. Barnes also enjoyed gathering pecans to make pies for the neighbors, as well as sewing clothes for her grandchildren.

Due to the severity of Mrs. Barnes's injury and the lack of familial and/or social support, a length of stay of two to three weeks was determined. During this time her treatment team will focus on improving those skills nec-

essary for Mrs. Barnes to return home and remain as independent as possible. The members of Mrs. Barnes's
treatment team include a doctor, a nurse, a physical therapist, an occupational therapist, a CTRS, a dietitian, and
a case manager.

Discussion Questions

1. Identify and discuss the different characteristics of
   individuals with fibromyalgia.
2. What cognitive, physical, social, and affective
   aspects of fibromyalgia and hip replacement will
   influence the development of Mrs. Barnes's program
   plan?
3. What are the desired outcomes of Mrs. Barnes's
   therapeutic recreation intervention?
4. Discuss the benefits of water activities with older
   adults and persons with physical disabilities such as
   arthritis.

In-Class Exercises

1. Identify Mrs. Barnes's strengths, interests, and areas
   of need. How will her strengths and interests be used
   in developing an individual program plan?
2. Develop a long-term goal with measurable short-
   term goals to address one of Mrs. Barnes's identified
   needs.
3. Select and analyze an activity that could be of
   interest to Mrs. Barnes and that addresses the stated
   goals.
4. Discuss some possible activity modifications for
   Mrs. Barnes based on her interest in the activities
   mentioned in the case study.
5. Create a health maintenance goal for Mrs. Barnes
   after her discharge. Discuss the role of the CTRS in
   community referral and reintegration.

Field Experiences

1. Write a report or prepare a presentation regarding
   the implications of recreation for individuals with

fibromyalgia and/or hip replacement. Students must compile information from library research, Internet resources, and personal interviews.

2. Visit a local transitional care or assisted living facility to learn more about this setting.

Selected References for Case Study

Arthritis Foundation. (no date). *PACE: People with arthritis can exercise* [Brochure]. Author.

Arthritis Foundation. [On-line]. Available: http://www.arthritis.org

Austin, D. R. (1999). *Therapeutic recreation: Process and techniques* (4th ed.). Champaign, IL, Sagamore.

Bickelew, S. P., Murray, S. E., Hewett, J. E., and Johnson, J. (1995). Self-efficacy, pain, and physical activity among fibromyalgia subjects. *Arthritis Care and Research, 8*(1), 43–50.

Birkel, D. (1998). Activities of the older adult: Integration of the body and mind. *Journal of Physical Education, Recreation, and Dance, 69*(9), 23–28.

Brandon, L. (1999). Promoting physically active lifestyles in older adults. *Journal of Physical Education, Recreation, and Dance, 70*(6), 34–37.

Broach, E., and Dattilo, J. (2000). Aquatic therapy. In J. Dattilo (Ed.), *Facilitation techniques in therapeutic recreation* (pp. 65–98). State College, PA: Venture Publishing, Inc.

Lovell, T., Dattilo, J., and Jekubovich, N. (1996). Effects of leisure education on individuals aging with disabilities. *Activities, Adaptations and Aging, 21*(2), 37–58.

Melcher, S. (1999). *Introduction to writing goals and objectives: A manual for recreation therapy students and entry-level professionals.* State College, PA: Venture Publishing, Inc.

Minor, M. A. (1991). Physical activity and management of arthritis. *Analysis of Behavioral Medicine, 13*(3), 117–124.

Peterson, C. A., and Stumbo, N. J. (2000). *Therapeutic recreation program design: Principles and procedures* (3rd ed.). Needham Heights, MA: Allyn & Bacon.

Rimmer, J. H. (1994). *Fitness and rehabilitation programs for special populations.* Dubuque, IA: Brown & Benchmark.

Schleien, S. J., Germ, P. A., and McAvoy, L. H. (1996). Inclusive community leisure services: Recommended professional practices and barriers encountered. *Therapeutic Recreation Journal, 30*(4), 260–273.

Smith, R. W., Austin, D. R., and Kennedy, D. W. (1996). *Inclusive and special recreation: Opportunities for persons with disabilities* (3rd ed.). Dubuque, IA: Brown & Benchmark.

CASE 9 - THERAPEUTIC RECREATION ACTIVITY CLUB

The Therapeutic Recreation Activity Club is an after school program for 10–15 participants, ages 6–22, with disabilities. Participants attend daily and meet after school from 3:00 p.m. to 6:00 p.m. at a recreation center operated by the city. A CTRS is responsible for programming and supervising the program. Five of the participants are described below.

Mattie is a 15-year-old White female with aggressive conduct disorder and mild to moderate mental retardation. She is very active and physically fit. She enjoys arts and crafts and playing with a younger participant who is more disabled than herself. Mattie often gets frustrated when staff give other children one-to-one attention. She is a truancy risk and when angry, may become violent. She currently takes Clondine and lithium. Her parents want her to be able to secure and maintain a job and become more independent.

Tommy is a 13-year-old White male with early onset schizophrenia, undifferentiated type. He began his off-and-on again involvement with state hospitals for evaluation, diagnosis, and placement at the age of four. He loves to play basketball and does so daily in the after school program. Occasionally, Tommy earns a "privilege" and is allowed to stay in the recreation center and play basketball while the rest of the group goes outside to the park. He is compliant, although at times he can be verbally combative. He does not like to participate in arts and crafts, but will if made to do so. Tommy no longer wants to participate in the after-school program because he says he is not a "retard." He has recently been mainstreamed at school, and his classmates often tease him and call him retarded and stupid. Tommy currently takes 1,200 mg. of lithium and 2 mg. of Risperdal daily.

Tommy is verbally and physically abusive to his father and stepmother at home, and they are looking for an out-of-home placement (e.g., state institution, group home) for him. Tommy, unfortunately, is aware of their desire and often interrupts with stories of what his life will be like when he moves to his mother's house in California.

Ricky is a nonverbal, incontinent, 13-year-old African American male with static encephalopathy. Ricky functions at a three- to six-month-old cognitive developmental level. He can ambulate with maximum assistance from staff, but uses a wheelchair most of the time. He is unable to feed himself, but he is working on feeding at school. Ricky enjoys assisted walking, playing with certain toys, and watching movies.

Kyle is a 12-year-old White male with Wolf-Hirschorn Syndrome, 4p−, a chromosomal deficiency of the fourth strand on the p chromosome. Comparable to Down syndrome, individuals with 4p− have similar physical characteristics: large protruding eyes, cleft palate, limited pronation and supination of the wrists, smaller than average height and weight, mental retardation, and various developmental delays (e.g., walking, talking, toileting, self-feeding). Kyle is nonverbal. However, he is able to communicate via seven signs. He is ambulatory and is almost independent in feeding. Kyle enjoys being chased by staff and jumping on the trampoline. Kyle needs maximum assistance with fine-motor activities and dressing due to limited range of motion (ROM) in his wrists.

Miguel is a 13-year-old Hispanic male with mild to moderate mental retardation who has a tendency to take items out of the refrigerator or the garbage and eat them. Miguel thoroughly enjoys playing with Kyle, jumping on the trampoline, and participating in arts and crafts. He understands English fairly well, and is able to speak in broken sentences. When he does not want to participate in an activity or gets into trouble, he responds by stating, "I don't know."

Discussion Questions

You are the CTRS for the after-school program offered by the city. You are responsible for planning and leading the daily programs for the participants described above.

1. What should be the focus of the program?
2. What similar or common needs exhibited by these participants indicate the viability of using particular interventions. Identify the needs and the specific interventions.
3. Discuss the differences between chronological and developmental age and how both should be considered in program design and implementation. When planning activities, should you plan for the highest functioning, middle, or lowest functioning individual? How will you handle the differences in participants' ages?
4. Miguel returns from the rest room. He has an empty bag in his hand and is eating something. The CTRS asks, "What are you eating?" Miguel replies, "I don't know." The CTRS repeats his question much louder. Miguel repeats his response in the same tone and volume. The angry CTRS yells, "Spit it out." Miguel spits on him. How could this situation have

been handled differently? Considering the language barrier, is it possible Miguel did not understand what the CTRS was asking him to do? What techniques could be used by the CTRS to manage Miguel's eating behavior?

5. What techniques could be used when Mattie or Tommy refuse to participate in activities? When they become aggressive?

In-Class Exercises

1. For the following diagnoses, list the diagnostic features pertinent to this case:

   a. Aggressive conduct disorder.

   b. Mild to moderate mental retardation.

   c. Schizophrenia, undifferentiated type.

2. Select one of the three individuals with a diagnostic feature described in number 1. For this individual:

   a. Identify a problem that needs to be changed.

   b. Determine what outcome is desired (long-term goal).

   c. Develop one short-term goal (a step toward achieving the long-term goal).

   d. Identify the action the CTRS will take to help the participant achieve the short-term goal.

3. Develop a leisure education activity in which each of the above described individuals can participate.

4. Generate a list of activities that Kyle and the rest of the group could participate in that will improve ROM in Kyle's wrists and also benefit the rest of the participants. For one of the activities, complete an activity analysis and indicate if it is the "best" activity to improve ROM in Kyle's wrists.

5. Select an intervention technique about which you have some question, in the use of which you are inexperienced, whose validity you question, or whose use you do not understand. Present this technique in class, raising your questions and illustrating the technique by showing ways in which it can be used to achieve specific goals.

Role-Playing

One person assumes the role of Mattie (or Tommy) and another the CTRS. Act out how the CTRS can interact successfully with Mattie (or Tommy) before, during, and after she (or he) becomes aggressive. After the role-play, discuss what the CTRS did well and what the CTRS could do to improve interactions with Mattie (or Tommy).

Field Experiences

Visit an after-school program for persons with varying disabilities. Discuss programming goals and challenges with the CTRS. Discuss the role of parents and guardians in the program. Consider the benefits of segregated versus inclusive programs. Volunteer with the CTRS to learn more about the individuals with disabilities and therapeutic recreation.

Selected References for Case Study

American Psychiatric Association. (1994). *Diagnostic and statistical manual of mental disorders* (4th ed.). Washington, DC: Author.

burlingame, j., and Skalko, T. K. (1997). *Idyll Arbor's glossary for therapists.* Ravensdale, WA: Idyll Arbor.

Bullock, C. C., and Mahon, M. J. (1997). *Introduction to recreation services for people with disabilities: A person-centered approach.* Champaign, IL: Sagamore.

Dattilo, J. (1999). *Leisure education program planning: A systematic approach* (2nd ed.). State College, PA: Venture Publishing, Inc.

Dattilo, J., and Murphy, W. D. (1987). *Behavior modification in therapeutic recreation: An introductory learning manual.* State College, PA: Venture Publishing, Inc.

Hogberg, P., and Johnson, M. (1994). *Reference manual for writing rehabilitation therapy treatment plans.* State College, PA: Venture Publishing, Inc.

Peniston, L. C. (1998). *Developing recreation skills in persons with learning disabilities.* Champaign, IL: Sagamore.

Schleien, S. J., and Fahnestock, M. K. (1996). Severe multiple disabilities. In D. R. Austin and M. E. Crawford (Eds.), *Therapeutic recreation: An introduction* (pp. 153–183). Needham Heights, MA: Allyn & Bacon.

Schleien, S. J., Ray, M. T., and Green, F. P. (1997). *Community recreation and people with disabilities: Strategies for inclusion.* Baltimore, MD: Brookes.

Therapeutic Recreation Directory—Activity and Treatment Ideas. [On-line]. Available: http://www.recreationtherapy.com/tractv.htm

CASE 10 - KENJI

Kenji is an 11-year-old Japanese American male who is comatose secondary to a brain injury incurred in an automobile accident. Kenji is medically stable at an acute medical facility near his home. Within one week of his admission to this facility, Kenji had no response to verbal or tactile stimuli, but did respond to pain by withdrawal of bilateral lower and left upper extremities. His pupils were reactive to light but visual tracking was not present. Kenji was determined to be at Rancho Los Amigos Level of Cognitive Functioning II.

Kenji's parents were interviewed on the day of his admission by the social service worker to introduce them to the medical facility, assess Kenji's academic and social history, and begin discharge planning. Kenji's long-term rehabilitation outcome is discharge to his home with an academic program provided by the school district and with outpatient physical, occupational, speech, and recreational therapies as needed.

Although Kenji has been receiving a variety of therapies since his third day of admission, a decision was made to implement a more formalized sensory stimulation program. The purpose of this program is to facilitate neuronal reorganization by providing meaningful stimuli that will produce a response and decrease sensory deprivation.

Discussion Questions

1. Is sensory stimulation an appropriate intervention for Kenji? Why or why not?
2. What general considerations should be made in developing a sensory stimulation program for Kenji? (Consider, for example, social history, stimulation schedule, sensory hierarchies, documentation, family involvement, and so on.)
3. Why is it important to know about Kenji's preinjury activities and personality characteristics? Why would it be helpful to assemble a list of Kenji's favorite foods, musical preferences, television programs, hobbies, and so on?
4. Kenji's parents are first-generation Japanese, who moved to the United States when Kenji's father accepted a position with an automobile company. How might specific cultural characteristics influence the implementation of a sensory stimulation program?

In-Class Exercises

1. Outline a sensory stimulation program for Kenji and specify items that could be included in a personalized sensory stimulation kit. Identify specific items and techniques for tactile, kinesthetic, olfactory/gustatory, auditory, and visual stimulation.
2. Accurate documentation of stimulus and response is essential with this intervention. Develop a stimulation program documentation flow sheet that will facilitate documentation of Kenji's progress in the sensory stimulation program. Areas to consider include stimuli utilized, favorable responses to stimuli, and unfavorable responses to stimuli.

3. Describe the role that Kenji's family could play in the implementation of the sensory stimulation program. Do the same for staff members involved in the day-to-day care of Kenji. How can you ensure that all family members/staff are following the sensory stimulation schedule?
4. Make a list of all the key words you could use in an Internet search to learn more about brain injury and a person's ability to function. Using your list, conduct your search.

Selected References for Case Study

Brain Injury Association, Inc. [On-line]. Available: http://www. biausa.org

Davis, A. E., and White, J. J. (1995). Innovative sensory input for the comatose brain-injured patient. *Critical Care Nursing Clinics of North America, 7*(2), 351–361.

Hagen, C., Malkmus, D., and Durham, P. (1979). *Rehabilitation of the head injured adult: Comprehensive physical management.* Downey, CA: Professional Staff Association of Rancho Los Amigos Hospital.

Johnson, D., and Roethig-Johnston, K. (1989). Early rehabilitation of head-injured patients. *Nursing Times, 85*(4), 25–28.

NOVA Online (1997). *Coma.* [On-line]. Available: http://www. pbs.org/wgbh/nova/coma

Sheldon, K., and Dattilo, J. (1997). Multiculturism in therapeutic recreation: Terminology clarification and practical suggestions. *Therapeutic Recreation Journal, 31*(3), 148–159.

Wilhite, B., Keller, M. J., Gaudet, G., and Buettner, L. (1999). The efficacy of sensory stimulation with older adults with dementia-related cognitive impairments. *Annual in Therapeutic Recreation, 8,* 43–45.

Wilson, S. L., Powell, G. E., Brock, D., and Thwaites, H. (1996). Vegetative state and responses to sensory stimulation: An analysis of 24 cases. *Brain Injury, 10*(11), 807–818.

CASE 11 - HARRISON

The setting for this case is a 24-bed inpatient rehabilitation facility within a nonprofit regional hospital. The rehabilitation center provides services for a variety of populations which include patients with diagnoses of cerebral vascular accident, traumatic brain injury, Guillian-Barre syndrome, as well as cardiac and orthopedic rehabilitation needs. Upon discharge from the program, most patients return home to a rural community with initial assistance from family members.

Harrison is a 32-year-old White male diagnosed with human immunodeficiency virus (HIV) related myopathy. He had been diagnosed HIV-positive three years prior to inpatient stay and has not taken antiretrovirals since the diagnosis. After noting progressive weakness in his thighs, accompanied by low back pain and pain in the lower extremities, Harrison consulted his primary care physician. He was admitted to the hospital, and tests were diagnostic of myopathy. His weakness was profound, as he was unable to move any extremities except for his fingers and toes. He was able to move his shoulder blades and hips minimally, but could not roll over in the bed. During the course of his rehabilitation stay, Harrison developed dysphagia, which became progressive in nature.

Upon completion of a leisure interest survey, it was determined that the patient had previously worked 40 hours a week in the computer field. Harrison enjoys cooking, eating out, attending collegiate sporting events, hiking, watching television, and playing on the computer. He lives with his significant other and has two pet cats.

The primary team goals were to assist the patient, significant other, and family with proper skills for transferring, bladder and bowel management, oral motor exercises, and upper and lower body positioning and stretching.

Additional goals related to educational sessions regarding activities of daily living and the development of a therapeutic recreation program plan.

Discussion Questions

1. Identify and discuss various therapeutic recreation interventions that might be appropriate for Harrison.
2. How might the diagnosis of dysphagia interfere with Harrison's leisure interests? What compensatory efforts might help Harrison select high priority activities and optimize personal and environmental resources for participating in these activities?
3. What are some other complicating factors related to HIV that must be considered when developing an individual therapeutic recreation program plan for Harrison?
4. Harrison's family members and his significant other tolerate each other, but do not get along very well. How could you successfully involve all of them in the development of Harrison's therapeutic recreation program plan?
5. How might Harrison's condition be expected to change over time? Using the *Optimizing Lifelong Health and Well-Being Through Therapeutic Recreation* model, explain how the CTRS can work with Harrison and his friends/family to maintain optimal functioning and fulfillment over time. What indicators might Harrison and his friends and family use to evaluate his quality of life?

In-Class Exercises

Identify factors affecting the lives of people with HIV/Acquired Immunodeficiency Syndrome (AIDS). Differentiate between institutional factors such as policies and personal factors such as customs and cultural patterns. Examine yourself in terms of your own feelings and attitudes in regard to people who have HIV/AIDS. What is the role of the CTRS in mitigating stigma and discrimination concerning this group of individuals?

Selected References for Case Study

AIDS Global Information Service. [On-line]. Available http://
www.aegis.com

Carter, M. J., Van Andel, G. E., and Robb, G. M. (1995). *Therapeutic recreation: A practical approach* (2nd ed.). Prospect Heights,
IL: Waveland.

Grossman, A. H. (1995). Using a systems approach leisure
education model for HIV/AIDS prevention education. In H. Ruskin
and A. Sivan (Eds.), *Leisure education towards the 21st century* (pp.
159–166). Provo, UT: Brigham Young University.

Grossman, A. H. (1997). Concern, compassion, and community:
Facing the daunting worldwide challenges of HIV/AIDS. *Therapeutic Recreation Journal, 31*(2), 121–129.

Grossman, A. H., and Caroleo, O. (1996). Acquired immunodefi-
ciency syndrome (AIDS). In D. R. Austin and M. E. Crawford (Eds.),
Therapeutic recreation: An introduction (2nd ed.) (pp. 285–301).
Needham Heights, MA: Allyn & Bacon.

Grossman, A. S., and Keller, M. J. (1994). New and growing
populations for therapeutic recreation to serve: Trends in the HIV/
AIDS epidemic. *Journal of Leisurability, 21*(4), 3–13.

Reid, E. (Ed.). (1995). *HIV and AIDS: The global interconnec-
tion.* West Hartford, CT: Kumarian.

Wilhite, B., Keller, M. J., and Caldwell, L. (1999). Optimizing
lifelong health and well-being: A health enhancing model of therapeutic recreation. *Therapeutic Recreation Journal, 33*(2), 98–108.

Audiovisual Resources

Fanlight Productions. (1996). *AIDS work: Six healthcare
workers face the AIDS crisis.* [videotape]. Available from Fanlight
Productions, 47 Halifax Street, Boston, MA 02130.

CASE 12 - WALTER BYRD

You met Walter Byrd, a 72-year-old male with a diagnosis of right cerebral vascular accident (CVA) with left hemiparesis, in chapter one, case 11 (page 60). Mr. Byrd has limited use in his left arm and leg, difficulty in coordination and standing balance, poor endurance, slight aphasia, poor attention span, and visuospatial neglect. Mr. Byrd and his wife enjoy taking walks at the marina and socializing with friends and patrons there. They also enjoy listening to music, reading, and gardening. Mr. Byrd stated that his favorite activity was fishing.

Discussion Questions

1. What types of activities could you select to:
   a. Increase standing balance?
   b. Decrease left-side neglect?
   c. Increase endurance?
   d. Increase verbal ability?
   e. Retrain cognitive and perceptual abilities?
2. Write a measurable outcome addressing each of the five areas noted above using the activities you selected for Mr. Byrd. Discuss the criteria used to make the above activity selections. Discuss general activity adaptations that may facilitate Mr. Byrd's optimal involvement in the selected activities.
3. Identify several community reintegration programs that might benefit Mr. Byrd. Discuss why you selected these programs. What type of accommodation will be necessary to facilitate Mr. Byrd's optimal participation?

In-Class Exercises

1. With a partner, practice simulating left-side neglect by using a patch on the left eye and a sock on the right hand. Play a game of dominoes, alternating roles as leader and patient.
2. Working in groups of three or four, critique each other's measurable outcomes developed in question 2 above. Consider whether the outcomes are appropriate (effective) and feasible (efficient).

Selected References for Case Study

Auerbach, J., and Benezra, A. (1998). Therapeutic recreation and the rehabilitation of the stroke patient. *Loss, Grief, and Care, 8*(1/2), 123–127.

Broach, E., Dattilo, J., and Loy, D. (2000). Therapeutic use of exercise. In J. Dattilo (Ed.), *Facilitation techniques in therapeutic recreation* (pp. 355–384). State College, PA: Venture Publishing, Inc.

National Stroke Foundation. [On-line]. Available: http://www. stroke.org.

Peterson, C. A., and Stumbo, N. J. (2000). *Therapeutic recreation program design: Principles and procedures* (3rd ed.). Needham Heights, MA: Allyn & Bacon.

Sherrill, C. (1998). *Adapted physical activity, recreation and sport: Crossdisciplinary and lifespan* (5th ed.). Boston, MA: WCB McGraw-Hill.

Therapeutic Recreation Directory—Activity and Treatment Ideas. [On-line]. Available: http://www.recreationtherapy.com/tractv.htm

Audiovisual Resources

Adaptive Equipment. [videotape]. Available from Indiana University, Department of Recreation and Park Administration, HPER Building, Room 133, Bloomington, IN 47405-4711.

CASE 13 - JAY CUMMINGS

Jay Cummings, a 42-year-old African American male, has pursued running as a way to achieve and maintain physical fitness, be with friends, and reduce stress. He has recently experienced a spinal cord injury. He has decided that he would like to continue running with adaptations.

Role-Playing

1. Using the *Optimizing Lifelong Health and Well-Being Through Therapeutic Recreation* (OLH-TR) model, role-play an interaction between the CTRS and Jay during which:

   a. Jay realizes that accomplishing his goal of running again may require considerably more time and energy than before his injury,

   b. The CTRS and Jay brainstorm what he will need to know or do to optimize his personal and environmental skills and capabilities, and

   c. The CTRS and Jay discuss what compensatory strategies may be needed in order for Jay to participate in running.

   As a group, critique the exchange between the CTRS and Jay.

2. Some time has passed and Jay begins to wonder if he wants to continue running. With two new students, role-play an interaction between the CTRS and Jay during which Jay decides if he wants to continue running, or if he wants to limit his running while expanding participation in other physical domains. As a group, critique the exchange between the CTRS and Jay. Discuss the strengths and limitations of the OLH-TR model as applied to individual therapeutic recreation program planning. Propose recommendations for how the model may be modified so that it provides a stronger framework for therapeutic recreation practice.

Selected References for Case Study

Baltes, P. B., and Baltes, M. M. (1990). Selective optimization with compensation. In P. B. Baltes and M. M. Baltes (Eds.), *Successful aging: Perspectives from the behavioral sciences* (pp. 1–34). New York, NY: Cambridge University.

Binkley, A. L. (1999). OLH-TR model critique: A practitioner's view. *Therapeutic Recreation Journal, 33*(2), 116–121.

Dattilo, J., Caldwell, L., Lee, Y., and Kleiber, D. A. (1998). Returning to the community with a spinal cord injury: Implications for therapeutic recreation specialists. *Therapeutic Recreation Journal, 32*(1), 13–27.

Freysinger, V. J. (1999). A critique of the "optimizing lifelong health through therapeutic recreation" (OLH-TR) model. *Therapeutic Recreation Journal, 33*(2), 109–115.

Lee, Y., Dattilo, J., Kleiber, D. A., and Caldwell, L. (1996). Exploring the meaning of continuity of recreation activity in the early stages of adjustment for people with spinal cord injury. *Leisure Sciences, 18*(3), 209–225.

National Spinal Cord Injury Association. [On-line]. Available: http://www.spinalcord.org

Wilhite, B., Keller, M. J., and Caldwell, L. (1999). Optimizing lifelong health and well-being: A health-enhancing model of therapeutic recreation. *Therapeutic Recreation Journal, 33*(2), 98–108.

Chapter Three
Implementing Individual Therapeutic Recreation Program Plans

The tasks undertaken during the assessment and planning phase result in a paper program according to Carter, Van Andel, and Robb (1995). It is during the implementation phase of the individualized program planning, that the "paper plan becomes an action plan" (Carter et al., 1995, p. 135). This paper program, however, is useless unless therapeutic recreation specialists, along with clients, implement it in such a way that it will achieve the established short-term and long-term goals. As therapeutic recreation specialists continually collect information about clients' recreation needs, reactions, and feelings, they may discover that clients are not achieving their desired behavioral changes. Thus, therapeutic recreation specialists must monitor with clients their progress and adjust or refine the individual therapeutic recreation program plan as needed to accommodate clients' needs and to facilitate desired (predetermined) outcomes. The success or failure of individual therapeutic recreation program plans depends heavily upon the personal and professional philosophy and skills of therapeutic recreation specialists (Austin and Crawford, 1996; Carter et al., 1995; Howe-Murphy and Charboneau, 1987; O'Morrow and Reynolds, 1989). Selected tasks and skills that are crucial to successful implementation are highlighted in this chapter.

Documentation and Recordkeeping

The implementation of individual therapeutic recreation program plans requires systematic, ongoing collection of information. As Navar (1984) pointed out, therapeutic recreation specialists must "do what you say" (implement the program as planned) as well as "say what you do" (maintain accurate records when monitoring, evaluating, and revising the program). Documentation is important because it provides a record of the necessity of intervention, the resources necessary to meet needs, the process of intervention, and the results (Corcoran and Vandiver, 1996; Peterson and Stumbo, 2000; Schalenghe, 1987). Such documentation is vital because therapeutic recreation specialists must be accountable for providing quality and appropriate services with clients.

Documentation also facilitates communication with clients, their family members, fellow therapeutic recreation specialists, interdisciplinary team members, and quality management committee members. Good communication ultimately improves the quality of services and aids in the achievement of planned outcomes because it helps to keep clients' individual plans relevant to their goals. The ongoing information provided through documentation is used to identify variations within the planned program (e.g., related to clients or families, staff, setting), and facilitate necessary program revisions. Quality management and improvement personnel use concurrent and retrospective review of documented information to ensure that high-quality services are being delivered (Wagner, Kennedy, and Prichard, 1996).

Therapeutic recreation specialists must also document program implementation to comply with various legal and regulatory standards. The National Therapeutic Recreation Society has designed (1) *Standards of Practice for Therapeutic Recreation Services and Annotated Bibliography* (NTRS, 1995) and (2) *Guidelines for the Administration of Therapeutic Recreation Services* (NTRS, 1990) to help therapeutic recreation specialists carry out effective programs. The American Therapeutic Recreation Association has also developed recommended *Standards for the Practice of Therapeutic Recreation and Self-Assessment Guide* (1993). Additional standards have been developed by federal or state regulatory agencies such as the Health Care Financing Administration (HCFA); various health-care accreditation agencies, including the Joint Commission on Accreditation of Healthcare Organizations (JCAHO), the Commission on Accreditation of Rehabilitation Facilities (CARF), and the Accreditation Council for Services for Mentally Retarded and other Developmentally Disabled Persons (AC-MR/DD); researchers evaluating the efficacy of therapeutic recreation interventions; and a variety of third-party (e.g., insurance companies) and fourth-party (e.g., managed care organizations) payers. The aim of these regulatory standards is to protect clients and give some assurance that services are being rendered in an effective and efficient manner.

Following the development of individualized therapeutic recreation plans, clients begin participating in already existing, newly developed, or one-on-one therapeutic recreation programs (Carter et al., 1995). A major concern of therapeutic recreation specialists during program implementation is to gather and record data that indicate how clients are progressing toward their goals. Generally, specialists gather subjective and objective information which corresponds to stated expectations or outcomes. The nature and extent of recordkeeping often varies from agency to agency.

Much of the recordkeeping and documentation required when implementing therapeutic recreation plans is now contained in computerized information systems (burlingame, 1998). Clinical or medical information systems (CISs/MISs) may include the therapeutic recreation plan and progress notes (O'Morrow and Carter, 1997). Meditech markets a variety of computerized documentation systems used in many institutionally based settings (Medical Information Technology, 1998). These systems organize and simplify tasks such as patient identification and scheduling, patient care management, and reimbursement. Personal computers used for documentation may be found at clients' bedsides (O'Morrow and Carter, 1997). Additionally, some therapeutic recreation specialists are using personal and/or hand-held computers to allow for immediate inputting of documentation information.

Navar (1984) pointed out that individual recordkeeping is primarily a concern of therapeutic recreation specialists working in institutional (e.g., hospitals, rehabilitation centers, long-term care facilities) settings. Nevertheless, specialists working in community settings generally maintain attendance records, activity summaries, evaluations, incident reports, and minutes from staff meetings. In addition, specialists maintain individual progress records for skill-based activities such as an American Red Cross swimming course or a SCUBA course. As lengths of stay in acute institutional settings continue to decline, therapeutic recreation specialists working in a variety of community settings may be increasingly required to document clients' continued progress toward the achievement of outcomes that are necessary to preserve the immediate and long-term health and well-being of clients.

In addition to the initial assessment and individual therapeutic recreation program plans discussed in chapters one and two, progress notes are required to document both progress toward expected outcomes and the effectiveness of interventions. The progress note is the result of the clinical method of recording information about clients into their chart or file (Navar, 1984). Internally and externally developed standards for therapeutic recreation practice provide guidelines regarding what and when to chart. In institutional settings, documentation is usually organized chronologically and maintained in an individual record or "chart." This written information provides evidence that intervention with a client has occurred, the results of these interventions, the need to continue the interventions, and the adjustments made in the program content or process. Since interventions and outcomes are predetermined when using critical pathways, documentation may consist of simply initialing each item (Rickerson and burlingame, 1998). More detailed charting occurs when there are variances (discussed in chapter two) to the interventions or outcomes (Rickerson and burlingame, 1998).

Most agencies have schedules for when and how often client progress, regression, or lack of change is noted. Rath and Page (1996) suggested that this documentation should occur, at a minimum, once every seven days. Periodically, information from a number of individual progress notes should be summarized and reported in conjunction with an individual program plan. O'Morrow and Reynolds (1989), however, cautioned against rigid limits on what, how much, and when to record. In their view, useful, relevant and timely documentation "is a professional and not a clerical activity" (O'Morrow and Reynolds, 1989, p. 150).

Progress notes should contain information pertinent to specific documentation standards for the agency and other stakeholders including regulatory and accrediting bodies, insurance companies, and managed care organizations. Examples of possible content as suggested by Austin (1999), Rath and Page (1996), and Wagner et al. (1996) include:

1. clients' functional status;
2. progress toward desired goals;
3. clients' limiting factors (e.g., low endurance, speech problems);
4. clients' strengths (e.g., individual cooperation, family support);

5. level and frequency of participation in activities;
6. interaction patterns with staff and peers;
7. new patterns of behavior (including noncompliant behaviors);
8. physical observations such as appearance and personal hygiene, posture, facial expressions, and movement;
9. information provided by clients or caregivers;
10. assessment of further progress expected;
11. new or revised measurable short-term goals;
12. plans for future actions related to a client's progress toward desired goals; and
13. expected length of treatment.

Progress notes should be written in a format that coincides with the method used to develop the individual therapeutic recreation program plan. For example, if the individual therapeutic recreation program plan was written using the SOAP method described in chapter two, progress notes are written in a specific format and referred to as SOAP notes. SOAP notes include subjective data (what a client says about the problem), objective data (what others say about, observe in, or find in the problem), assessment of the problem (based on subjective and objective data), and a plan for addressing the problem, now and in the future. A similarly structured approach should be used for the PIE and DAP formats also described in chapter two. Additionally, therapeutic recreation professionals may use a narrative format for recording clients' progress.

Progress notes should prove that individual program plans are being followed, and record clients' progress. They should provide accurate and complete records of clients' responses to interventions. Progress notes should be written clearly, objectively, and precisely in a behavioral language that describes exactly clients' words, actions, and conditions. For example, a therapeutic recreation specialist describes behavior when she writes, "The individual was observed crying during the evening meal." In another example, a specialist should state that a client participated in an activity "three times a week" rather than "often." When writing progress notes, the therapeutic recreation specialist should resist interpreting clients' behavior. For example, avoid writing a statement such as, "The client is depressed." Precisely stated, objective documentation provides a better understanding of a client's actions than do interpretations or generalizations. If therapeutic recreation specialists feel it is appropriate to include their professional interpretation regarding clients' behavior, they must identify the interpretation as their own and include the behavioral observations that led to this interpretation.

Rath and Page (1996) provided the following example of documenting client progress using a SOAP format:

S "Shut up. I'm going to beat you up!"

O Patient became oppositional during transition to fourth floor activity following provoking by a peer. He threw open the door and pushed past a staff member, verbalizing as above. Patient required escort to quiet room and basket-hold restraint.

A Patient continues to display low frustration tolerance, exploding aggressively at the slightest provocation. This aggression is targeted indiscriminately toward both staff and peers.

P Therapeutic recreation staff will continue to assist patient in identifying coping mechanisms via positive leisure outlets for his aggression. (p. 37)

Other specific guidelines and tips for writing progress notes are provided by Wagner et al. (1996) and Peterson and Stumbo (2000).

The Team Approach

Providing optimal care and treatment and managing outcomes cannot be achieved by just one profession, discipline, or service area. In health and human services today, it is common for many professional specialists to offer a variety of services to clients simultaneously. The interdisciplinary team combines these individual professional efforts to produce a single coordinated result. Team members work together to identify clients' needs, develop plans to meet these needs, periodically evaluate clients' responses to the plans, problem-solve barriers that may be preventing progress toward desired outcomes, and revise the plans accordingly. In addition to this interdependence among disciplines, several other descriptions of how teams function have been suggested:

Chapter Three

1. sharing a common goal or purpose,
2. consolidating knowledge and coordinating activities,
3. specifying tasks based on expertise of team members,
4. developing and monitoring intervention plans, and
5. communicating (Brill, 1990; Landrum, Schmidt, and McLean, 1995; O'Morrow and Reynolds, 1989).

The composition of a team, as well as the roles its members play, may vary. Team membership may be determined by factors such as the specific setting in which therapeutic recreation is delivered, the goal the team hopes to accomplish, and the length of time the team expects to work together. Likewise, team members' roles will be determined in large measure by clients' problems. A current trend is for interdisciplinary teams to be organized according to particular disabilities, diagnoses, or medical goals (e.g., product line or program model approach) (Smith, 1995). With this approach, the importance of interchangeable roles is stressed and two different disciplines often deliver designated interventions together, or "co-treat," to achieve desired outcomes (Brill, 1990; Smith, 1995). Usually a case manager or coordinator is assigned to be responsible for monitoring all aspects of clients' status and progress, and to ensure that interventions are modified in a timely manner as needed

(Landrum et al., 1995). Increasingly, therapeutic recreation specialists are serving in the capacity of case manager. For example, in one Veterans' Affairs domiciliary program for homeless veterans, therapeutic recreation specialists are responsible for serving as case managers for a specified number of residents.

While the team concept seems appropriate and logical, certain aspects of group dynamics can stalemate the team and render it less effective. For instance, the pooling of knowledge and expertise characteristic of the team approach should enhance the quality and efficiency of individual program planning. A team member, however, may perceive a need to defend his or her role, profession, or area of expertise and this may hinder the maximizing efforts of other team members. Nonetheless, therapeutic recreation team members will often need to establish themselves as representing a specific body of knowledge and skill that is an essential part of the team and the service to clients. Another problem that may arise from the team concept is a blurring of roles that results in a failure to distinguish among team tasks, producing ineffective and inefficient situations where no one team member accepts responsibility or feels accountable for the end result. Team conflict may also occur because of the very nature of interdependency. Even in the best team relationships, there are inevitable differences of opinions, approaches, and perceptions.

Effective team relationships depend heavily on good communication. In short, team members must want to communicate—to give, receive, and respond to information. This effort can be enhanced if team members explain specific professional terminologies and methodologies so that each member understands. When team members openly communicate, share responsibility for planning, and are accountable for carrying out team activities, the potential achievement of clients' goals is maximized.

Working with Volunteers

Volunteers offer a wealth of diversity in backgrounds and skills (Smith, Austin, and Kennedy, 1996) and are being used in therapeutic recreation services to extend, enhance, and expand a variety of team functions, programs, and resources (O'Morrow and Carter, 1997). For example, the use of volunteer advocates, companions, and aides as one strategy for community reintegration and inclusion has necessitated intensive volunteer training and higher levels of volunteer competence (O'Morrow and Carter, 1997; Schleien, Ray, and Green, 1997). In addition, it is expected that volunteers will become integral to implementing therapeutic recreation services which are increasingly outpatient-, home-, and community-based (O'Morrow and Carter, 1997).

Guidelines for volunteer management are provided by the National Therapeutic Recreation Society in its *Guidelines for Administration of Therapeutic Recreation Services* (NTRS, 1990). These guidelines include:

1. written selection procedures;
2. written outline of mandatory orientation and training program;
3. written procedures for supervision and evaluation;
4. written position description;
5. best use of volunteers' talents, training, and interests;
6. volunteer manual including regulations, policies, and procedures;
7. ongoing training and education;
8. program for formal recognition; and
9. restraint from using volunteers in place of paid personnel.

With appropriate and conscientious volunteer management, using volunteers to help implement therapeutic recreation programs can be a win-win situation. Volunteers can derive the various benefits that motivate them to pursue volunteerism, and agencies and clients can receive valuable expertise and resources.

Staff Development

Whether staff are paid or choose to volunteer their time and expertise, a need exists to confirm, maintain, and upgrade their knowledge and skills. As pointed out by O'Morrow and Carter (1997), staff training and education are part of the demand for the continuous quality improvement of therapeutic recreation programs and services. In addition, the rapid rate of change and innovation occurring in health and human service settings emphasizes the need to prepare staff for continuous professional growth so that their knowledge and skills remain current (O'Morrow and Carter, 1997).

As with volunteer management, professional standards documents prepared by the American Therapeutic Recreation Association (1993) and the National Therapeutic Recreation Society (1990, 1995) provide therapeutic recreation specialists with guidelines for developing and implementing staff development programs. Common to these guidelines is the need to articulate written policies (i.e., plans) that assess the educational needs of staff, provide opportunities for staff training and development, evaluate the effectiveness of these programs, and offer suggestions for improvement of staff development efforts. Staff development opportunities may be offered through both formal and informal means including orientation programs, probationary hiring periods, in-service training programs, professional development programs, and retraining opportunities (O'Morrow and Carter, 1997; Robbins, 1995).

Risk Management and Legal Liability Concerns

When individual program plans are implemented, therapeutic recreation specialists must consider all possible risks and ensure a reasonable level of client safety. Van der Smissen (1990) identified three major areas of risk management:

1. supervision of participants,
2. conditions of the environment, and
3. manner of conducting activities.

Personal injury or property loss may arise from poor professional judgment, lack of adherence to current safety standards, inadequate supervision, infrequent inspections and repair of areas and facilities, and poor design of program formats and conduct (Jordan, 1996; Peterson and Hronek, 1992; Siegenthaler, 1996). Specialists must respond to these concerns when implementing individual therapeutic recreation program plans. Can adequate and appropriate supervision be provided? Are facilities and equipment in safe operating condition, and free from hazards? Will the planned approaches allow reasonably safe participation? Though part of the recent attention to managing risks has been caused by an increasing emphasis on minimizing legal liability, Siegenthaler (1996) suggests that risk management is essential to the provision of quality services. That is, when participation risks are kept at a minimum, a higher level of enjoyment and quality of care are possible.

Van der Smissen (1990) reported that 80% of litigation involving programmatic situations in recreation and sports involved supervision issues, and a majority were based on a charge of negligence. Borkowski (1993) stated that proper supervision requires leading clients in a necessary warm-up, providing instruction about the activity, establishing safety rules, and informing clients of potential risks and hazards. Jordan (1996) added that as the potential risk of injury increases, so should the level of supervision. Sometimes charges of inadequate supervision are based on the competence of leaders. Competence of leaders may be measured by knowledge, age, experience, and credentials (van der Smissen, 1990). For therapeutic recreation specialists, applicable credentials, such as Certified Therapeutic Recreation Specialist, first-aid and CPR, as well as certificates of completion for training in ropes course instruction, aquatic therapy, universal precautions, professional management of aggressive behavior, and so on, help to verify the competence of leaders (Jordan, 1996; Siegenthaler, 1996).

Voelkl (1988) suggested a three-step process for managing risk. First, therapeutic recreation specialists, aided by all staff involved in the implementation of programs, must identify all possible risks to the clients, staff, and facility. Once risks have been identified, specialists should determine the best approach to eliminating or minimizing the risks. Finally, therapeutic recreation specialists must develop a plan describing how the risks will be handled. As in the case of individual program plans, risk management plans should help specialists decide whether to continue, modify, or terminate the activity or program.

A variety of forms may be used by therapeutic recreation specialists in an effort to inform clients of potential risks, demonstrate the agency's concern for the well-being of clients, and minimize the potential for charges of negligence. These include parental or guardian permission forms, medical history forms, accident or incident report forms, assumption of risk/agreement to participate forms, release or waiver forms, and photo release forms (Jordan, 1996).

Least Restrictive Environments

Some implementation issues relate to the characteristics of clients'
environments that enable their full participation in activities of
choice. Therapeutic recreation specialists are increasingly identifying
with the term *inclusive leisure services* (see, for example, Dattilo,
1994; Schleien, et al., 1997; Smith, et al., 1996) to describe a variety
of recreation and leisure options available to individuals with disabilities in their communities. Sherrill (1994) challenged professionals to consider the appropriateness of the least restrictive environment (LRE) philosophy when conceptualizing inclusive services and
programs. The least restrictive setting is that one which is the least
"different," or closest to the mainstream of society. Sherrill defined
the LRE philosophy as an integration or an inclusion-with-support-
services conceptual framework based on the belief that assessment,
planning, implementation, and evaluation should be individualized
and personalized through a continuum of placement options and
services. For example, Abu Yilla, a Paralympic athlete, described the
LRE continuum he employs in his life:

> I study and work in a fully integrated environment.
> When I compete, I am in the realistically segregated
> environment of wheelchair basketball. When I recreate, I
> can be at almost any point in the LRE continuum. (1994,
> p. 18)

Schleien et al. (1997) pointed out that recreation and leisure
within the LRE "refers to the acquisition and performance of leisure
skills by people with disabilities in normalized community environments" (p. 85). It is believed that within this environment clients
have the best opportunities to maximize their individual abilities.
Clients and therapeutic recreation specialists should strive to develop
recreation and leisure skills that are naturally occurring, frequently
demanded, have a specific purpose, are age appropriate, and are
comparable to the skill performance of peers without disabilities
(Schleien et al., 1997).

A continuum of recreation and leisure options is progressive and
sequential, and could include segregated services, "special" or
physically integrated services, and socially or fully integrated

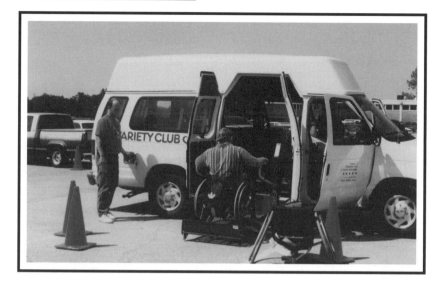

(inclusive) services. As described in the Optimizing Lifelong Health and Well-Being Through Therapeutic Recreation model of therapeutic recreation service delivery presented in chapter two, it is possible for clients to participate in different levels of recreation inclusion simultaneously, based on individual needs and readiness (Wilhite, Keller, and Caldwell, 1999). Therapeutic recreation specialists strive to develop a range of opportunities offered in situations and settings with as few restrictions as possible, preferably in settings also used by persons without disabilities. These recreation opportunities are those that are valued and supported by clients, their family members, friends with or without disabilities, and other significant individuals. While it is not necessary or desirable for families and friends to share each recreation interest of clients, it is desirable that they share some common interests. This inclusion continuum will enable individuals to have as satisfying and as interdependent leisure lifestyles as possible.

Legislation

Legislation passed in the 1960s and 1970s coincided with the emphasis on least restrictive environment and inclusion philosophies, challenging the "separate but equal" concept. For example, the Architectural Barriers Act of 1968 (PL 90-480), the Rehabilitation

Act of 1973 (PL 93-112) as amended in 1974 (PL 93-516), and the Education for All Handicapped Children Act (PL 94-142) as amended in 1986 (PL 99-457), guaranteed access for individuals with disabilities to facilities and activities that are available to the general public. All of these acts ensure access to services in the least restrictive and most appropriate environment.

In 1989, the Americans with Disabilities Act (ADA) was introduced in the U.S. Senate and House of Representatives and signed into law by President George Bush on July 26, 1990. This piece of legislation is an omnibus civil rights statute that prohibits discrimination against people with disabilities in private sector employment, all public services, public accommodations, transportation, and telecommunications. It is broader in scope and impact than the aforementioned laws and its provisions extend to the private sector as well. In signing the ADA into law, the federal government sent a strong message that inaccessibility, whether physical, programmatic, or administrative, intentional or unintentional, is discrimination. The ADA provides comprehensive guidelines on banning discrimination against people on the basis of disability.

Amendments to the Education for All Handicapped Children Act in 1990 renamed the act the Individuals with Disabilities Education Act (IDEA) (PL 101-476). This Act guarantees all students with disabilities a free and appropriate public education that emphasizes special education and related services. Related services are those that are necessary to help students, from birth to 21 years of age, benefit fully from special education services. These services are reimbursable under IDEA. Recreation, occupational therapy, speech pathology, physical therapy, counseling, and transportation are examples of related services specified in the law. The reauthorized act included:

1. recreation as a related service that should be available to all students through public education programs,
2. a rationale for the provision of recreation programs to meet the individualized needs of students with disabilities, and
3. an emphasis on least restrictive environments in which recreation services are offered in physical and social environments that optimize opportunities for students to develop to their greatest potential. (Gerrard, 1994)

Additionally, new emphasis was placed on the transition and assistive technology needs of students. In the 1997 reauthorization of IDEA, recreation includes assessment of recreation and leisure function, leisure education and therapeutic recreation services, and recreation in school and community agencies (Arnhold and Auxter, 1999; Bullock and Mahon, 1997).

Outreach, Transition, and Referral

In the early years of organized recreation in the United States, concern was directed toward those members of society who found themselves temporarily displaced or out of the mainstream. These individuals were primarily disadvantaged youth and adults, many of whom were immigrants in transition from rural agricultural settings to urban industrial ones. Recreation was considered socially purposeful and necessary to improve the quality of life for these individuals perceived as having unique needs. There seemed to be a feeling of moral responsibility for individuals who were having difficulty fitting society's norms. Programs, such as those offered on the playgrounds and in the settlement houses, were easily accessible to the people they were intended to serve.

As the profession of recreation has grown, however, it seems to have lost some of its earlier philosophical and moral commitments and concern for the "common good" (Lahey, 1991, 1996), and its focus on "outreach." Recreation professionals seem to assume all citizens are equally prepared to enter the public arena and seek desired recreation services. Yet, in reality, participation may be limited because of chronic or temporary disability, lack of transportation, unawareness or nonacceptance of opportunity, and/or economic circumstances. Many professionals in community recreation programs consider themselves underfunded. Hence they may have avoided specific attempts to bring "hard-to-reach" citizens into mainstream community recreation services. Perhaps of greatest concern is the possibility that because therapeutic recreation has claimed to be the primary professional discipline concerned with the recreation needs of people with disabilities, community recreation professionals have felt little responsibility to provide recreation to all persons within communities, specifically, those with disabilities. Current downsizing efforts in community recreation and park programs may actually be using an inclusion philosophy as justification for failing to provide an array of participation alternatives for everyone, including individuals with disabilities (Wilhite, Adams Mushett, and Calloway, 1996). However, most people with disabilities in our society are not served by therapeutic recreation specialists, but by community recreation personnel (Carter, 1991; Smith et al., 1996).

Therapeutic recreation specialists working in institutionally based settings and general and therapeutic recreation professionals working in community-based settings share a responsibility in regard to clients' transition from institutional to community-based settings whether from inpatient to outpatient services or from outpatient to inclusionary settings (Carter et al., 1995). This responsibility implies that all recreation professionals assume an active role in facilitating the community recreation involvement of populations such as individuals with disabilities living in urban or rural areas who may be isolated, and individuals, who because of chronic illness, disability, or frailness caused by advanced age, spend a disproportionate amount of time in their homes. Individuals with disabilities who are in an ethnic or cultural minority, and thus face even greater obstacles relative to community acceptance and involvement, may also be members of this population. The expertise of therapeutic recreation specialists can be used to provide consultation, technical assistance, and training to community recreation personnel regarding specific access issues such as attitudes, adaptations, human resources, architectural barriers, communication, and transportation. In addition, therapeutic recreation specialists can function as consumer advocates and help to ensure that the rights and needs of people with disabilities remain in the forefront of community recreation service delivery.

O'Morrow and Reynolds (1989) state "a major obstacle to participation in leisure experiences following discharge is the poor link between the rehabilitation facility and community recreation agencies" (p. 188). This "poor link" could result in lack of future client progress or even regression (Navar, 1984). Referral systems help clients pursue leisure opportunities as they move from institutions into communities. In many cases, these networks are developed through joint efforts by therapeutic recreation specialists working in hospitals, state facilities for people with mental retardation, nursing homes, psychiatric facilities, rehabilitation centers, and correctional institutions, and their community recreation counterparts. To aid in this process, some communities have developed directories of agencies offering leisure services and resources. The development of effective discharge and referral systems will demand a greater emphasis in the future.

Identifying and Utilizing Community Resources

Implementing individual therapeutic recreation program plans often involves the use of community resources, and therapeutic recreation specialists must be knowledgeable about available community leisure opportunities and resources. For example, the telephone book, both the white and yellow pages, provides valuable information since it contains the telephone numbers and addresses of leisure service agencies and facilities. Also, retailers selling equipment for recreation activities, or private and commercial facilities, such as bowling alleys, golf courses, and tennis clubs, can usually provide information about classes and other leisure opportunities. Local libraries, many of which have developed community leisure directories or research files, are excellent sources for the names and locations of potential leisure service providers. Directories often contain names of associations, clubs, and organizations devoted to specific recreation interests or activities, as well as community centers and recreation facilities in the area. The library, itself, is a good resource, providing an abundance of information about potential recreation activities.

Many libraries also offer access to the Internet. The Internet has made it possible for therapeutic recreation specialists and clients to gain comprehensive and up-to-date information pertaining to community programs, activities, clubs, locations, accessibility, costs, transportation routes, parking, and so on. Many programs and activities listed on-line include an e-mail address to communicate with the organizers and sponsors. Finally, virtual reality recreation opportunities, as well as on-line interactive learning centers, make it possible for clients to "experience" selected recreation choices, or gain information from others who have past experiences with specific activities and/or programs.

Therapeutic recreation specialists will find it helpful to develop a leisure resource system or file management program that organizes the individuals and agencies according to the services they provide. The information contained in this system should include the contact person's name, agency or category affiliation (such as community recreation professionals, parents, school personnel, and civic group representatives), address, telephone number, and services provided. It should also include other useful program information such as costs, transportation requirements, registration deadlines, times of the week or month when a leader is available, education and background a resource person has to offer, and meeting time and location.

Technology

As noted earlier, much of the recordkeeping and documentation required in institutional settings is now computerized. Advances in technology have made it easier to manage information collected during program implementation. Computer-assisted management information systems (MISs) allow program monitoring data to be accumulated and displayed in a variety of ways. MISs generally serve two functions. One is to enhance storage, retrieval, and reporting mechanisms. A second function is to quantify data by condensing and analyzing large data sets into a few indicators that represent the most relevant feature of the information (Rossi and Freeman, 1993). Whatever data management approach or system is used, it should enable therapeutic recreation specialists and others to collect relevant data, organize it into information, and use this information to make program decisions (burlingame, 1998; O'Morrow and Carter, 1997; Landrum et al., 1995).

However, therapeutic recreation researchers, professionals, and students are just beginning to explore the frontiers of therapeutic recreation service delivery through technology (Mainville, 1997; Mainville and Valerius, 1999). The issues surrounding the conceptualization, development, evaluation, and application of computer-based and Internet-based therapeutic recreation interventions are multifaceted. At the present state of research and development in this area, it is unknown if computer- and Internet-based therapeutic recreation programming may be more feasible for certain types of clients and interventions than others. The therapeutic recreation

profession is just beginning to explore how the nature of clients' problems and preferences may influence the use of these interventions, which type of interventions (e.g., treatment or rehabilitation, education, recreation participation, leisure facilitation) may be most appropriate, and various arrangements that may be preferred (e.g., individual or group interventions). Many helping professionals believe, however, that computer-based and Internet-based interventions, as components of a total treatment program, may be useful for some clients and problems (Bradley, Holm, Steere, and Stromqvist, 1993; Mainville, 1998; Wagman, 1988).

Discussion of various ethical concerns is warranted. For instance, while some clients may prefer and benefit from computer-based or Internet-based interventions, others might feel that turning to a computer for assistance, rather than a human, is insulting and humiliating (O'Morrow and Carter, 1997; Wagman, 1988). In addition, concerns exist that clients who do use these interventions should not have their needs compromised by access, or by technical difficulties in using the requisite hardware or interacting with the software. Other ethical issues, such as those pertaining to confidentiality in transactions, conditions of referral, quality control, and research must be addressed in therapeutic recreation specialists' efforts to develop and implement such programs.

The potential usefulness of computer-based interventions is exciting, however. In addition to augmenting therapeutic recreation services in institutional settings (see, for example, McConatha, McConatha, Deaner, and Dermigny, 1995), computer-based and Internet-based interventions may help to provide services in urban or rural areas where such services have been extremely minimal or even absent. The progress made in the distributed learning arena, and increased access to these opportunities, should be very instructive to the profession as exploration of computer- and Internet-based interventions continues. As therapeutic recreation services move into day, outpatient, and home settings, the ability to continue and rein-force treatment and compliance, to individuals as well as their families or caregivers, through various "homework" assignments is appealing. These efforts may prove to be a convenient, efficient, and cost-effective way to extend the benefits of therapeutic recreation interventions. Using technology in this manner may also provide an opportunity for therapeutic recreation specialists to track the long-term benefits of therapeutic recreation interventions and participation in recreation and leisure.

Summary

Individual therapeutic recreation program plans remain just that—plans—until they are put into practice. Thus, the implementation phase of the individual therapeutic recreation program planning process could be considered the make-it-or-break-it phase. During this phase, therapeutic recreation specialists must monitor plans, make necessary revisions, and document client progress. The risks of participation must be minimized, and the quality of intervention maximized. Therapeutic recreation specialists should identify and use human, community, and technological resources that contribute to the achievement of successful leisure experiences in environments that optimize clients' individual abilities and interests.

During implementation, therapeutic recreation specialists work directly with clients. In the next chapter, *Leadership in Therapeutic Recreation*, guidelines for effective leadership will be highlighted.

Bibliography

Austin, D. R. (1999). *Therapeutic recreation: Process and techniques* (4th ed.). Champaign, IL: Sagamore.

Austin, D. R., and Crawford, M. E. (Eds.). (1996). *Therapeutic recreation: An introduction* (2nd ed.). Needham Heights, MA: Allyn & Bacon.

American Therapeutic Recreation Association. (1993). *Standards for the practice of therapeutic recreation and self assessment guide.* Hattiesburg, MS: Author.

Arnhold, R. W., and Auxter, D. A. (Eds.). (1999). Legislative update: IDEA regulations released and state improvement grant opportunities. *Palaestra, 15*(2), 7–8.

Bradley, G., Holm, P., Steere, M., and Stromqvist, G. (1993). Psychosocial communication and computerization. *Computers in Human Behavior, 9*, 157–169.

Borkowski, R. (1993). Avoiding the gavel. *Athletic Management, 5*(6), 22–26.

Brill, N. (1990). *Working with people: The helping process* (4th ed.). White Plains, NY: Longman.

Bullock, C. C., and Mahon, M. J. (1997). *Introduction to recreation services for people with disabilities: A person-centered approach.* Champaign, IL: Sagamore.

burlingame, j. (1998). The role of information technologies. In F. Brasile, T. K. Skalko, and j. burlingame (Eds.), *Perspectives in recreational therapy: Issues of a dynamic profession* (pp. 463–486). Ravensdale, WA: Idyll Arbor.

Carter, M. J. (1991). *Designing therapeutic recreation programs in the community.* Reston, VA: American Alliance for Health, Physical Education, Recreation and Dance.

Carter, M. J., Van Andel, G. E., and Robb, G. M. (1995). *Therapeutic recreation: A practical approach* (2nd ed.). Prospect Heights, IL: Waveland.

Corcoran, K., and Vandiver, V. (1996). *Maneuvering the maze of managed care: Skills for mental health practitioners.* New York, NY: The Free Press.

Dattilo, J. (1994). *Inclusive leisure services: Responding to the rights of people with disabilities.* State College, PA: Venture Publishing, Inc.

Gerrard, L. C. (1994). Inclusive education: An issue of social justice. *Equity and Excellence in Education, 27,* 58–67.

Howe-Murphy, R., and Charboneau, B. G. (1987). *Therapeutic recreation intervention: An ecological perspective.* Englewood Cliffs, NJ: Prentice Hall

Jordan, D. J. (1996). *Leadership in leisure services: Making a difference.* State College, PA: Venture Publishing, Inc.

Landrum, P. K., Schmidt, N. D., and McLean, A. (1995). *Outcome-oriented rehabilitation: Principles, strategies, and tools for effective program management.* Gaithersburg, MD: Aspen.

Lahey, M. P. (1991). Serving the new poor: Therapeutic recreation values in hard times. *Therapeutic Recreation Journal, 25*(2), 9–18.

Lahey, M. P. (1996). The commercial model and the future of therapeutic recreation. In C. Sylvester (Ed.), *Philosophy of therapeutic recreation: Ideas and issues, volume II* (pp. 20–29). Arlington, VA: National Recreation and Park Association.

Mainville, S. (1997). TR and the Internet. *Parks and Recreation, 32*(6), 71–73.

Mainville, S. (1998). *Leisure education for the prevention of alcohol abuse: The potential use of the Internet in therapeutic recreation.* Unpublished master's thesis, University of North Texas, Denton, Texas.

Mainville, S., and Valerius, L. (1999). Nothing but 'net: Therapeutic recreation and the web. *Parks and Recreation, 34*(5), 86–93.

McConatha, J. T., McConatha, D., Deaner, S. L., and Dermigny, R. (1995). Computer-based intervention for the education and therapy of institutionalized older adults. *Educational Gerontology, 21*, 129–138.

Medical Information Technology. (1998). *Meditech: Information systems for integrated healthcare delivery.* [On-line]. Available: http://www.meditech.com/pages/pl.htm

National Therapeutic Recreation Society. (1990). *Guidelines for the administration of therapeutic recreation services.* Alexandria, VA: National Recreation and Park Association.

National Therapeutic Recreation Society. (1995). *Standards of practice for therapeutic recreation services and annotated bibliography.* Arlington, VA: National Recreation and Park Association.

Navar, N. (1984). Documentation in therapeutic recreation. In C. A. Peterson and S. L. Gunn, *Therapeutic recreation program design: Principles and procedures* (2nd ed.) (pp. 212–266). Englewood Cliffs, NJ: Prentice Hall.

O'Morrow, G. S., and Carter, M. J. (1997). *Effective management in therapeutic recreation service.* State College, PA: Venture Publishing, Inc.

O'Morrow, G. S., and Reynolds, R. P. (1989). *Therapeutic recreation: A helping profession* (3rd ed.). Englewood Cliffs, NJ: Prentice Hall.

Peterson, C. A., and Stumbo, N. J. (2000). *Therapeutic recreation program design: Principles and practices* (3rd ed.). Boston, MA: Allyn & Bacon.

Peterson, J. A., and Hronek, B. B. (1992). *Risk management for park, recreation, and leisure services* (2nd ed.). Champaign, IL: Sagamore.

Rath, K. V., and Page, G. (1996). *Understanding financing and reimbursement issues.* Arlington, VA: National Recreation and Park Association.

Rickerson, N., and burlingame, j. (1998). Healthcare delivery systems. In F. Brasile, T. K. Skalko, and j. burlingame (Eds.), *Perspectives in recreational therapy: Issues of a dynamic profession* (pp. 205–220). Ravensdale, WA: Idyll Arbor.

Robbins, S. P. (1995). *Supervision today.* Englewood Cliffs, NJ: Prentice Hall.

Rossi, P. H., and Freeman, H. E. (1993). *Evaluation: A systematic approach.* Newbury Park, CA: Sage.

Schalenghe, R. W. (1987). Foreward. In B. Riley (Ed.), *Evaluation of therapeutic recreation through quality assurance* (pp. ix–x). State College, PA: Venture Publishing, Inc.

Schleien, S. J., Ray, M. T., and Green, F. P. (1997). *Community recreation and people with disabilities: Strategies for inclusion* (2nd ed.). Baltimore, MD: Brookes.

Siegenthaler, K. L. (1996). Supervising activities for safety: Avoid the negligence trap. *Journal of Physical Education, Recreation, and Dance, 67*(7), 29–30, 36.

Sherrill, C. (1994). Least restrictive environment and total inclusion philosophies: Critical analysis. *Palaestra, 10*(1), 25–35, 52–54.

Smith, R. W. (1995, May). Trends in therapeutic recreation. *Parks and Recreation, 30*(5), 66–71.

Smith, R. W., Austin, D. R., and Kennedy, D. W. (1996). *Inclusive and special recreation: Opportunities for persons with disabilities* (3rd ed.). Madison, WI: Brown & Benchmark.

van der Smissen, B. (1990). *Legal liability and risk management for public and private entities* (Vol. 2). Cincinnati, OH: Anderson.

Voelkl, J. E. (1988). *Risk management in therapeutic recreation: A component of quality assurance.* State College, PA: Venture Publishing, Inc.

Wagman, M. (1988). *Computer Psychotherapy Systems.* New York, NY: Gordon and Breach Science.

Wagner, D., Kennedy, B., and Prichard, A. (1996). *Recreational therapy: The next generation of reimbursement.* Hattiesburg, MS: American Therapeutic Recreation Association.

Wilhite, B., Adams Mushett, C., and Calloway, J. (1996). Sport and disability across the lifespan: Introduction to the special issue. *Therapeutic Recreation Journal, 30*(2), 106–113.

Wilhite, B., Keller, M. J., and Caldwell, L. (1999). Optimizing lifelong health and well-being: A health enhancing model of therapeutic recreation. *Therapeutic Recreation Journal, 33*(2), 98–108.

Yilla, A. B. (1994). Full inclusion: A philosophical statement. *Palaestra, 10*(4), 18.

CASE 1 - TREVOR CLEMSON

Trevor Clemson is a 34-year-old White male. He is diagnosed as having mild mental retardation with his adaptive skills in the moderate range. He has a history of paranoid schizophrenia. He resides in an intermediate care facility for people with mental retardation (ICF/MR) group home for adults with behavior problems. He receives Haldol injections, 100 mg. am q. 5 wks., and takes Cogentin 2 mg. q. p.m., and Prozac 20 mg. q. p.m.

Trevor's gross-motor abilities are within the normal range. He takes great pride in his physical abilities and appearance, and likes to look "fit." He likes to lift weights, a set of which he keeps in the basement of the home. He likes to dance to rap music, but does not do so often in front of others. Although in the past he would dress mostly in black with Kung Fu-like accessories, he is now dressing more appropriately for his job.

Trevor has very good fine-motor abilities, and is especially adept at perceptual tasks. His job in the community includes operating an embroidery machine, which requires very good eye-hand coordination. He can also draw well, but he is highly critical of his work.

Trevor displays academic abilities that are about equal to an eight year old. He can read and write, perform math problems, and is able to plan for the future. He is also able to make decisions about situations by weighing the consequences. He is able to use both the bus and subway independently, use the telephone, and make purchases independently. He is very adept in the kitchen and displays the ability to cook well.

Trevor's weaknesses are in his social functioning, although he has displayed some improvements over the last two years, possibly due to adjustments in his medications. He is quiet when around others, and prefers to engage in leisure activities alone. Although generally not very talkative, he is able to express his views on various topics.

Over the last two years, Trevor has had the freedom to sign himself out when he wants to leave the house, as long as he indicates when he will return. He began showing signs of regular alcohol consumption in October. Staff report that whenever he has any extra money, he uses it to buy beer. When he does not have access to alcohol, he expresses disappointment. In December he broke into a house and was arrested. He now must have a staff person with him at all times in the community. He greatly regrets his behavior because he now has little freedom.

It is felt that much of his recent behavior, including the alcohol consumption, may stem from his frustration in dealing with his present living situation. He is in a group home with individuals who require ongoing supervision and instruction in daily activities. There are no other residents with whom he can relate.

Trevor's cognitive abilities and variety of interests enable him to experience a high degree of independence during his leisure time. Because he is not willing to allow others to structure his life for him, he spends most of his time pursuing self-initiated spontaneous activities. Leisure activities that he enjoys are lifting weights, listening to music in his room, watching movies and sports on TV, visiting relatives independently, and traveling in the community independently.

Discussion Questions

1. You, a certified therapeutic recreation specialist, are the only team member at Trevor's annual team conference to indicate that he is having a problem with alcohol. Trevor denies that there is a problem, and staff members are vague about how often Trevor is drinking. How can you convince the other team members that this needs to be addressed, and what course of action would you recommend?
2. You also feel that Trevor may have been inappropriately placed in the group home. In preparation for opposition from other team members to the idea that

Trevor may not be suitably placed, what "home-work" could you do?

3. Discuss the legal liability issues and individual rights of Trevor regarding alcohol consumption.

In-Class Exercises

1. Discuss the differences between short-term and long-term goals as they relate to the development of an individual program plan. Develop a long-term goal for Trevor that addresses his alcohol consumption issues. Develop a short-term goal related to the long-term goal.

2. Invite professionals from a local mental retardation and mental health community agency who might serve on an interdisciplinary team for Trevor (e.g., social worker, mental health assistant, group home manager, CTRS, psychologist, nurse) to come to class and demonstrate the development of an individual program plan for Trevor.

3. Write progress notes to be shared with the interdisciplinary team, including all of your concerns about Trevor. Use this note as a point of discussion in the following role-play.

Role-Playing

Role-play the scenario described in question 2 above.

Selected References for Case Study

Benner, S. M. (1998). *Special education issues within the context of American society.* Belmont, CA: Wadsworth.

Gimmestad, K. (1995). A comprehensive therapeutic recreation intervention: A woman with schizophrenia. *Therapeutic Recreation Journal, 29*(1), 56–62.

Hogberg, P., and Johnson, M. (1994). *Reference manual for writing rehabilitation therapy treatment plans.* State College, PA: Venture Publishing, Inc.

Huang, W., and Cuvo, A. (1997). Social skills training for adults with mental retardation in job-related settings. *Behavior Modification, 21*(1), 3–44.

Melcher, S. (1999). *Introduction to writing goals and objectives: A manual for recreation therapy students and entry-level professionals.* State College, PA: Venture Publishing, Inc.

National Alliance of the Mentally Ill. [On-line]. Available: http://www.nami.org

National Clearinghouse on Alcohol and Drug Information. [On-line]. Available: http://www.health.org

National Institute on Alcohol Abuse and Addiction. (1995). The genetics of alcoholism. *Alcohol Alert, 18*[PH328]. Rockville, MD: U.S. Department of Health and Human Services.

Prestle, K., Card, J., and Menditto, A. (1998). Therapeutic recreation in a social-learning program: Effect over time on appropriate behaviors of residents with schizophrenia. *Therapeutic Recreation Journal, 32*(1), 28–41.

Project Life (no date). *Understanding mental illness: A guide to diagnosis, medications and therapeutic intervention* (3rd ed.). Columbia, MO: University of Missouri.

The ARC of the United States. [On-line]. Available: http://www.thearc.org

Audiovisual Resources

Documentation and Behavioral Observation. [videotape]. Available from Indiana University, Department of Recreation and Park Administration, HPER Building, Room 133, Bloomington, IN 47405-4711.

CASE 2 - TOM GOES FOR TWO

The city recreation department annually sponsors a competitive basketball league for children of all ages. Although the stated mission of the program is to provide all children of the community the opportunity to play, the program has traditionally been limited to nondisabled players. This year, however, the recreation director has been approached by a parent who explains that her eight-year-old son, Tom, who has a spinal cord injury and uses a wheelchair for mobility, would like to participate in the league. With the spirit that reflects the intent of the Americans with Disabilities Act (ADA), the director readily consents to the parent's request, and places Tom on a team. However, because the director has very little experience with working with people with disabilities, she contacts you, a CTRS, for assistance.

You immediately begin the process of integrating Tom into the basketball league. Through your assessment of Tom, his family, and peers, you find out that Tom regularly plays basketball with his older brother and the other children in his class at school. Tom is a good ball handler, and very mobile in his wheelchair (a chair designed for active sports use). He does not consider his disability to be a handicap. In fact, he considers himself to be a good basketball player. However, he does find it difficult to shoot and rebound because he cannot "out jump" the other players. This does not discourage him from playing.

Through your interviews with Tom's parents you find that they support all efforts to afford Tom a normalized lifestyle. They encourage his interactions with other children at school, and even approve of his somewhat rough play with his older brother. They are concerned, however, that Tom will eventually be ostracized by his peers because of his disability. At this point in time, his peers at school have accepted Tom as one of the gang, enjoy playing with him, and find it "kinda weird that you are asking all of these questions."

You follow your assessment with a thorough activity and environmental analysis of the basketball program. You first make note of the following "house rules":

1. Each game consists of four eight-minute quarters. The clock does not stop during the quarter unless a coach calls a time out.
2. There are 10 players on each team. Each player will play two quarters.
3. All games are half-court games. Play stops whenever the ball goes out of bounds or there is a change of possession (e.g., a defensive rebound, a steal). Play resumes by having one member of the team inbound the ball from center court.
4. Dribbling rules are loosely enforced, if at all.
5. The basket is set at eight feet above the floor. Two points are scored for each field goal, and one point for each free throw. There is a three-point line on the floor, but it is out of range of most of the players.

Next, you observe one of the games for the seven- to eight-year-old players, and talk to coaches, players, and referees. As a result, you discover:

1. The players are young enough to play for the sheer enjoyment of the game. In other words, the players are not concerned with winning and losing.
2. There is very little recognizable strategy involved in the game. Most plays include an in-bound pass and a mad dash for the basket. Much of the activity takes place underneath the basket. This is also the "danger zone" where players are jumping up and down without looking where they are going.
3. Parents of opposing players do not give 100% support of your intention to integrate Tom into the league.

Discussion Questions

1. What specific skills and experiences are involved in playing league basketball? Which of these skills and experiences can Tom participate in, and which present a problem for you as a programmer? How will you modify the game in order to integrate Tom into the league?
2. Discuss liability concerns and how you would address them.
3. How do current laws (e.g., ADA) address these situations? Was the recreation director legally obligated to attempt to integrate Tom into the program?
4. Assume that a similar situation arises with a league for 15–16 year-old players. Would you recommend the same integration and implementation strategy?
5. As the CTRS involved in this case, how would you conduct an assessment? Consider and list your questions; how would you approach your questions so Tom and his parents are comfortable? What do you really need to know and why? Discuss why you selected the content and format of the assessment.

In-Class Exercises

1. Plan a series of group games. After each game, have one student assume a specific disability (if you do not already have a class member who has a disability). Design a strategy to integrate the individual with a disability into the game, and replay the game. Discuss the effectiveness of the integration efforts, and the extent to which the quality of the experience changed as a result of the inclusion of a player with a disability.

2. Develop a risk management plan for the city recreation department's competitive basketball league for children that will now include participants with disabilities. When developing your plan, be sure to consider supervision of participants, conditions of the environment, and manner of conducting activities.

Role-Playing

1. Assume that the recreation director refused to integrate Tom into the league. One student assumes the role of the recreation director and other students assume the role of Tom's parents. A final student assumes the role of an advocate (CTRS) who has been called in to mediate between the two. Carry out a discussion on the legal, moral, and practical merits of integrating Tom into the league.

2. One student assumes the role of an advocate (CTRS), and all other students assume the roles of parents of opposing players who believe that the quality of the experience will be diminished through your efforts to integrate the activity. The CTRS should try to convince them that even though the nature of the experience might change, the quality of the experience will not.

3. Simulate a training workshop for coaches and officials.

Field Experiences

1. Attend a youth league basketball game. Note the skills required and how the players perceive the basketball experience. Note what appears to be important to the players and what they seem to enjoy. How is this different from adult basketball? How is the players' perception of the experience different from the experience as perceived by their parents?

2. Invite athletes with a physical disability to class to discuss this situation. Ask about their experiences in both integrated and segregated athletics. Explore their motivation to participate in both integrated and segregated athletics.

Selected References for Case Study

Carter, M. J. (1991). *Designing therapeutic recreation programs in the community*. Reston, VA: American Alliance for Health, Physical Education, Recreation and Dance.

Devine, M. A., McGovern, J. M., and Hermann, P. (1998). Inclusion in youth sports. *Parks and Recreation, 33*(7), 69–76.

Green, F. P., and DeCoux, V. (1994). A procedure for evaluating the effectiveness of a community recreation integration program. *Therapeutic Recreation Journal, 28*(1), 41–47.

McGovern, J. (1992). *The ADA self-evaluation: A handbook for compliance with the Americans with disabilities act by parks and recreation agencies*. Arlington, VA: National Recreation and Park Association.

Moon, M. S. (1994). *Making school and community recreation fun for everyone: Places and ways to integrate*. Baltimore, MD: Brookes.

National Center on Accessibility. [On-line]. Available: http://www.indiana.edu/~nca

O'Morrow, G. S., and Carter, M. J. (1997). *Effective management in therapeutic recreation service.* State College, PA: Venture Publishing, Inc.

Schleien, S. J., Germ, P. A., and McAvoy, L. H. (1996). Inclusive community leisure services: Recommended professional practices and barriers encountered. *Therapeutic Recreation Journal, 30*(4), 260–273.

Schleien, S. J., Ray, M. T., and Green, F. P. (1997). *Community recreation and persons with disabilities: Strategies for inclusion* (2nd ed.). Baltimore, MD: Brookes.

Spyer, B. (1998). Wheelchair sports as social interaction. In G. L. Hitzhusen and L. Thomas (Eds.), *Global therapeutic recreation V* (pp. 172–184). Columbia, MO: University of Missouri.

U.S. Department of Justice ADA. [On-line]. Available: http://www.usdoj.gov/crt/ada/adahom1.htm

CASE 3 - ADVOCATE OR ADVERSARY?

David is the coordinator of therapeutic recreation services for Lancaster County Parks and Recreation Department. The department serves a population base of 185,000 in a rural area in the Midwest. Despite having limited resources, the department prides itself as being progressive and quick to respond to citizen needs. It is that reputation which attracted David to the job as the first coordinator of therapeutic recreation services three years ago. Through hard work and dedication, David has slowly been able to provide an outreach program to the area's population of individuals with disabilities and initiate a county-wide advisory group to help develop inclusive recreation activities.

Things seemed to be going smoothly until one day when David arrived at the office, he was told that the Director of the Department wanted to see him immediately. David knew the minute he saw the Director's face that there was trouble. The Director informed David that at the previous night's County Supervisor's meeting, "his" advisory board showed up in force and demanded that all the county's playground equipment be immediately retrofitted so that the playgrounds would be accessible to children with disabilities. According to the Director, the group told the supervisors that if they failed to act, the group would file a federal lawsuit under the provision of the Americans with Disabilities Act (ADA).

"You organized these people," the Director yells at David. "You get them to back off! There is no way we can even start to comply with these demands, especially since less than 10% of the population in the county is disabled. You have until the end of the week to get them to change their minds."

Discussion Questions

1. Does the advisory group have a legal case against the county according to ADA guidelines?
2. Do all county playgrounds have to comply with ADA guidelines?
3. Is David responsible for the actions of the group?
4. What role should advisory groups have in the political process?
5. What is the role of an advocate?
6. What is the role and scope of responsibilities for an advisory board?
7. What should David do in the limited time that the Director has given him to solve the problem?

In-Class Exercises

1. Invite a member(s) of a therapeutic recreation advisory committee and a CTRS to come to class and discuss this case.
2. Discuss who should make up a TR advisory committee for a county parks and recreation department.

Draft a set of policies and procedures for a TR
advisory committee. Would the set of policies and
procedures have helped David with his current
situation; why or why not?

Role-Playing

Hold a County Supervisor's meeting where advocates
for the rights of people with disabilities show up to
petition for equal access to public facilities including
playgrounds. Consider inviting local officials to participate in the role-play.

Selected References for Case Study

Axlerod, N. (1991). *Creating and renewing advisory boards:
Strategies for success.* Washington, D.C. National Center for Nonprofit Boards.

Beneficial Designs. [On-line]. Available: http://www.
beneficialdesigns.com

Carver, J. (1990). *Boards that make a difference: A new design
for leadership in nonprofit and public organizations.* San Francisco,
CA: Jossey-Bass.

Center for Universal Design. [On-line]. Available: http://www2.
ncsu.edu/ncsu/design/cud

Christiansen, M. L., and Vogelsong, H. (Eds.). (1996). *PLAY IT
SAFE: An anthology of playground safety* (2nd ed.). Ashburn, VA:
National Recreation and Park Association.

National Center on Accessibility. [On-line]. Available: http://
www.indiana.edu/~nca

Recreation Access Advisory Committee, U.S. Architectural and
Transportation Barriers Compliance Board. (1994). *Recommendations*

for accessibility guidelines: Recreational facilities and outdoor developed areas. Washington, DC: U.S. Government Printing Office.

Schleien, S. J. (1993). Access and inclusion in community leisure services. *Parks and Recreation, 28*(4), 51–66.

Strensrud, C. (1993). *A training manual for Americans with disabilities act compliance in parks and recreation settings.* State College, PA. Venture Publishing, Inc.

U.S. Consumer Product Safety Commission. (1991). *Handbook for public playground safety.* Washington, DC: U.S. Government Printing Office.

U.S. Department of Justice ADA. [On-line]. Available: http://www.usdoj.gov/crt/ada/adahom1.htm

CASE 4 - JACK FINE

Jack Fine is a 38-year-old White investment analyst working for a small investment company, Chapman and Associates. His position requires frequent travel and a lot of wining and dining potential clients. Jack finds the traveling somewhat lonely and, therefore, often finds himself in the hotel bars and lounges drinking and look- ing for conversation. Throughout the past 18 months of work, he and his wife have noticed that Jack has become reliant upon his drinks, even when not at work. Jack has tried to go to Alcoholics Anonymous meetings and church support groups in his community. Unfortunately, Jack is more often out of town and out of contact with the groups; as a result, he has not benefitted from the interaction.

Jack approached his employer, who is also a good friend, for help. He does not want to lose his position, but fears that he will have to quit to save his health. Jack's em- ployer does not want to lose a good employee. The cost of replacing and retraining alone would be astronomi- cal, not to mention the effects it could have on the cli- ents that have grown to trust and rely on Jack. Chapman and Associates did some research on behalf of Jack and found a new, indirect delivery of therapeutic recreation services that could help.

A CTRS met with Jack to complete an initial assessment. Jack used to be involved in church activities with his wife. He enjoyed playing cards, baseball, fishing, shopping, dining, computer games, running, and rock climbing. Six years ago, Jack started working for Chapman and Associates and within one year, all his activities stopped. He attributed this to his frequent trips and responsibilities at work. It was determined that he needed leisure education that he could access during his travels. Due to Jack's trips, further contact with the CTRS would take place over the Internet.

Discussion Questions

1. What are the advantages and disadvantages to communicating with Jack over the Internet?
2. Is there a difference in leisure education if you are orienting the person to the community in which he or she lives or orienting to the entire world?
3. How could you educate someone about leisure using indirect contact?
4. Is leisure education an appropriate intervention for Jack? Why or why not? Explain in detail.
5. Should other professionals be consulted in Jack's situation? If so, how?
6. What legal and/or ethical issues should be considered in this case?
7. Jack has been working with you, the CTRS. Prepare a progress note for him. You will make assumptions about his involvement, progress toward goals, his strengths and weaknesses, his support or lack of, and future directions for both him and you.

In-Class Exercises

1. Choose an activity and, using the Internet, prepare a leisure education program for a client in another country.

2. Using an Internet browser such as Yahoo, type in *virtual* and *reality* and *vacation* and explore potential vacation spots on-line. Discuss how Jack and the CTRS might use this resource.

3. After working with Jack for three months, it becomes clear to you, the CTRS, that Jack needs strong support to be engaged in activities. You believe a volunteer leisure companion would be ideal. Consider what you need to do to create a win-win situation for Jack and his leisure companion. Prepare an outline of points to consider in creating a volunteer leisure companion program.

Selected References for Case Study

Bradley, G., Holm, P., Steere, M., and Stromqvist, G. (1993). Psychosocial communication and computerization. *Computers in Human Behavior, 9*, 157–169.

Broida, J. K., and Germann, C. (1999). Enhancing accessibility through virtual environments. *Parks and Recreation, 34*(5), 94–97.

Dattilo, J. (1999). *Leisure education program planning: A systematic approach* (2nd ed.). State College, PA: Venture Publishing, Inc.

Dattilo, J., and Williams, R. (2000). Leisure education. In J. Dattilo (Ed.), *Facilitation techniques in therapeutic recreation* (pp. 165–190). State College, PA: Venture Publishing, Inc.

Deiser, R. B., and Voight, A. (1998). Therapeutic recreation and relapse prevention intervention. *Parks and Recreation, 33*(5), 78–83.

Faulkner, R. W. (1991). *Therapeutic recreation protocol for treatment of substance addictions.* State College, PA: Venture Publishing, Inc.

Jaklevic, M. C. (1996). Internet technology moves to patient-care front lines. *Modern Healthcare, 26*(11), 47–50.

LaFee, S. (1993). Virtual reality: Technology opens doorway to worlds imagined and beyond. *Mainstream, 17*(6), 13–20.

Mainville, S. (1997). TR and the Internet. *Parks and Recreation, 32*(6), 70–73.

Mainville, S., and Valerius, L. (1999). Nothing but 'net: Therapeutic recreation and the Web. *Parks and Recreation, 34*(5), 86–93.

McConatha, J. T., McConatha, D., Deaner, S. L., and Dermigny, R. (1995). A computer-based intervention for the education and therapy of institutionalized older adults. *Educational Gerontology, 21*, 129–138.

McCormick, B., and Dattilo, J. (1995). "Sobriety's kind of like freedom": Integrating ideals of leisure into the ideology of Alcoholics Anonymous. *Therapeutic Recreation Journal, 29*(1), 18–29.

National Clearinghouse on Alcohol and Drug Information. [On-line]. Available: http://www.health.org

National Institute on Alcohol Abuse and Alcoholism. [On-line]. Available: http://www.niaaa.nih.gov

Rifkin, L. G. (1994). The importance of leisure to the recovery process. In D. M. Compton and S. E. Iso-Ahola (Eds.), *Leisure and mental health, volume one* (pp. 191–201). Park City, UT: Family Development Resources.

Audiovisual Resources

Computer Applications in TR. [videotape]. Available from Indiana University, Department of Recreation and Park Administration, HPER Building, Room 133, Bloomington, IN 47405-4711.

CASE 5 - JOHN PIERCE

Junctions, Inc. is a day support, nonfacility established program that focuses on community participation and inclusion based on an interdependent model of community support. A community service board refers adults with mental retardation to the program. As the adults are referred, they are matched with a Junctions' program "coach." The coach and adult work and recreate side-by-side in various community settings developing relationships and skills necessary for full community inclusion. Each consumer has individualized goals and a program plan. Objectives of the program are to provide skill and leisure training and educational opportunities; to empower individuals to realize personal freedoms, rights and responsibilities; and to apply normalization and least restrictive environment concepts in attitude and practice. The program is a classroom without walls and focuses on enabling adults to become connected to their community and to themselves.

John Pierce, a 36-year-old African American male with moderate mental retardation, was referred to the Junctions' program. He had been placed in different state institutions since he was seven years old. During a period of deinstitutionalization, John was taken out of the state facility where he was residing, and placed at a group home where he still resides. Before being referred to Junctions, John spent most of his time during the day at the group home watching television alone.

Five years later, John was referred by the community service board to the Junctions' program with problems of inability to communicate needs and wants, inappropriate social behaviors of aggression and self-inflicted abuse, and an inability to function in the community without supervision. During the next five years, a coach worked with John to assist him with these challenges. During this time, it became apparent to John's coach that a favorite activity of John's was looking at magazines and books. John's coach recommended to the supervisor of the Junctions' program that a good goal for John would be for him and his coach to frequently visit the local library. Eventually John might be able to volunteer at the local library to possibly develop job readiness skills for future employment in a library setting. John agreed to the goal and had been visiting as well as volunteering at the local library for approximately nine months. John's volunteer duty was to check out and stamp books with the return date. During this nine-month time period, the group home staff noticed John was experiencing increased agitation. This was not communicated to the Junctions' program.

In October, John's coach and John were visiting another library during peak hours; it was crowded with families and children. John, in the presence of his coach, had a behavioral outburst in the periodical section reading area. During this episode, John threw a library table and broke it, but caused no harm to himself or others. John's coach de-escalated the situation and tried to escort John out of the library. The librarian became alarmed when she perceived that the coach didn't have control of the predicament and telephoned the police department. When the police arrived at the scene, they asked John to leave the library and not to return until his behavior was under control. The librarian told John as he was leaving, "Don't come back at all."

A few days later, the supervisor of the Junctions' program, John's coach, and John met with the librarian to discuss the incident. The supervisor of the Junction's program discussed issues such as John's right to access and choice as well as possible job skills he was working on while volunteering. The librarian stated that the Junction's clients "may not be welcomed because several members of the local community complained about the presence of "retarded persons." The librarian suggested that "retarded people" go to the library at "non-prime time" hours, which she specified, because these hours of operation could be less stressful not only for the members of the community but also for John. At the end of the meeting it was decided that John should either come at nonpeak hours as stipulated by the library, or use another library in the vicinity.

Discussion Questions

1. What is deinstitutionalization and how has it affected people with disabilities? Society?
2. What philosophical issues are addressed in this case?
3. What legal issues are involved? What are John's rights?
4. What are John's responsibilities in this incident? Could the incident have been prevented?
5. Whose responsibility is it to handle liability issues related to community reintegration?
6. John's coach is preparing an in-service training program for the librarians. Suggest topics to be covered and explain why you selected them.
7. Think about the role of the CTRS in outreach, transition, and referral. Discuss this role as it relates to John.
8. From the case study, discuss the implications of good public relations as well as protection of the rights of the consumer (John).
9. Discuss the importance of positive behavioral support to individuals with disabilities as well as noncrisis intervention issues.

In-Class Exercises

Prepare an incident report and progress note for John after his visit to the library. What should be included? Should goals or interventions be altered based on the incident? How do you balance one incident as it relates to ongoing behaviors?

Role-Playing

1. Role-play the meeting with the librarian, supervisor of the Junctions' program, John's coach, and John. During the role-playing episode, take into consideration the following questions:
   a. What are some other resolutions that could arise from the meeting?

     b. What are the librarian's responsibilities? John's coach? The supervisor of Junctions? Group Home personnel?

     c. What could the coach have done to prevent the situation that occurred?

2. A team meeting with John, John's coach, John's case manager (a licensed social worker), the group home manager, and a psychologist with Junctions, Inc. is also held. Role-play this meeting. Focus on the importance of documentation and communication between and among service providers.

Selected References for Case Study

Benner, S. M. (1998). *Special education issues within the context of American society*. Belmont, CA: Wadsworth.

Browder, D. M. (1991). *Assessment of individuals with severe disabilities: An applied behavior approach to life skills assessment*. Baltimore, MD: Brookes.

Certo, N., Schleien, S., and Hunter, D. (1983). An ecological assessment inventory to facilitate community recreation participation by severely disabled individuals. *Therapeutic Recreation Journal, 17*(3), 29–38.

Howe-Murphy, R., and Charboneau, B. G. (1987). *Therapeutic recreation intervention: An ecological perspective*. Englewood Cliffs, NJ: Prentice Hall.

Huang, W., and Cuvo, A. (1997). Social skills training for adults with mental retardation in job related settings. *Behavior Modification, 21*(1), 3–44.

Mahon, M. J. (1994). The use of self-control techniques to facilitate self-determination skills during leisure in adolescents and young adults with mild and moderate mental retardation. *Therapeutic Recreation Journal, 27*(2), 58–72.

Meyer, L. H., Peck, C., and Brown, L. (1991). *Critical issues in the lives of people with severe disabilities*. Baltimore, MD: Brookes.

Rynders, J., and Schleien, S. (Eds.). (1991). *Together successfully: Creating recreational and educational programs that integrate people with and without disabilities*. Arlington, TX: Association for Retarded Citizens.

CASE 6 - CAMP HORIZON

Camp Horizon is a three-week summer day camp for abused and neglected children under the care or supervision of Child Protective Services (CPS). The camp is conducted by the therapeutic recreation section of the city parks and recreation department and paid for by CPS.

Camp Horizon provides individualized goal-oriented programs designed to address issues related to self-esteem, social skill development, anger management, assertiveness, and positive leisure skill development. Participants achieve goals through participation in games, sports, arts and crafts, nature and outdoor education, drama and role-play, team-building activities, and a ropes challenge course. Both a pre- and post-assessment is conducted and results are forwarded to CPS. CPS also receives weekly progress notes that include progress toward goals, attendance sheets, assessments and results, and all incident and accident reports. Upon conclusion of camp, all documentation becomes the property of CPS.

Campers in Camp Horizon participate in leisure education and trust-building activities each day. In the afternoon, they participate in an integrated camp. The therapeutic recreation section also conducts a half-day summer camp for participants with disabilities. Camp Horizon participants and participants from the day camp for individuals with disabilities are integrated in afternoon activities (12:00 noon–4:30 p.m.).

Discussion Questions

1. How and when do you prepare the Camp Horizon and day camp participants for inclusion in the afternoon programs? What are some issues that need to be discussed before the integrated afternoon sessions begin? How do you respond to questions asked by Camp Horizon participants about the day camp participants and vice versa?

2. Is the inclusive arrangement described in this case desirable? Why or why not? If not, discuss changes you would make.

3. Discuss staff development and training needs that are necessary to ensure the successful integration of Camp Horizon and day camp participants.

4. Discuss liability issues related to participants in Camp Horizon and the day camp.

5. Camp Horizon is in a community where volunteers—young, middle age, and older—are plentiful. The director of parks and recreation has asked you to prepare a position paper as to whether or not volunteers should be used with Camp Horizon. Defend your position. If you decide volunteers should be used, consider areas where policies, procedures, and training will be needed.

In-Class Experiences

1. Invite a representative from CPS and the therapeutic recreation section of your local parks and recreation department to discuss the pros and cons of integrating Camp Horizon and the day camp.

2. Select five members of the class to prepare and conduct an in-service training program. The trainers are to assume that class members will all be camp counselors at Camp Horizon. Challenge the trainers to be creative and get the class involved in the learning experience.

Selected References for Case Study

Bullock, C. C., and Mahon, M. J. (1997). *Introduction to recreation services for people with disabilities: A person-centered approach*. Champaign, IL: Sagamore.

Bullock, C. C., and Mahon, M. J., and Welch, L. K. (1992). Easter Seals' progressive mainstreaming model: Options and choices in camping for children and adults with disabilities. *Therapeutic Recreation Journal, 26*(4), 61–70.

Modell, S. J., and Imwold, C. H. (1998). Parental attitudes toward inclusive recreation. *Parks and Recreation, 33*(5), 88–93.

National Clearinghouse on Child Abuse and Neglect Information. [On-line]. Available: http://www.calib.com/nccanch

Schleien, S. J., Germ, P. A., and McAvoy, L. H. (1996). Inclusive community leisure services: Recommended professional practices and barriers encountered. *Therapeutic Recreation Journal, 30*(4), 260–273.

Schleien, S. J., Ray, M. T., and Green, F. P. (1997). *Community recreation and persons with disabilities: Strategies for inclusion* (2nd ed.). Baltimore, MD: Brookes.

Smith, R. W., Austin, D. R., and Kennedy, D. W. (1996). *Inclusive and special recreation: Opportunities for persons with disabilities* (3rd ed.). Madison, WI: Brown & Benchmark.

CASE 7 - KYLE

You were introduced to Kyle, a participant in the Therapeutic Recreation Activity Club after school program, in chapter two, case 9 (page 132). He is 12 years old and has a chromosomal deficiency (Wolf-Hirschorn Syndrome, 4p–) leading to mental retardation and various developmental delays. You are the CTRS for the city parks and recreation department and Kyle's parents have asked you to attend the admission, review, and retention

(ARR) meeting at Kyle's school. In attendance at this educational planning meeting are the principal, Kyle's teacher, the special services coordinator for the school district, the adaptive physical education (APE) teacher, the occupational therapist (OT) for the school district, and Kyle's parents.

During the meeting, the APE teacher shares with the committee the results of Kyle's assessment. Kyle scored very low in the following areas: jumping, sit-ups, running, catching, and throwing. You strongly disagree with the assessment results. You have worked with Kyle for three years and know he can do everything in the APE teacher's assessment.

Kyle's parents tell the ARR committee that they want the OT to work with Kyle on toileting and dressing. They also explain that he is only able to pronate and supinate his wrists to a 45-degree angle. The OT tells Kyle's parents that he only qualifies for 30 minutes of OT per week.

Discussion Questions

1. Consider the concepts of least restrictive environment and inclusion. Make a list of ideas or questions you might share at Kyle's upcoming ARR committee meeting.
2. Kyle will soon be transferring to high school. What outreach, transitional, and service options should be considered for Kyle so he will be successful in high school. Be as creative as possible.

Role-Playing

Role-play the above scenario. You know that the school has to provide services for Kyle that the family requests. Thirty minutes of OT per week is not enough to improve Kyle's range of motion and address his dressing and toileting needs. In addition, you continue to be concerned about the physical assessment results presented by the APE teacher. You are at the meeting as an advocate for Kyle. Should you speak up and demand services for Kyle? Would therapeutic recreation services be appropriate for Kyle? Would they be allowed or legitimate (refer to the Individuals with Disabilities Education Act regulations)? If so, how would you go about having them included in his individual education plan? Try to arrange to have an OT, APE, special education teacher, and parent of a child with a disability available as consultants during preparation for the role-play and debriefing following the role-play.

Selected References for Case Study

Bullock, C. C., and Johnson, D. E. (1998). Recreational therapy in special education. In F. Brasile, T. K. Skalko, and j. burlingame (Eds.), *Perspectives in recreational therapy: Issues of a dynamic profession* (pp. 107–124). Ravensdale, WA: Idyll Arbor.

Peniston, L. C. (1998). *Developing recreation skills in persons with learning disabilities.* Champaign, IL: Sagamore.

Rainforth, B., York, J., and Macdonald, C. (1992). *Collaborative teams for students with severe disabilities: Integrating therapy and educational services.* Baltimore, MD: Brookes.

Sable, J., Powell, L., and Aldrich, L. (1993/94). Transdisciplinary principles in the provision of therapeutic recreation services in inclusionary school settings. *Annual in Therapeutic Recreation, 4,* 69–81.

Schleien, S. J., Meyer, L. H., Heyne, L. A., and Brandt, B. B. (1995). *Lifelong leisure skills and lifestyles for persons with developmental disabilities.* Baltimore, MD: Brookes.

Audiovisual Resources
Learning to Play; Playing to Learn: Recreation as a Related Service. [videotape]. Available from Center for Recreation and Disability Studies, 730 Airport Road, #204, University of North Carolina at Chapel Hill, CB#8145, Chapel Hill, NC 27599-8145.

CASE 8 - HARRISON

You were introduced to Harrison in chapter two, case 11 (page 139). Harrison is a 32-year-old White male diagnosed with human immunodeficiency virus (HIV) related myopathy. Upon discharge from an inpatient rehabilitation program, Harrison is expected to return home to a rural southeastern community with initial assistance from family members. Harrison had previously worked 40 hours a week in the computer field. He enjoys cooking, eating out, attending collegiate sporting events, hiking, watching television, and playing on the computer. He lives with his significant other and has two pet cats. During the course of his rehabilitation stay, Harrison developed dysphagia, which became progressive in nature.

In-Class Exercises

1. Develop an outline for an educational resource packet for the patient, family members, friends, and significant other. Suggested contents could include nutritional information, sex education information, community resource information (e.g., available area support groups), and therapeutic touch interventions.

2. Devise a program for preparing a volunteer to deliver therapeutic recreation services to Harrison in his home. What would the volunteer need to know and how would he or she obtain that knowledge?

3. Using the Internet, search for information on HIV/AIDS and dysphagia.

4. Brainstorm a variety of ways that technology could be used to help Harrison maintain quality of life.

5. Write a discharge plan for Harrison. Consider the nature of Harrison's disabling condition, past leisure activities, available support, and location of his home.

Selected References for Case Study

AIDS Global Information Service. [On-line]. Available: http://www.aegis.com

Grossman, A. H. (1995). Using a systems approach leisure education model for HIV/AIDS prevention education. In H. Ruskin and A. Sivan (Eds.), *Leisure education towards the 21st century* (pp. 159–166). Provo, UT: Brigham Young University.

Grossman, A. H. (1997). Concern, compassion, and community: Facing the daunting worldwide challenges of HIV/AIDS. *Therapeutic Recreation Journal, 31*(2), 121–129.

Grossman, A. H., and Caroleo, O. (1996). Acquired immunodeficiency syndrome (AIDS). In D. R. Austin and M. E. Crawford, *Therapeutic recreation: An introduction* (2nd ed.) (pp. 285–301). Needham Heights, MA: Allyn & Bacon.

Grossman, A. H. (1995). Using a systems approach leisure education model for HIV/AIDS prevention education. In H. Ruskin and A. Sivan (Eds.), *Leisure education towards the 21st century* (pp. 159–166). Provo, UT: Brigham Young University.

Grossman, A. H., and Keller, M. J. (1994). New and growing populations for therapeutic recreation to serve: Trends in the HIV/AIDS epidemic. *Journal of Leisurability, 21*(4), 3–13.

Huber, J., and Schneider, B. E. (Eds.). (1992). *The social context of AIDS*. Newbury Park, CA: Sage.

Scherer, M. J. (1996). *Living in a state of stuck: How technology impacts the lives of people with disabilities* (2nd ed.). Cambridge, MA: Brookline.

CASE 9 - A STROLL ON OUR OWN

As a CTRS supervising an after-school program, you have trained and assigned your internship student, Steve, to conduct the program on his own. On a very cold day in December, Mattie, who has a compulsive aggressive disorder (introduced in chapter two, case 9, page 131), and Paul, a participant with Down syndrome, arrived at the recreation center. When Mattie and Paul got off the bus, they did not see Steve, so they put their books and jackets down inside and left the center.

Steve was in the gymnasium with two other participants at the time Mattie and Paul arrived, and did not notice that they had been in the center. Steve called the school district's transportation department to find out if Mattie and Paul had been dropped off at the recreation center. He learned that they had been dropped off earlier.

Approximately 45 minutes passed before Steve noticed Mattie's and Paul's jackets in the recreation center. He then searched the area around the center and the park across the street. After the participants had been gone for one hour, Steve decided he needed to call you, his supervisor, and Mattie's and Paul's parents. Steve then called the transportation department again to double check that these participants were dropped off at the recreation center. Steve called the police only after Mattie's mother requested he do so.

Meanwhile, Mattie and Paul had walked, in freezing weather without jackets, two and one-half miles down a busy street to a park. Mattie asked a man who was riding a bicycle through the park if he had a phone she could use. This man walked Mattie and Paul across the street to a grocery store. The manager at the grocery store called the police.

Mattie's and Paul's parents meet you, the CTRS, at the store and give their statements to the police. Paul's father stated that "This situation needs to be brought to the attention of someone higher, like the city manager."

He also tells you that Paul will never return to the after-school program. Mattie's parents want to know how this could have happened and what will be done to keep it from happening again.

Discussion Questions

1. As the supervisor of this program, how should you deal with your internship student to make this a positive learning experience? Is this situation serious enough to terminate his internship?
2. What policies and procedures could be put into place to insure that this incident will not be repeated?
3. Can the parents of these two participants ever feel comfortable leaving their children in your care again? How can you facilitate this?

In-Class Exercises

Make a list of the mistakes that were made in this scenario, and the ramifications of each.

Role-Playing

Role-play the exchange between Mattie's and Paul's parents and the supervisor of the after-school program. As the supervisor, explain to the parents how this incident happened and what you are going to do about it.

Selected References for Case Study

American Therapeutic Recreation Association. (1993). *Standards for the practice of therapeutic recreation and self-assessment guide.* Hattiesburg, MS: Author.

American Therapeutic Recreation Association. (1998). *Guidelines for internships in therapeutic recreation.* Hattiesburg, MS: Author.

National Therapeutic Recreation Society. (1995). *Standards of practice for therapeutic recreation services and annotated bibliography.* Arlington, VA: National Recreation and Park Association.

National Therapeutic Recreation Society. (1997). *NTRS intern-ship standards and guidelines for therapeutic recreation.* Arlington, VA: National Recreation and Park Association.

O'Morrow, G. S., and Carter, M. J. (1997). *Effective management in therapeutic recreation service.* State College, PA: Venture Publishing, Inc.

Siegenthaler, K. L. (1996). Supervising activities for safety: Avoid the negligence trap. *Journal of Physical Education, Recreation, and Dance, 67*(7), 29–30, 36.

CASE 10 - TO LOOK AT HER YOU'D NEVER KNOW

Caroline, introduced in chapter two, case 3 (page 107), is a 30- to 40-something, White female. She is an intelligent, well-educated woman who works as a trial lawyer. After experiencing suicidal thoughts, Caroline sought help from her primary care physician (PCP) who diagnosed her as "anxious and probably depressed," and referred her to a psychiatrist at Glacier Ridge Hospital System (GRHS). The psychiatrist, Dr. Kincaid, used both psychotherapy and psychotropic medications with Caroline. After a few sessions, Dr. Kincaid presented a diagnosis of major depressive disorder with associated anxiety.

Associated with the GRHS was the Glacier Ridge Outpatient Mental Health Center (GROMHC). Given the complexity of symptoms and Caroline identifying herself as being "blindsided by [her] illness, as though it crept up and sprung out [at her]," Dr. Kincaid additionally referred Caroline to group therapy at GROMHC. Caroline's health maintenance organization (HMO) required that the PCP be in constant contact with the specialist (psychiatrist) regarding Caroline's status, as the HMO covered 50% of the cost of each of her outpatient individual therapy sessions for up to 18 months. In addition, the HMO also covered 50% of inpatient and outpatient group therapy for up to 24 months.

Discussion Questions

1. Healthcare reform is being debated among many circles. What are HMOs and the philosophy behind them? How do HMOs differ from other insurers?

2. What are "co-pays" and the rationale for them? Caroline's HMO is typical of many others in that she has only a $5.00 co-pay no matter what the cost of treatment is for any general or specific physical health problems that she may have. Equally typical, after the first visit, Caroline has a 50% co-pay (at $135.00/hr.) for the treatment of mental health problems. What does this suggest about access to mental healthcare for persons who are economically disadvantaged?

3. As this text goes to press, Congress is debating the merits of a Patient's Bill of Rights that would address concerns, such as raised in this scenario, regarding managed care. Discuss the current status of this bill. Discuss the pros and cons of this bill.

4. While shopping one Saturday, you saw a volunteer of GROMHC. She asked you how Caroline was doing and mentioned it was so sad to see such an intelligent woman so depressed. How would you respond to the volunteer? Should any action be taken regarding the volunteer's behavior?

In-Class Exercises

Search the Internet for information on managed care. Summarize the primary issues being discussed at the various web sites you locate. Discuss the implications of the issues for the design and delivery of therapeutic recreation services.

Selected References for Case Study

Goodman, M., Brown, J. A., and Deitz, P. M. (1996). *Managing managed care II: A handbook for mental health professionals* (2nd ed.). Washington, DC: American Psychiatric Press.

Lahey, M. P. (1996). The commercial model and the future of therapeutic recreation. In C. Sylvester (Ed.), *Philosophy of therapeutic recreation: Ideas and issues, Volume II* (pp. 20–29). Arlington, VA: National Recreation and Park Association.

Rickerson, N., and burlingame, j. (1998). Healthcare delivery systems. In F. Brasile, T. K. Skalko, and j. burlingame (Eds.), *Perspectives in recreational therapy: Issues of a dynamic profession* (pp. 205–220). Ravensdale, WA: Idyll Arbor.

Wagner, D., Kennedy, B., and Prichard, A. (1996). *Recreational therapy: The next generation of reimbursement.* Hattiesburg, MS: American Therapeutic Recreation Association.

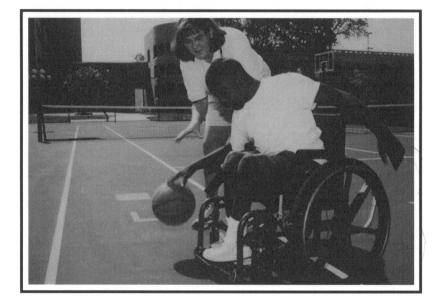

Chapter Four
Leadership in Therapeutic Recreation

Leadership is considered by many to be the key to the success of planned recreation interventions. The way therapeutic recreation specialists interact with clients may either enhance or detract from their therapeutic recreation experiences (Jordan, 1996). If we do not fulfill leadership responsibilities with great care, clients may be harmed (Pope and Vasquez, 1991). Personal qualities and professional skills necessary for successful leadership are highlighted in this chapter.

Influencing Change

Tannenbaum and Massarik (1957) define leadership as "interpersonal influence, exercised in situations and directed, through the communication process, toward the attainment of a specified goal or goals" (p. 3). Thus, in a broad sense, leadership in therapeutic recreation means influencing clients toward goal accomplishment.

It is in change that the opportunity for growth, development, and fulfillment of our clients' potentials lies (Brill, 1990). Planned change requires deliberate action. If therapeutic recreation specialists are to intervene effectively and enable clients to grow and develop, they first need to recognize their potential as agents of change (Anthony, 1985; Brill, 1990; Howe-Murphy and Charboneau, 1987). As change agents, therapeutic recreation specialists engage themselves, clients, families, and the community in a process of assessing, planning, implementing, and evaluating desired individual and environmental change. What characteristics must therapeutic recreation specialists possess to function effectively as change agents?

First and foremost, therapeutic recreation specialists must seek both personal and professional self-awareness and clarify their basic values and philosophical underpinnings. Therapeutic recreation specialists' own emotional health is essential to successful and ethical leadership. They must seek answers to personal questions such as:

- Who am I?
- How do I think and feel about myself?
- How do I deal with my human needs?
- What are my strengths?
- What is important to me?
- How do I choose to live my life? and
- How am I influenced by my gender and culture?

If they know themselves, their abilities, and limitations, they will better understand the characteristics relevant to their role as helping professionals.

To facilitate behavior change, therapeutic recreation specialists must also understand clients, whose lives are to be changed, the nature of professional relationships, and the medium serving as both the means to and the goal of that change. To maximize intrinsic motivation, self-determination, and enjoyment, therapeutic recreation specialists must possess unwavering belief in the value and dignity of all human life, regardless of individual variation, and an awareness of the interdependence of human beings. In addition, specialists must cherish the meaning, purpose, and value of leisure and recreative experiences in their own and others' lives. These irreplaceable, satisfying human experiences are vital for achieving and maintaining personal well-being. These experiences may also provide a springboard for personal and environmental change. Last, therapeutic recreation specialists must constantly accept and affirm accountability for their own behaviors.

Improving Techniques Used in Therapeutic Recreation Relationships

The achievement of optimal health and well-being through leisure and recreation depends heavily on the development of behaviors, skills, and knowledge that enable clients to make choices and to gain full enjoyment, satisfaction, and benefit from these choices. To help clients develop, therapeutic recreation specialists must be effective communicators.

Communicating Effectively

Collective efforts directed toward achieving a desired goal imply communication, which occurs when those involved in the process of change exchange information and ideas, and achieve a common or shared understanding (Austin, 1999; Brill, 1990). Therefore, the ability to communicate effectively is essential if therapeutic recreation specialists are to be successful leaders.

Interviews and discussions are two essential modes of communication used in professions such as therapeutic recreation (Brill, 1990). Interviews are structured face-to-face meetings, usually between two people. Discussions are characterized as informed conversation among a group of people (Brill, 1990). The larger the group, the greater the possibility for miscommunication. Thus, small discussion groups are recommended. Since both interviews and discussions occur within the framework of a purposeful, therapeutic relationship, they should be driven by general and specific goals. While discussions tend to be a more democratic style of communicating than interviewing, both have a beginning, middle, and ending structure. As Brill (1990) described, the beginning helps to establish a common understanding, the middle focuses on feelings, behaviors, and events, and the ending summarizes what has taken place and what will occur next. In evaluating these types of communication, therapeutic recreation specialists must consider how they move the helping relationship forward toward clients' ultimate goals, as well as how they meet immediate ones (Brill, 1990; Okun, 1992).

What are some of the skills required for effective communication? Perhaps the most important skill, and a necessary precondition of the helping relationship, is the ability to attend to clients (Carkhuff, 1993; Hackney and Cormier, 1994). *Personal attentiveness* can be communicated through various nonverbal behaviors. For example, the therapeutic recreation specialist communicates interest when facing clients in a relaxed, forward-leaning body position and using natural eye contact (not an unwavering stare), meaningful gestures such as head nodding and smiling, and animated facial expressions to convey concentration and interest. These behaviors should be appropriate within the context and culture of the situation and should not be exaggerated (Brill, 1990; Hackney and Cormier, 1994). For example, "looking directly at a person, or not meeting the gaze directly, may be considered rude or taboo in a particular culture or family group" (Brill, 1990, p. 66). Physical touch, which has tremendous potential for displaying empathy and support, can also be misinterpreted. Thus, specialists must be constantly aware of individual, familial, and cultural differences among clients to ensure that their own nonverbal behavior does not say something quite different from what they intend.

Observation is another skill important to effective communication. Carkhuff (1993) and Okun (1992) indicate that most of what therapeutic recreation specialists need to know about clients they learn by observing their physical, emotional, and intellectual characteristics. For instance, observing body build, posture, and grooming helps ascertain whether a client has a high or low physical energy level, while observing certain postures and behavioral and facial expressions helps determine a client's feelings. As Carkhuff (1993) explains, drooped shoulders and head might indicate "down" feelings while a rigid posture might indicate tension. Slow or overly swift body movements or gestures may also indicate low affect or tension, respectively. Certain facial expressions can convey a variety of emotions such as happiness, anger, interest, or confusion. These same areas—posture, behavior, and facial expressions—often provide clues about clients' intellectual readiness. The slouched posture could indicate a lack of readiness for intellectual tasks, while certain facial expressions often convey the level of interest in a task or experience or the ability to concentrate.

Another important way therapeutic recreation specialists can increase their ability to understand clients' communication is by *listening* carefully to what they say. While it may seem an easy, passive activity, listening is actually hard work and requires intense concentration. Meaningful responses to clients' statements depend on the therapeutic recreation specialist's ability to hear and understand what is being said and to uncover underlying messages (Okun, 1992). Listening improves when leaders know why they are listening, and in the therapeutic recreation process, the main reason for listening is to gather or share information needed to ameliorate problems and achieve goals. To get or give this information, specialists must focus both on the words used by clients and on the tone, volume, and manner of presentation.

Thus, effective listening demands a strong focus on clients, during which therapeutic recreation specialists must try to rid themselves of external and internal distractions. To the extent possible, this means finding a place to interact that is private and free from excessive noises or visual distractions. Perhaps more importantly, listening implies "being with" clients psychologically, which means temporarily suspending personal judgments about the information being conveyed, eliminating stereotypes or preconceived beliefs about the client, refusing to be preoccupied with personal concerns, or simply avoiding the tendency to daydream about future plans or tasks.

Certain verbal behaviors, such as "mm-hmm," "I see," and "Go on" encourage clients' communication and demonstrate continued interest (Hackney and Cormier, 1994). Therapeutic recreation specialists must avoid verbal interruptions or changes in topics that cut off or interfere with a client's expression. Also, since there may be a propensity for therapeutic recreation specialists to talk too much during personal interactions, silence is often an important aspect of verbal attentiveness. When used with good judgment, silence indicates a willingness to listen, allows communicators to collect their thoughts, and provides time for important observation and reflection.

Learning

Therapeutic recreation specialists work with clients to help them acquire and develop the attitudes, skills, and knowledge necessary to achieve and maintain their own optimal health and well-being through leisure and recreation. Russell (1986) distinguishes these three types of learning in the following way. *Attitude* is affective learning, and refers to the feelings that influence one's leisure behaviors and preferences. *Skill* is psychomotor learning and refers to one's ability to perform or engage in an activity. *Knowledge* is cognitive learning and includes an understanding of the concepts, information, or abstractions necessary to participate in an activity or experience. Certain basic principles will help facilitate learning, whether working with individual clients or groups (Austin, 1999; Flatten, Wilhite, and Reyes-Watson, 1987; Jordan, 1996; Peniston, 1998; Russell, 1986).

First, therapeutic recreation specialists must value and support individual *variation*. Effective leaders consider each person individually, recognizing diverse values, interests, and abilities. Personal attentiveness to variations will help specialists select the most appropriate approaches and techniques. To accommodate individual variation, therapeutic recreation specialists should not expect all clients to learn the same things, or learn things at the same rate or in the same manner.

Individual variation also implies that clients travel at their own pace and that their readiness for involvement will vary. Some clients will be ready to participate in therapeutic recreation experiences while others will only go through the motions or will not participate at all. For instance, a client who has been inactive for a long time will require much encouragement and may participate during one activity and not during the next. Therapeutic recreation specialists, in attempting to structure the learning process so that clients will be

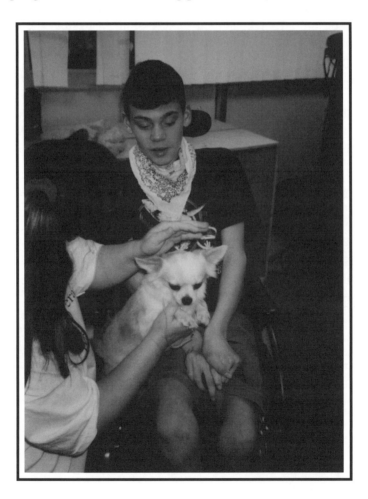

motivated to seek involvement and self-direction, must meet clients at their current level of readiness and gradually help them move in desired directions. Regardless of specialists' efforts, however, some days will be unsuccessful and efforts to learn will not be fulfilled. In this situation, it may be best to allow clients to be observers, or perhaps, to end the activity early and reschedule for another time.

Second, therapeutic recreation specialists must recognize that clients develop skills through involvement or *doing*. Therefore, clients should be involved in learning as early in the therapeutic recreation process as possible. To accomplish this, specialists should limit verbal explanations and use approaches that are multisensory, combining seeing, hearing, touching, smelling, tasting, and moving.

Since practice facilitates learning and the acquisition of skills, repeating activities and practicing skills are important aspects of *doing*. Through repetition and practice, specialists guide efforts and make corrections when necessary.

Therapeutic recreation specialists should remember, however, that they are functioning in an educator and facilitator role, and carefully determine when and when not to assist. In the therapeutic recreation process, the ultimate leadership goal is to help clients recognize their own capabilities and encourage them to assume greater responsibility for and control over their lives in general and their leisure in particular.

A related principle pertains to meaningfulness. Clients' involvement is stimulated as they become aware of the personal relevance of the experience. Their learning will be enhanced when they realize the personal benefits to be gained through involvement and when they are encouraged to seek those activities and experiences most likely to provide the desired benefits. Here planning "with" and not "for," clients is all-important. Experiences are meaningful when clients help determine, to the extent possible, the content of the experience and the processes used to engage in the experience.

The third area is *constructive feedback and positive reinforcement*. Feedback reinforces learning. Clients need support and encouragement when they are performing as desired, as well as when they are not. Therapeutic recreation specialists must recognize the importance of attempts to learn and acknowledge them with comments that enable clients to make necessary corrections while still appreciating their progress. For some clients, it is important for specialists to recognize partial success and reinforce all behavior that can be interpreted as an approximation of the desired activity (Peniston, 1998; Schleien, Meyer, Heyne, and Brandt, 1995). Specialists should use their best judgment when providing positive reinforcement, however. Overpraising or praising something that obviously did not turn out well is belittling and provides inaccurate feedback from which clients measure their progress. Clients' efforts should be acknowledged realistically.

A crucial component of providing feedback and reinforcement is the determination of realistic expectations. Persons with a disability, having experienced failure more often than their nondisabled peers, may have learned to expect to fail in new situations or experiences and need opportunities to experience success in the new leisure interests and skills they are developing. However, they also need to realize that regardless of best efforts, success in an experience or activity may not be achieved quickly.

Avoiding Burnout

As with any job, therapeutic recreation specialists will discover rewards and challenges to their work. When people experience burnout, however, they can no longer find enough satisfaction from the rewards of their work to balance the challenges (Brill, 1990). Helping professionals such as therapeutic recreation specialists may be at increased risk of experiencing burnout (Austin, 1999), which may be manifested in physical or emotional illness, addiction, anger, inefficiency, personal problems, exhaustion, inattention, impatience, and intolerance.

Spielman and Blaschko (1998) suggest that there are three major causes of burnout that must be considered: personal characteristics, dysfunctional workplaces, and stress inherent in even the best work settings. In the case of burnout, prevention is always better than cure. Thus, therapeutic recreation specialists should learn to recognize the beginning symptoms of burnout and initiate steps to address it. Becoming aware of sources of stress and seeking effective coping strategies is one approach to preventing burnout. Accordingly, therapeutic recreation specialists should be receptive to the comments and behaviors of clients, colleagues, friends, and family who may perceive burnout symptoms before they do. Sometimes, explor-

3 causes of burnout
  personal characteristics
  dysfunctional workplaces
  stress

Become more
  aware of the
  sources of stress

ing possible work changes, such as shifting responsibilities, may help prevent burnout. Ultimately, as discussed earlier, therapeutic recreation specialists must find a personal way of living that is sufficiently satisfying to enable them to distance themselves from their work in appropriate ways. Ironically, recreation and leisure services professionals often fail to do this. As McGuire, Boyd, and Tedrick (1995) suggested, therapeutic recreation specialists must become better at "practicing what they preach" by taking opportunities for restoration and development through recreation and leisure.

Informal caregivers, such as family members and friends of clients, are also at risk for experiencing burnout, and thus for neglecting their own health and well-being. As the preference for in-home care has increased, so has the demand on caregivers, especially women (Rogers, 1997). Negative consequences of caregiving that have been documented include reduced free time and social involvement, guilt related to one's ability to care, lowered life satisfaction, increased depression, neglect of exercise and proper diet, and increased use of tobacco, alcohol, and drugs (Aronson, 1992; Keller, and Tu, 1994; Rogers, 1997). Caregivers appear to want recreation and leisure in their lives, but because of various barriers and stigmas related to caregiving, they reduce or forsake it altogether (Bedini and Guinan, 1996). When caregivers are provided respite opportunities, their discretionary time increases (McCallion and Toseland, 1995). Unfortunately, caregivers tend to use this time for purposes other than leisure or social experience (Bedini and Phoenix, 1999).

Therapeutic recreation specialists who learn to take care of themselves can serve as role models for other therapeutic recreation specialists as well as for informal care providers. Effective helping will be enhanced when helpers keep themselves healthy, and when they educate others around them regarding healthy behavior (Spielman and Blaschko, 1998).

Selected Teaching Strategies

Therapeutic recreation specialists must also determine teaching strategies that are most effective in the development and acquisition of attitudes necessary for interdependent leisure participation, social interaction and recreation activity skills, and knowledge of and ability to use leisure resources. Examples of teaching strategies are discussed in the following paragraphs.

Task Analysis

Teaching or presenting an activity is aided by a technique known as task analysis: the breaking down of a recreation activity into all the necessary parts or steps and sequencing the steps for appropriate interactions within the activity. Activity analysis, discussed in chapter two, helps therapeutic recreation specialists determine which activities are most likely to contribute to the accomplishment of clients' objectives and help them to optimize personal and environmental resources. Task analysis gives a precise description, in observable and measurable terms, of each response or skill that is required to participate in the selected activity (Fine, 1996).

Task analysis is associated with a procedure known as *chaining*, which links the individual parts or steps of the selected activity. *Forward chaining* occurs when the steps are arranged and taught from the first to the last step. In *backward chaining*, the last step is listed and taught first and the steps are arranged from last to first (Fine, 1996; Schleien et al., 1995; Sherrill, 1998).

If a particular step in a sequence is not being performed well, therapeutic recreation specialists may break that step into a further sequence of steps, a procedure referred to as *branching*. The new sequence of steps or branch can be performed within the total sequence or can be practiced in isolation. If the branch is practiced in isolation, the step is then integrated with the total sequence after it has been mastered by the client (Gaylord-Ross and Holvoet, 1985).

Task analysis provides therapeutic recreation specialists with detailed knowledge of what clients must learn to do, step by step, in order to accomplish the activity objective. It also allows specialists to individualize their presentation by developing a skill sequence appropriate for each client.

Leader Assistance

Teaching or leading involves a combination of physical (e.g., tactile guidance), visual (e.g., modeling, gestures, diagrams), and verbal (e.g., auditory) prompts. In other words, therapeutic recreation specialists can "tell" individuals what to do, "show" them what to do, "physically help" them perform the activity, or use a combination of these prompts (Crawford and Mendell, 1987; Schleien et al., 1995;

Sherrill, 1998). Clients and situations vary, calling for the use of various prompts, such as physical or verbal cues, gestures, directions, examples, demonstrations, and guidance. Therapeutic recreation specialists should experiment with these prompting methods to discover the ones which will facilitate successful client participation. Decisions regarding when and how much to prompt a client depend on both the individual and the situation. In general, however, clients should perform as much of the task as possible with a minimum amount of assistance. Gradually, more restrictive prompts can be replaced with less restrictive ones.

Assistance may also be provided by peers or family members. Peer interactive approaches may include peer tutors, peer buddies, and/or special friends (Brimer, 1990). *Peer tutors* assist therapeutic recreation specialists by teaching specific skills, recording clients' progress, or attempting to modify certain behaviors. *Peer buddies* interact socially with clients but still assume primary responsibility for directing the activities in which both are taking part. In contrast, *special friends* emphasize friendship, leisure integration, and social interaction on an equal basis.

Leadership Issues

Therapeutic recreation specialists encourage clients to develop self awareness and to assume responsibility for achieving and maintaining optimal health and well-being through leisure and recreation. However, therapeutic recreation clients, because of the nature of their problems and/or life situation, may have increased vulnerability. Thus, certain transactions among specialists, clients, families, and the environment may negatively affect clients' self-awareness and self-responsibility. The fundamental ethical challenge faced in therapeutic recreation specialists' day-to-day work with clients is how to be helpful without being hurtful—the principle of beneficence or nonmaleficence (McFarlane, Keogh Hoss, Jacobson, and James, 1998; Pope and Vasquez, 1991). This type of caring is basic to all leadership interactions.

Codes of ethics established by both the American Therapeutic Recreation Association (1990) and the National Therapeutic Recreation Society (1990) serve as guides to ethical relationships and transactions with clients. These codes also provide criteria for evaluating the ethics of actual practice, and the adjudication of unethical practice complaints. These codes are understandably general since they must meaningfully apply to a variety of clients, situations, and circumstances. Nonetheless, therapeutic recreation specialists must be able to reliably interpret and apply these ethical principles in their practice. McFarlane and colleagues (1998) suggest six steps for making decisions regarding ethical relationships and transactions:

1. identify the behavior,
2. determine the professional relevance,
3. differentiate personal and/or professional ideals and values,
4. consider legal duties,
5. assess ethical obligations, and
6. define action.

Leadership issues that therapeutic recreation specialists should consider, and that may well present ethical dilemmas, are dependency, learned helplessness, self-fulfilling prophecy, confidentiality, client motivation, and client diversity.

Dependency

All individuals in a therapeutic helping relationship may naturally feel a certain amount of dependency on therapeutic recreation specialists (Corey, Corey, and Callanan, 1993; Hackney and Cormier, 1994), and people with serious illnesses or severe disabilities may experience feelings of dependency to an even greater extent. A certain amount of dependency is important to successful intervention since positive change will more readily occur when clients allow themselves to be influenced by those involved in the intervention (Brill, 1990). If, however, clients become too dependent, they may avoid accepting personal responsibility for meeting their needs and thus delay progress toward optimal health and well-being. Unfortunately, therapeutic recreation specialists, through efforts to support and nurture clients and their families and friends, may unintentionally foster overdependence. Clients may be psychologically attracted to this dependency state because of the attention they receive and the release from self-responsibility they experience. Moreover, therapeutic recreation specialists may be psychologically attracted to this type of relationship because it satisfies needs for acceptance, power, control, usefulness, and importance. Dependency may also arise because of lack of opportunity or lack of knowledge of opportunities (Brill, 1990). If dependency continues, clients learn to be helpless, relying on others rather than on themselves (Austin, 1999). Therapeutic recreation specialists must be aware of clients' dependency issues so that they help clients meet their needs in ways which positively affect personal growth and development.

Learned Helplessness

Often, people who are vulnerable feel powerless or helpless (Brill, 1990). This is especially common for clients in the initial phases of therapeutic recreation. The nature of specific disabilities, the suddenness of their onset or the unpredictability of their manifestations, clients' personalities, and society's reaction to the disability may all contribute to a feeling that there is nothing clients can do about the situation. It is important for therapeutic recreation specialists to realize that this feeling of helplessness is learned through certain transactions between clients and their environments, and may appear when coping with overpowering situations (Iso-Ahola, 1980; Seligman, 1975, 1992). Clients may perceive unsuccessful transactions as resulting from a lack of ability and come to believe that efforts cannot engender success. Therapeutic recreation specialists' responsibility is to maximize clients' abilities and the supportive properties of various environments so that they can develop feelings of competence rather than feelings of inadequacy. Therapeutic recreation content and process should allow for maximum client input, decision making, and choice so that clients can increase personal control and cease to feel helpless.

Therapeutic recreation specialists must also help clients recognize and accept the limiting realities of their particular illnesses or disabilities, primarily by making them realize that in everyone's life and environment there are events and situations which can be controlled and those which cannot. The development of realistic goals of intervention will help clients identify abilities as well as limitations.

Self-Fulfilling Prophecy

Therapeutic recreation specialists should not question whether they will influence change, but rather how. This idea is clearly demonstrated in the self-fulfilling prophecy—a concept based on the belief that clients will, within reason, exhibit the behaviors expected of them. Much of clients' identity and thus their behaviors are based on how they are treated by others. If therapeutic recreation specialists expect clients to fail, they may find it extremely difficult to succeed. On the other hand, if specialists recognize and encourage clients' ability for personal growth, they are more likely to achieve desired behavioral changes.

Confidentiality

Therapeutic recreation specialists are exposed to confidential information partially because they work in settings where the communication of confidential information is necessary. In addition, the very nature of therapeutic recreation activity often creates an atmosphere in which clients feel free to communicate confidential information to specialists. Therapeutic recreation specialists have an ethical responsibility to respect the confidences and the right to self-determination of their clients (burlingame, 1998).

Confidential information is any written or verbal communication to, or observations by therapeutic recreation specialists which are not clearly intended to be shared with another person. When clients reveal private information, therapeutic recreation specialists should not disclose this information except for the reasons for which it was intended (Corey et al., 1993). Exceptions occur when required by law, or when the client's well-being or the welfare of others is clearly and immediately at stake (Corey et al., 1993; Levy, 1993). For example, most states have laws which require that therapeutic recreation specialists who suspect any form of child abuse report it to the appropriate agency (Corey et al., 1993). Examples of confidential information include:

1. the fact that a person is or has been a client;
2. information given in confidence by a client in the course of receiving treatment;

3. information given in confidence by family, friends, and colleagues;
4. any opinion, summary, or instruction concerning the client given by the treatment team or other agency personnel in the course of treatment; and
5. personal information, which, if told to others, could possibly be detrimental to the best interests of the client.

A study conducted by Sylvester (1982) provided insight regarding how some therapeutic recreation specialists interpret the limits of confidentiality. Sylvester reported that when a client's well-being was in jeopardy, the responding therapeutic recreation specialists did not perceive confidentiality as unconditional. The general feeling expressed was that the safety of others was more important than the need for absolute confidentiality. Matters of confidentiality also appeared to be situation specific, and in some situations, specialists felt it was ethical to breach confidentiality. For example, if the responding therapeutic recreation specialists felt certain clients' behaviors, such as dishonest or illegal acts, were serious, they were less protective of confidentiality than if they considered the behaviors to be less critical. But in other cases, such as situations involving sexual matters, the specialists were in disagreement. Sylvester

concluded that in essence, confidentiality is a matter of individual choice influenced heavily by the values of each therapeutic recreation specialist.

Debates regarding the limits of confidentiality are ongoing and this important topic will continue to be of great concern to the therapeutic recreation profession and individual therapeutic recreation specialists. However, as noted by Austin (1999), "it is critical that therapeutic recreation specialists are clear about their positions with regard to confidentiality" (p. 235).

Client Motivation Strategies

It can be troubling and frustrating when clients passively or actively resist intervention efforts. This resistance, however, may be a natural reaction of clients as they attempt to move beyond or change familiar ways of behaving and thinking. Brill (1990) suggests five possible reasons clients may resist services:

1. they have sought help involuntarily,
2. their past helping relationships were not good,
3. they are currently incapable of healthy relationships,
4. they tend to resist all power and authority, and/or
5. structured helping relationships run counter to their cultural experience and values.

Clients who are not motivated are not likely to experience desired positive changes. It may be necessary to confront them with the demonstrable facts of their resistance, and discuss the effects that this lack of motivation is having on goal attainment. During this time, it may be helpful to clarify intervention expectations and to reinforce why their participation is important (i.e., the necessity of their participation as it relates to desired areas of change). It may also be helpful to reemphasize how desired changes will contribute to a higher level of well-being and, if appropriate, relocation to a less restrictive environment. Motivation may also be increased when participation and outcome expectations are realistically achievable. Realistic expectations enable clients to actually perceive movement toward desired change even if these accomplishments may, at quick glance, appear inconsequential. Last, for those clients who seem to resist formal helping relationships, it may be more motivating and effective to support and use their natural helping relationships such as family and friends.

Client Diversity Issues

Client diversity affects every aspect of therapeutic recreation practice

Clients' various experiences within their own lifestyle and culture help to determine their language, values, attitudes, and behaviors, and establish patterns of living with and relating to others (Brill, 1990). Clients exhibit differences in values, social behaviors, educational level, socioeconomic level, language, religion, and so on. Likewise, therapeutic recreation specialists' characteristics and behaviors are culture-bound (Brill, 1990). This diversity affects every aspect of therapeutic recreation practice.

Society seems to be moving beyond the melting pot concept to a more pluralistic one where different groups exist side-by-side while retaining characteristics of their own culture (Godbey, 1997; Jordan, 1996; Kraus, 2000). Still, differences between members of minority groups and members of the predominant culture can be troublesome in therapeutic relationships. Therapeutic recreation specialists must develop ways of communicating effectively in light of these differences. They may need to become skillful in differentiating between changes which are desired by their clients and which will lead to improvement in some aspect of their lives, and those which are merely in sync with specialists' own values and cultural/lifestyle orientation. They also need to be aware of barriers to establishing helping relationships such as lack of language fluency, reluctance to seek help from formal care providers, lack of role models, mistrust, and poor knowledge of resources. Acknowledgment of past and present relationships between cultures; an awareness of self values, prejudices, and cultural identity; a willingness to proceed slowly and be open to various learning styles; and a continual focus on the well-being of clients will help to establish effective and ethical communication and practice with diverse populations (Brill, 1990; Corey et al., 1993; Goldenberg and Wilhite, 1996).

A difficult question to answer is whether therapeutic recreation specialists must share the same background of clients in order to be effective. Corin (1994) suggested that practitioners of similar background attract clients to treatment early and help to maintain them in treatment. Brill (1990) points out that like experience may provide unique learning. But, unless accompanied by other knowledge, it is limited in its ability to be useful in a helping relationship and "may actually lead to a narrowing rather than a broadening of insight" (Brill, 1999, p. 185). Regardless of perceived commonalities, specialists must "emerge from their own 'cultural tunnel'" (Valerius, Hodges, and Perez, 1997, p. 61) and strive continually to try to understand the world-views of their clients (Goldenberg and Wilhite, 1996; Sue and Sue, 1990). While they do not have to accept these views as their own, they need to be able to work with these differing perspectives in a nonjudgmental manner (Sue and Sue, 1990). Therapeutic recreation specialists are bound by the ethical principle of justice to represent and treat all subgroups within society equitably. If therapeutic recreation specialists are convinced that they cannot be objective or helpful in working with certain clients, it may then be best, and most ethical, to relinquish care to another specialist. Another helpful approach may be to develop and use a referral network for special client populations.

Self-Advocacy

In the past several decades, governmental, professional, and public awareness and concern for persons with disabilities have been heightened. People with disabilities are becoming more assertive and insistent in their demands for access to education, employment, recreation, and independent living. They have participated in a broad range of group and individual efforts to improve conditions, campaign for their rights, preserve service benefits, and educate the public regarding their abilities. Yet dependency, rather than self-advocacy, has historically been the expected role of people with disabilities. Therefore, these individuals may lack advocacy skills and knowledge of how to influence decision makers.

The need to help clients become self-advocates is now greater than ever before. The restructuring of health services in response to healthcare reform has placed more emphasis on promoting clients' participation as informed and active consumers and as agents of change in their treatment (Corcoran and Vandiver, 1996; Wilhite, Keller, and Caldwell, 1999). This development has occurred at the same time that individuals with disabilities have begun demanding a greater voice in determining appropriate health and human service interventions (Coyle, Boyd, Kinney, and Shank, 1998). Still, clients may have to be educated regarding the benefits of therapeutic recreation services, especially in regard to health promotion and disease prevention, as well as regarding their basic human and legal rights.

Certain rights are guaranteed by law to people with disabilities. Velleman (1990) lists the "Big Ten Civil Rights of People With Disabilities" as the right to:

1. a barrier-free environment,
2. appropriate housing and independent living,
3. transportation and travel,
4. financial assistance,
5. healthcare,
6. insurance,
7. certain social services,
8. work,
9. education, and
10. consumer involvement.

In a setting where purposeful intervention occurs, such as in therapeutic recreation, people with disabilities and their parents or guardians, where appropriate, maintain these basic, legal rights and more. For example, people receiving therapeutic recreation services have the right to receive proper assessment and evaluation as well as the right to due process. Due process includes the right to be involved in the development of individual program plans, to be adequately informed regarding the goals of these plans (i.e., informed consent), to obtain information regarding the process by which these plans may be challenged in an impartial hearing, and to privacy. In addition to these legal rights, clients have the human right to be treated with respect and full recognition of their dignity and individuality.

Clients also have the right, to the maximum extent possible, to self-determination, to be in control of their futures, and to choose freely from meaningful and appropriate options. Self-determination implies that clients have the right to refuse or challenge participation or treatment, and in various court cases, the constitutional right to refuse treatment has been upheld. Self-determination also implies that clients have the right to dignity of risk—the right to experience both success and failure during participation in therapeutic recreation services.

Advocacy may be best approached as a partnership between therapeutic recreation specialists and other helping professionals and their clients. When these professionals support their clients by teaching advocacy procedures and by adhering to program concepts such as self-determination, dignity of risk, freedom of choice, and personal responsibility, these clients are empowered to assume increased responsibility for achieving and maintaining optimal health and well-being.

Summary

Therapeutic recreation specialists, because they are almost always involved in working directly with the recipients of their services, must establish and maintain cooperative relationships with clients and their families and caregivers. Understanding the importance of leadership and learning about effective helping strategies will enable specialists to have a positive effect on client outcomes. And, it is only within a context of caring—specifically, caring about clients' optimal health and well-being—that therapeutic recreation specialists' leadership status and power are justified (Pope and Vasquez, 1991).

The process of assessing, planning, and implementing individualized therapeutic recreation services is only as valuable as it is successful. Evaluation is needed to determine whether the services were implemented as planned and whether they accomplished what they intended to accomplish. Evaluation is discussed in chapter five, *Client Evaluation in Therapeutic Recreation*.

Bibliography

American Therapeutic Recreation Association (1990). *Code of ethics*. Hattiesburg, MS: Author.

Anthony, P. (1985). The recreation practitioner as change agent and advocate for disabled persons. *Leisurability, 12*, 19–23.

Aronson, J. (1992). Women's sense of responsibility for the care of old people: "But who else is going to do it?" *Gender and Society, 6*(1), 8–29.

Austin, D. R. (1999). *Therapeutic recreation: Processes and techniques* (4th ed.). Champaign, IL: Sagamore.

Bedini, L. A., and Guinan, D. M. (1996). The leisure of caregivers of older adults: Implications for CTRS in nontraditional settings. *Therapeutic Recreation Journal, 30*(4), 274–288.

Bedini, L. A., and Phoenix, T. L. (1999). Recreation programs for caregivers of older adults: A review and analysis of literature from 1990–1998. *Activities, Adaptation and Aging, 24*(2), 17–34.

Brimer, R. W. (1990). *Students with severe disabilities: Current perspectives and practices.* Mountain View, CA: Mayfield.

Brill, N. I. (1990). *Working with people: The helping process* (4th ed.). White Plains, NY: Longman.

burlingame, j. (1998). Confidentiality. In F. Brasile, T. K. Skalko, and j. burlingame (Eds.), *Perspectives in recreational therapy: Issues of a dynamic profession* (pp. 265–285). Ravensdale, WA: Idyll Arbor.

Carkhuff, R. R. (1993). *The art of helping* (7th ed.). Amherst, MA: Human Resource Development.

Corcoran, K., and Vandiver, V. (1996). *Maneuvering the maze of managed care: Skills for mental health practitioners.* New York, NY: The Free Press.

Corey, G., Corey, M. S., and Callanan, P. (1993). *Issues and ethics in the helping professions.* Pacific Grove, CA: Brooks/Cole.

Corin, E. (1994). The social and cultural matrix of health and disease. In R. E. Evans, M. L. Barer, and T. R. Marmor (Eds.), *Why are some people healthy and others not? The determinants of health of populations* (pp. 93–132). Hawthorne, NY: Aldine de Gruyter.

Coyle, C., Boyd, R., Kinney, W., and Shank, J. (1998). The changing nature of therapeutic recreation: Maintaining consistency in the face of change. *Parks and Recreation, 33*(5), 57–63.

Crawford, M. E., and Mendell, R. (1987). *Therapeutic recreation and adapted physical activities for mentally retarded individuals.* Englewood Cliffs, NJ: Prentice Hall.

Fine, A. H. (1996). An overview of behavioral management strategies. In A. H. Fine and N. M. Fine (Eds.), *Therapeutic recreation for exceptional children: Let me in, I want to play* (pp. 367–76). Springfield, IL: Charles C. Thomas.

Flatten, K., Wilhite, B., and Reyes-Watson. (1987). *Recreation activities for the elderly.* New York, NY: Springer.

Gaylord-Ross, R. J., and Holvoet, J. F. (1985). *Strategies for educating students with severe handicaps.* Boston, MA: Little, Brown, and Company.

Godbey, G. (1997). *Leisure and leisure services in the 21st century.* State College, PA: Venture Publishing, Inc.

Goldenberg, L., and Wilhite, B. (1996). What is a moose? Becoming culturally sensitive leaders. *Camping Magazine, 68*(4), 38–40.

Hackney, H., and Cormier, S. (1994). *Counseling strategies and interventions* (4th ed.). Boston, MA: Allyn & Bacon.

Howe-Murphy, R., and Charboneau, B. G. (1987). *Therapeutic recreation intervention: An ecological perspective.* Englewood Cliffs, NJ: Prentice Hall.

Iso-Ahola, S. E. (1980). *The social psychology of leisure and recreation.* Dubuque, IA: Wm. C. Brown.

Jordan, D. J. (1996). *Leadership in leisure services: Making a difference.* State College, PA: Venture Publishing, Inc.

Keller, M. J., and Tu, S. F. (1994, October). *The relationships between leisure and perceived burden of spouse caregivers of persons with Alzheimer's disease.* Paper presented at the meeting of the National Recreation and Park Association, Minneapolis, MN.

Kraus, R. (2000). *Leisure in a changing America: Trends and issues for the 21st century* (2nd ed.). Needham Heights, MA: Allyn & Bacon.

Levy, C. S. (1993). *Social work ethics on the line*. New York, NY: Haworth.

McCallion, P., and Toseland, R. W. (1995). Supportive group interventions with caregivers of frail older adults. *Social Work with Groups, 18*(1), 11–25.

McFarlane, N., Keogh Hoss, M. A., Jacobson, J. M., and James, A. (Eds.). (1998). *Finding the path: Ethics in action*. Hattiesburg, MS: American Therapeutic Recreation Association.

McGuire, F., Boyd, R., and Tedrick, R. T. (1995). Preventing caregiver burnout. *Recreation Focus, 3*(1), 4.

National Therapeutic Recreation Society. (1990). *Code of ethics*. Alexandria, VA: National Recreation and Park Association.

Okun, B. F. (1992). *Effective helping: Interviewing and counseling techniques* (4th ed.). Pacific Grove, CA: Brooks/Cole.

Peniston, L. C. (1998). *Developing recreation skills in persons with learning disabilities*. Champaign, IL: Sagamore.

Pope, K. S., and Vasquez, M. J. T. (1991). *Ethics in psychotherapy and counseling: A practical guide for psychologists*. San Francisco, CA: Jossey-Bass.

Rogers, N. B. (1997). Centrality of the caregiving role and integration of leisure in everyday life: A naturalistic study of older wife caregivers. *Therapeutic Recreation Journal, 31*(4), 230–243.

Russell, R. V. (1986). *Planning programs in recreation*. St. Louis, MO: C. V. Mosby.

Schleien, S. J., Meyer, L. H., Heyne, L. A., and Brandt, B. B. (1995). *Lifelong leisure skills and lifestyles for persons with developmental disabilities*. Baltimore, MD: Brookes.

Seligman, M. E. P. (1975). *Helplessness: On depression, development, and death.* San Francisco, CA: Freeman.

Seligman, M. E. P. (1992). *Learned optimism: How to change your mind and your life.* New York, NY: Alfred A. Knopf.

Sherrill, C. (1998). *Adapted physical activity, recreation and sport: Crossdisciplinary and lifespan.* Boston, MA: WCB McGraw-Hill.

Spielman, M. B., and Blaschko, T. M. (1998). Healthy caring. In F. Brasile, T. K. Skalko, and j. burlingame (Eds.), *Perspectives in recreational therapy: Issues of a dynamic profession* (pp. 165–191). Ravensdale, WA: Idyll Arbor.

Sue, D. W., and Sue, D. (1990). *Counseling the culturally different: Theory and practice* (2nd ed.). New York, NY: Wiley.

Sylvester, C. (1982). Exploring confidentiality in therapeutic recreation practice: An ethical responsibility in need of response. *Therapeutic Recreation Journal, 16*(3), 25–33.

Tannenbaum, R., and Massarik, F. (1957). Leadership: A frame of reference. *Management Science, 4*(l), 1–9.

Valerius, L., Hodges, J. S., and Perez, M. A. (1997). Cultural tunnel syndrome: A disabling condition. *Parks and Recreation, 32*(5), 60–64.

Velleman, R. A. (1990). *Meeting the needs of people with disabilities: A guide for librarians, educators, and other service professionals.* Phoenix, AZ: Oryx Press.

Wilhite, B., Keller, M. J., and Caldwell, L. (1999). Optimizing lifelong health and well-being: A health enhancing model of therapeutic recreation. *Therapeutic Recreation Journal, 33*(2), 98–115.

CASE 1 - LEAVE ME ALONE

You worked with Walter Byrd, a 72-year-old male with a diagnosis of right cerebral vascular accident, in chapter one, case 11 (page 60), and chapter two, case 12 (page 142). After completing the assessment, the CTRS scheduled and began treatment with Mr. Byrd. The CTRS noticed that when he would come close to Mr. Byrd, he would wince or flinch. He also noticed that the patient would not attempt to engage in any of the therapeutic recreation sessions without a family member's encouragement and that he was often frustrated with his performance. Following the second week of treatment, the CTRS noticed that Mr. Byrd began to have episodes of crying when he was approached for therapeutic recreation. The CTRS became alarmed and reported this behavior to a senior CTRS, and it was agreed that maybe Mr. Byrd was simply being labile secondary to his stroke.

Following the second week of treatment, the CTRS appeared on the unit to escort Mr. Byrd to the therapeutic recreation clinic. This particular day, however, Mr. Byrd began to utter racial slurs to the CTRS, who was of a different race than himself. Although shocked and hurt by the remarks, the CTRS tried to downplay the incident. However, other members of the staff also heard the remarks of Mr. Byrd and began to gather around. To add to the situation, this day Mr. Byrd put his foot down, literally. He took his right foot off of his wheelchair's footrest and placed it on the floor, so he could not be wheeled to the therapeutic recreation clinic. Members of the staff who gathered, who were also the same race as Mr. Byrd, began to apologize for his remarks and behavior. The CTRS left the unit and returned to the therapeutic recreation clinic and spoke to the director of the department about the incident. It was decided that Mr. Byrd would no longer be treated by this CTRS, but by a CTRS of his same race. When Mr. Byrd's family was told of this incident, they denied any knowledge of him having any hatred toward anyone or any racial or ethnic group.

Mr. Byrd received therapeutic recreation treatment from another CTRS. He made positive physical gains and was soon discharged from the rehabilitation center.

Discussion Questions

1. What would you have done if you were the first CTRS treating Mr. Byrd? What would you do or say to Mr. Byrd if you were the second CTRS treating him? Is switching the CTRS the right thing to do here (consider Mr. Byrd's rights as a patient or client)? Imagine that the therapeutic recreation department had no personnel of the same race as Mr. Byrd. Would you deny or withhold therapeutic recreation services?

2. Would you get input from the rest of the team treating Mr. Byrd? Would you address this issue in the predischarge interdisciplinary team meeting? If so, how?

In-Class Exercises

Ask CTRSs of different racial and ethnic backgrounds to present a panel discussion on client diversity issues. Ask each student to prepare at least two questions to share with the panel.

Role-Playing

1. Consider the feelings and emotional state of Mrs. Byrd. Develop a series of questions that she might ask the interdisciplinary team concerning the progress of her husband. Role-play this discussion

with one individual as Mrs. Byrd and the other individuals as various members of the interdisciplinary team.
2. Role-play the above scenario in which Mr. Byrd begins to use racial slurs and refuses to participate in therapeutic recreation activities. Discuss Mr. Byrd's and the other therapists' behavior.

Field Experiences

1. Visit a therapeutic recreation program with a diverse population. Ask questions about working with clients of different racial, ethnic, cultural, and lifestyle backgrounds. Consider the answers to your questions in how you would work with individuals with diverse backgrounds.
2. During the next week, observe nonverbal behaviors of as many different people as possible: on buses, in restaurants, waiting rooms, class, and so on. Share your findings and see if students can agree upon racial-related or ethnicity-related differences in nonverbal behaviors.

Selected References for Case Study

Brill, N. I. (1990). *Working with people: The helping process* (4th ed.) White Plains, NY: Longman.

Corey, J., Corey, M. S., and Calanan, P. (1993). *Issues and ethics in the helping professions* (4th ed.). Pacific Grove, CA: Brooks/Cole.

Goldenberg, L., and Wilhite, B. (1996). What is a moose? Becoming culturally sensitive leaders. *Camping Magazine, 68*(4), 38–40.

Jordan, D. J. (1996). *Leadership in leisure services: Making a difference.* State College, PA: Venture Publishing, Inc.

Kraus, R. (2000). *Leisure in a changing America: Trends and issues for the 21st Century* (2nd ed.). Needham Heights, MA: Allyn & Bacon.

Okun, B. F. (1992). *Effective helping: Interviewing and counseling techniques* (4th ed.). Pacific Grove, CA: Brooks/Cole.

Pope, K. S., and Vasquez, M. J. T. (1991) *Ethics in psychotherapy and counseling: A practical guide for psychologists.* San Francisco, CA: Jossey-Bass.

Valerius, L, Hodges, J. S., and Perez, M. A. (1997). Cultural tunnel syndrome: A disabling condition. *Parks and Recreation, 32*(5), 60–64.

> *The composite character in the case study was created from four inmates who have received services at Crawford Correctional Institute (CCI), presented in chapter two, case 1 (page 98). Although this case may seem exaggerated, it is a real representation of the mental health population at CCI. For a demographic attribute to be given to this composite character, it must have been demonstrated in at least two of the four inmates.*

CASE 2 - JAMES SHERMAN

James Sherman is a 25-year-old White male inmate of average build. He was recently sent to Crawford Correctional Institute (CCI) from another institution because of disciplinary problems. Counseling services at his former institution have rated him as a Level III mental health inmate. They also determined that his need for mental health services exceeded their resources.

A review of his institutional, mental health, and medical files revealed the following data. James is currently serving time for statutory rape and child molestation. His next parole review is scheduled in 2015. His maximum release date is in 2035. He has served one prior term for the following convictions: theft by taking a motor vehicle, violation of the controlled substance act, and driving under the influence. His sentences were served concurrently.

James and his two female siblings were raised by his mother, who has a history of mental illness. He currently

has only phone contact with his sisters. He has few pleas-
ant memories of his father, as he was physically abusive
and abandoned the family when James was four years
old. James reported to the staff that he was sexually
molested by his stepfather from the ages of six to eight
years. These acts were not reported to legal authorities.
He also reported extensive use of alcohol within his original family.

James stated that he began using inhalants around the
age of eight years. Over the next eight years he added
use of alcohol, marijuana, and crack cocaine to his leisure activities. He began showing signs of physical addiction to crack cocaine at the age of 17.

During the period just prior to his first conviction, James
reported working as a prostitute. He currently describes
his sexual orientation as homosexual.

A review of James' mental health file indicated the following data. His first report of mental illness occurred
when he was hospitalized at a state facility for self-mutilation and attempted suicide. He had one other psychiatric hospitalization for a second suicide attempt at age
16. His current diagnoses, as classified by the *Diagnostic and Statistical Manual of Mental Disorders* (4th Ed.)
(DSM-IV), are the following: Axis I: Schizophrenia paranoid type, polysubstance abuse; Axis II: Antisocial personality disorder, not otherwise specified, with borderline features; and Axis III: Post status traumatic brain
injury, received treatment for crack addiction during his
first incarceration. A history of his symptomatic behaviors include paranoia, auditory/visual hallucinations,
self-mutilation and suicide attempts x 2, increased
aggressivity, and acting out. James is currently receiving Haldol and Cogentin for the symptoms of his illness. He has a history of noncompliance with his medications.

James has an IQ of 99. He reports having completed the
eleventh grade in "free world" special education. During this incarceration, he has made one attempt to pass
the high school graduate equivalency exam. He is currently enrolled in preparatory courses for a second attempt.

During his initial interview with the CTRS, James appeared to have no physical limitations for activities. He was congenial and cooperative with the CTRS. He expressed interest in basketball, softball, drawing, painting, card games, reading, and weightlifting.

Discussion Questions

1. James' case contains several controversial areas including child molestation and sexual orientation. Almost every client a CTRS encounters will have some aspect which may not coincide with the therapist's personal value system. In order for positive interaction and behavioral change to occur, the CTRS must establish a therapeutic alliance with the client. How does a CTRS remain professional and achieve behavioral goals with a client whose behaviors are outside of the CTRS's value system? Is it ethical for a CTRS to refuse to work with a client due to personal bias? If so, what steps should the CTRS take to remain professional in this situation?

2. Recent changes in state and federal law have included the "three strikes and you're out" approach. How is the development of a client's treatment plan affected when the client is a "lifer," without hope of parole?

3. Within the inmate's informal societal structure, child molesters are considered of low status. They are often abused by their peers. Statistically, child molesters have one of the highest rates of recidivism. Hence, it is imperative that the various disciplines work together to address the needs of these individuals. What psychosocial deficits of this behavior can be addressed with therapeutic recreation? How would a CTRS formally address these deficits in treatment while maintaining the inmate's confidentiality within the general prison population?

In-Class Exercises

Examine your own personal culture (as expressed in family, peer, religious, and social groups) and its effect on your attitudes in regard to noncomformity with generally accepted social norms—for example, divorce, child abuse, dependency, homosexuality, crime, working wives, abortion, househusbands. Trace these attitudes to their origin and relate them to your ability (or inability) to get along with people who are different from you. Produce a chart tracing the development of these attitudes and be prepared to discuss them in class.

Role-Playing

1. James' assessment is complete and you, the CTRS, are conducting your first session playing cards with James. Role-play this session with James discussing his past experiences as described in the case. After the role-play, discuss aspects of communication skills (e.g., personal attentiveness, observation, listening) that were helpful or unhelpful during the session. The CTRS and James will also provide feedback on what was experienced as helpful or unhelpful. What did you learn about communication skills? What do you think needs to be changed?

2. You are the supervisor of the CTRS working with James. The CTRS is active in her church and is a strong practicing Christian. She uses her vacation to participate in missionary work. You enter the recreation area, and James and the CTRS have two unopened board games in front of them and it is half-way through the session. You hear the CTRS say, "Jesus Christ will save you from your past sins and renew you. Please claim Jesus as your personal savior." The CTRS sees you and says, "James, we will talk more later. Do you want to play Aggravation or a new game today?" [Select one person to be James, another to be the CTRS, and one to serve as the CTRS's supervisor. Role-play the incident outlined above.] What would you do immediately? What would you do later? Role-play the scenario once where the CTRS becomes defensive when approached by the supervisor, and once where this

does not happen. If possible, ask an experienced
CTRS to play the role of the supervisor. Were there
any differences? If so, what and why?

Selected References for Case Study

American Correctional Association. [On-line]. Available: http://
www.corrections.com/aca

American Psychiatric Association. (1994). *Diagnostic and
statistical manual of mental disorders* (4th ed.). Washington, DC:
Author.

Brill, N. J. (1990). *Working with people: The helping process*
(4th ed.). White Plains, NY: Longman.

Grinspoon, L., and Bakalar, J. (1988). Substance use disorders.
In A. M. Nicholi (Ed.), *The new Harvard guide to psychiatry* (pp.
259–274). Cambridge, MA: Bellknap.

Gunderson, J. B. (1988). Personality disorders. In A. M. Nicholi
(Ed.), *The new Harvard guide to psychiatry* (pp. 346–349). Cambridge, MA: Bellknap Press.

McCall, G. E. (1996). Corrections and social deviance. In D. R.
Austin and M. E. Crawford (Eds.), *Therapeutic recreation: An
introduction* (2nd ed.) (pp. 78–94). Needham Heights, MA: Allyn &
Bacon.

Munson, W. (1991). Juvenile delinquency as a societal problem
and social disability: The therapeutic recreator's role as ecological
change agent. *Therapeutic Recreation Journal, 25*(3), 19–28.

Nikkel, R. E. (1994). Areas of skill training for persons with
mental illness and substance use disorders: Building skill for successful community living. *Community Mental Health Journal, 30*(1),
61–72.

Stumbo, N., and Bloom, C. (1990). The implications of traumatic brain injury for therapeutic recreation services in rehabilitation settings. *Therapeutic Recreation Journal, 24*(3), 64–79.

Tsuang, M. T., Faraone, S. V., and Day, M. (1988). Schizophrenic disorders. In A. M. Nicholi (Ed.), *The new Harvard guide to psychiatry* (pp. 259–274). Cambridge, MA: Bellknap.

Wankel, L., and Berger, B. (1990). The psychological and social benefits of sport and physical activity. *Journal of Leisure Research, 22*(2), 167–182.

Audiovisual Resources

Therapeutic Communication. [videotape]. Available from Indiana University, Department of Recreation and Park Administration, HPER Building, Room 133, Bloomington, IN 47405-4711.

Effective Listening. [videotape]. Available from Indiana University, Department of Recreation and Park Administration, HPER Building, Room 133, Bloomington, IN 47405-4711.

Nonverbal Communication. [videotape]. Available from Indiana University, Department of Recreation and Park Administration, HPER Building, Room 133, Bloomington, IN 47405-4711.

CASE 3 - MILDRED SUMMERS

In chapter one, case 3 (page 32), you assessed the needs of Mildred Summers, a 90-year-old widow who lives alone in her own home. In chapter two, case 5 (page 118), you developed a coordinated healthcare plan for Mrs. Summers. Recently, Mrs. Summers, who has been receiving home healthcare for about two years, has been experiencing noticeable changes in her physical and cognitive functional skills. Review the case of Mildred Summers and answer the following questions.

Discussion Questions

1. After considering what specific therapeutic recreation interventions might be appropriate for Mrs.

Summers, determine which strategies the CTRS could employ to foster her perceptions of control and freedom.

2. What strategies might the CTRS use when Mrs. Summers becomes aggravated and resists intervention?

3. Describe the issues of dependency that are involved with Mrs. Summers' daughter.

In-Class Exercises

Ask a CTRS and several older adults to come to class and share their views on selected leadership issues (e.g., dependency, learned helplessness, self-fulfilling prophecy, respect/dignity, self-determination, quality of life).

Selected References for Case Study

Austin, D. R. (1999). *Therapeutic recreation processes and techniques* (4th ed.). Champaign, IL: Sagamore.

Beattie, M. (1987). *Codependent no more*. New York, NY: Harper & Row.

Carter, M. J., Browne, S., LeConey, S. P., and Nagle, C. J. (1991). *Designing therapeutic recreation programs in the community*. Reston, VA: American Alliance for Health, Physical Education, Recreation, and Dance.

Carter, M. J., Van Andel, G. E., and Robb, G. M. (1995). *Therapeutic recreation a practical approach* (2nd ed.). Prospect Heights, IL: Waveland.

Delta Society. (1994). *Handbook for animal-assisted activities and animal-assisted therapy*. Renton, WA: Author.

Dychtwald, K., and Flower, J. (1990). *Age wave: The challenges and opportunities of an aging America*. New York, NY: Bantam Books.

Foret, C. M., and Keller, M. J. (1993). A society growing older: Its implications for leisure. *Leisure Today/JOPERD, 64*(4), 29–59.

Lewis, C. B. (1990). *Aging: The healthcare challenge* (2nd ed.). Philadelphia, PA: F. A. Davis.

Searle, M. S., Mahon, M. J., Iso-Ahola, S. E., Sdrolias, H. A., and van Dyck, J. (1995). Enhancing a sense of independence and psychological well-being among the elderly: A field experiment. *Journal of Leisure Research, 27*(2), 107–124.

Teague, M. L., and MacNeil, R. D. (1992). *Aging and leisure: Vitality in later life* (2nd ed.). Dubuque, IA: W. C. Brown & Benchmark.

CASE 4 - THERAPEUTIC RECREATION ACTIVITY CLUB

The Therapeutic Recreation Activity Club is an after-school program for participants with disabilities ages 6–22. You were introduced to several participants in this program in chapter two, case 9 (page 131):

Mattie is a 15-year-old White female with aggressive conduct disorder and mild to moderate mental retardation. She often gets frustrated when staff give other children attention, is a truancy risk and, when angry, may become violent.

Tommy is a 13-year-old White male with early-onset schizophrenia. Tommy no longer wants to participate in the after-school program because he says he is not a "retard." He has recently been mainstreamed at school and his classmates often tease him and call him "retarded" and "stupid."

Kyle is a 12-year-old White male with Wolf-Hirschorn Syndrome, 4p–. Kyle is nonverbal; however, he is able to communicate via seven signs. He is ambulatory and is almost independent in feeding. Kyle needs maximum assistance with fine-motor activities and dressing.

Miguel is a 13-year-old Hispanic male with mild to moderate mental retardation who has a compulsivity to take items out of the refrigerator, or the garbage, and eat them. Miguel thoroughly enjoys playing with Kyle.

Discussion Questions

1. Discuss some ways to help Mattie become more independent in a controlled and supervised environment.

2. How could you respond to Tommy when he begins to tell you he isn't "retarded" and therefore does not need to be in the after-school program? Discuss how people with disabilities can, and sometimes do, establish hierarchies of power and value with individuals who appear or act least disabled at the top and those who are more severely disabled at the bottom. How can you address this and other symbolic meanings of disability?

3. Miguel and Kyle are enjoying being together while creating an arts and crafts project. The project is making a Mother's Day card. How could Miguel help Kyle with his fine-motor skills which are needed to complete this simple project? Consider activity and task analyses, learning, and motivation.

4. As the CTRS responsible for the Therapeutic Recreation Activity Club, you saw a request for proposals (RFP) to help teens with disabilities serve in mentorship roles for children with disabilities. Please think about if and how Mattie, Tommy, Kyle, and Miguel could serve as mentors. This would be a new program area for your after-school program. Please outline how you would go about preparing the RFP: consider the rationale for the program, the actual program goals and how they would be implemented, costs, and how you would evaluate the program. It may be helpful to contact CTRSs who have been successful in obtaining funding to support new programs.

Role-Playing

Role-play the situations described in discussion questions 2 and 3. After the role-play, discuss various leadership techniques that could be useful in these situations.

Selected References for Case Study

Bullock, C. C., and Mahon, M. J. (1997). *Introduction to recreation services for people with disabilities: A person-centered approach.* Champaign, IL: Sagamore.

Dattilo, J. (1996). Mental retardation. In D. R. Austin and M. E. Crawford (Eds.), *Therapeutic recreation: An introduction* (pp. 130–152). Needham Heights, MA: Allyn & Bacon.

Dattilo, J. (1999). *Leisure education program planning: A systematic approach* (2nd ed.). State College, PA: Venture Publishing, Inc.

Lavay, B. W., French, R., and Henderson, H. L. (1997). *Positive behavior management strategies for physical educators.* Champaign, IL: Human Kinetics.

Peniston, L. C. (1998). *Developing recreation skills in persons with learning disabilities.* Champaign, IL: Sagamore.

Schleien, S. J., and Fahnestock, M. K. (1996). Severe multiple disabilities. In D. R. Austin and M. E. Crawford (Eds.), *Therapeutic recreation: An introduction* (pp. 153–183). Needham Heights, MA: Allyn & Bacon.

Schleien, S. J., Ray, M. T., and Green, F. P. (1997). *Community recreation and people with disabilities: Strategies for inclusion.* Baltimore, MD: Brookes.

Audiovisual Resources

Feedback in Learning and Performance Situations. [videotape]. Available from Indiana University, Department of Recreation and Park Administration, HPER Building, Room 133, Bloomington, IN 47405-4711.

CASE 5 – IS IT TIME TO MOVE ON?

Gloria Edgewater is a therapeutic recreation supervisor at the Johnson Heights Rehabilitation Center. In this position, her primary duties are organizing and scheduling adult activities and overseeing the work of two other CTRSs. She is directly responsible to James Higgins, who is the coordinator of all therapeutic activities at the Center.

Gloria is very energetic, enthusiastic, and creative. She is flexible and easily adapts to situations that require change. Her relationship with the staff and clients is excellent, and her leadership with her fellow supervisors is effective. James is very much aware of Gloria's ability to direct the adult department, and he has delegated a considerable amount of authority and responsibility to her over the last three years.

James has been with the Center for over 14 years. He is dedicated, but somewhat conservative. When he first came into the organization, he rose quickly from a specialist's position to supervisor, and later to coordinator. However, four years ago, when the Director of Therapy Activities (position overseeing physical, recreation, and occupational therapists) opened up, he was passed over. The rumor had it that he was dependable and likeable, but he was not aggressive enough for the top job.

On a number of occasions, Gloria had made suggestions to James about new programs and activities, but either these suggestions were not considered or they were met with James' opposition. This is very frustrating to Gloria because she knows that the Director of Therapy Activities is always looking for ways for the different units to improve their services. Gloria did notice, however, that when the Director makes suggestions to James, they are instituted immediately.

Gloria is beginning to get very annoyed and impatient and has decided that if her suggestions are not going to be considered, it is time for her to look for a new job

Discussion Questions

1. How can Gloria effectively deal with James?
2. What strategies can Gloria employ to get James to consider and accept her suggestions?
3. If Gloria went directly to the Director of Therapy Activities, what problems do you think she would encounter with the Director? With James?
4. If Gloria decides to go directly to the Director, should she first seek James' permission to do so? Why?
5. What are, in your opinion, possible reasons that James gives little consideration to Gloria's suggestions?
6. Does Gloria have an obligation to let James know how she feels?
7. What confidentiality issues, if any, are present in this case? How would you address these issues?

Role-Playing

Hold a meeting among James, the Director, and Gloria in which the issues of this case are discussed in an open and honest way.

Selected References for Case Study

Covey, Stephen. (1989). *The 7 habits of highly effective people.* New York, NY: Simon & Schuster.

Hitt, William D. (1988). *The leader-manager: Guidelines for action.* Columbus, OH: Battelle Press.

Kraus, R., and Curtis, J. (2000). *Creative management in recreation, parks, and leisure services* (6th ed.). St. Louis, MO: McGraw-Hill.

Myers, Scott. (1991). *Every employee a manager* (3rd ed.). San Diego, CA: University Associates.

O'Morrow, G. S., and Carter, M. J. (1997). *Effective management in therapeutic recreation service.* State College, PA: Venture Publishing, Inc.

Reece, Barry. (1987). *Effective human relations in organizations.* Boston, MA: Houghton Mifflin.

CASE 6 -

EDDIE AND VERA HARRIS

Eddie and Vera Harris are 73 years old and have been married for 49 years. The couple currently resides in a small, one-story condominium purchased 12 years ago when they retired as owners of a small restaurant. Prior to retirement, Eddie's life was focused almost entirely on his work. He worked 50–60 hours a week, and rarely took vacations. The couple enjoyed traveling after retirement until three years ago, when Eddie started to experience substantial health problems stemming from his diabetes. During Eddie's last visit to his physician, the physician noticed that Eddie and Vera were having difficulty coping with the disability. Eddie seemed despondent, and Vera seemed nervous and stressed. The physician was concerned that the couple is overly focused on Eddie's disease. As a result, he referred the couple to a CTRS with a recommendation that the CTRS help the couple find some pleasure in their lives.

Eddie has lost much of his sight in spite of four laser surgeries. In addition, Eddie has experienced substantial sensory loss in his lower legs, to the extent that he no longer has feeling below the knees. As a result, Eddie's balance is very poor and he frequently falls. He uses a walker in the couple's house, but refuses to use the walker in public because he feels it is too humiliating. In addition to the sensory loss in his legs, Eddie has lost much of the feeling in his hands and fingers. As a result, he no longer independently dresses or uses the toilet.

In addition to the physical complications of diabetes, Eddie has experienced some emotional problems. A few times each month Eddie wakes up during the wee hours of the morning and experiences what Vera calls a "panic attack." The only way Vera can get him to stop the panic attack is to get him out of bed and dressed and take him for a one- to two-hour ride in the car.

Vera is extremely frustrated by the caregiving situation. She feels exhausted each time her husband has a panic attack. She also feels that there is no escape from the caregiving situation. Eddie does not want anyone to help with his care but her. The couple's house is full of lovely paintings that Vera has painted. She is no longer able to paint because each time she starts to paint, her husband calls to her to do something for him. He also does not let her leave the house to attend any of the meetings of the various social organizations of which she is a member. Vera misses her favorite leisure activities tremendously, but does not want to upset her husband. Eddie's most troubling behavior is his threats to commit suicide. When Eddie is having a particularly bad day, he will tell Vera that he is "just going to take a few pills and end it all." Vera is not sure whether he is serious and feels tremendous pressure to keep him wanting to live.

Eddie is frustrated by his disability. He feels that there is nothing meaningful for him to do anymore and believes that the future holds no promise. He frequently indicates that his "life is over," he "has nothing to contribute," and he is "just waiting for the end." Eddie's family physician has indicated that Eddie's vision will deteriorate further, and eventually he will have to use a wheelchair. When asked about how his disability has affected Vera, Eddie only says that Vera is all he has now. It seems that Eddie is so focused on his disability that he cannot even focus on how it has impacted his wife's life.

The only leisure experiences Eddie and Vera described during the interview with the CTRS were occasional outings. The television is on in their house almost all day, but neither of them seem to enjoy watching it. Sometimes they go out for dinner; however, the amount of work involved transporting and assisting Eddie reduces Vera's enjoyment. Vera indicated that prior to their retirement, the couple had promised to spend all of their leisure time together once they retired. Vera attempted to keep this promise, even though it did not bring her much satisfaction.

Discussion Questions

1. Eddie believes that his life is over because he has "nothing left to offer." Discuss societal views of older adults and their contributions to society. What are some potential reasons why Eddie feels that his life has little meaning?

2. Discuss some of the dilemmas therapeutic recreation specialists face when confronted with an individual who is considering suicide. How are issues such as confidentiality challenged when a specific third party, or the public more generally, is perceived to be at risk?

3. What is the function of therapeutic recreation when serving an older adult who has a progressively debilitating disease?

4. Are there any circumstances in which you feel suicide is a viable solution? How might your feelings about suicide impact your professional practice?

5. Are CTRSs prepared to treat the complex needs of this couple outside of a treatment team? What training, education, or ethical issues are we facing as the need for our services increases in this area?

6. Discuss the leadership issue of learned helplessness and how this may be impacting both Eddie and Vera.

In-Class Exercises

1. Invite a marriage and family therapist to class who has experience working with older adults to discuss the emotional, social, and relationship issues surrounding aging, particularly as it pertains to loss of function, caregiving-receiving roles, and suicide.

2. Invite a CTRS who conducts a support or leisure education group with older adult caregivers to discuss the role of therapeutic recreation in working with couples like Eddie and Vera.

Role-Playing

In groups of three, role-play a CTRS interviewing an older adult who is expressing feelings similar to Eddie's. One student is an observer. When playing the role of observer, write down all verbal and nonverbal behaviors. After each member of the triad has played all roles, work together to produce a list of helpful and unhelpful verbal and nonverbal behaviors. Discuss why a particular behavior seemed helpful to one person and not another. What was comfortable and uncomfortable for you as a "helper?" How did you feel as a "helpee?" What did you learn about your helping behaviors? What do you think you might want to change?

Field Experiences

1. Contact a local mental health center and gather information about the prevalence of suicide among older adults. Prepare a report that indicates the incidence of suicide among older adults, groups at risk for suicide, and potential suicide symptoms.
2. Identify what services are available in your community to assist suicidal older adults.

Selected References for Case Study

American Foundation for Suicide Prevention. [On-line]. Available: http://www.afsp.org

Caregiver's Resource Homepage. [On-line]. Available: http://www.caregiver911.com

Howe, C. Z. (1988). Selected social gerontology theories and older adult leisure involvement: A review of the literature. *The Journal of Applied Gerontology, 6*(4), 448–463.

Hughes, S., and Keller, M. J. (1992). Leisure education: A coping strategy for family caregivers. *Journal of Gerontological Social Work, 19*(1), 115–128.

Levine, R. E., and Merrill, S. C. (1987). Psychosocial aspects of the environment. *Topics in Geriatric Rehabilitation, 3*(1), 27–34.

Mannell, R. C. (1993). High-investment activity and life satisfaction among older adults: Committed, serious leisure, and flow activities. In J. R. Kelly (Ed.), *Activity and aging* (pp. 125–145). Newbury Park, CA: Sage.

Maynard, M. (1993). Achieving emotional well-being for the aged through leisure programs. In *The best of the therapeutic recreation journal: Aging* (pp. 76–79). Arlington, VA: National Recreation and Park Association.

Mental Health Infosource. [On-line]. Available: http://mhsource.com

Mosher-Ashley, P. M., and Barrett, P. W. (1997). *A life worth living: Practical strategies for reducing depression in older adults.* Baltimore, MD: Health Professions.

Okun, B. F. (1992). *Effective helping: Interviewing and counseling techniques* (4th ed.). Pacific Grove, CA: Brooks/Cole.

Patrick, G. D. (1994). The uses of recreation in geropsychiatry. In M. J. Keller and N. Osgood (Eds.), *Dynamic Leisure Programming* (3rd printing) (pp. 85–97). Arlington, VA: National Recreation and Park Association.

Pratt, C. (1991). A model community education program on depression and suicide in later life. *Gerontologist, 31*(5), 692–695.

Smith, J., and Couch, R. H. (1990). Adjustment services and aging. *Vocational Evaluation and Work Adjustment Bulletin, 24*(4), 133–138.

Audiovisual Resources

Therapeutic Communication. [videotape]. Available from Indiana University, Department of Recreation and Park Administration, HPER Building, Room 133, Bloomington, IN 47405-4711.

Effective Listening. [videotape]. Available from Indiana University, Department of Recreation and Park Administration, HPER Building, Room 133, Bloomington, IN 47405-4711.

Nonverbal Communication. [videotape]. Available from Indiana University, Department of Recreation and Park Administration, HPER Building, Room 133, Bloomington, IN 47405-4711.

CASE 7 - SHARON PARSONS

Sharon Parsons, a 31-year-old White female, was voluntarily admitted to the inpatient psychiatric unit of Greenlawn Mental Health Hospital with the diagnosis of major depressive disorder, severe. She reported during her evaluation that she was experiencing increasing job stress related to an impending hearing on sexual harassment charges that she had filed against a male co-worker and relationship difficulties with her significant other. Several days prior to admission, she began experiencing suicidal thoughts, and upon devising a plan to end her life, she presented herself to the hospital for assistance.

The inpatient unit of Greenlawn treats a diverse population of patients suffering from a wide variety of psychiatric disorders. The facility utilizes an interdisciplinary approach to treatment in an attempt to provide comprehensive care. Each patient is assigned a treatment team consisting of a psychiatrist, a psychologist, a social worker, a chemical dependency counselor, a registered nurse, and a CTRS. The role of the CTRS is vital to the patient's treatment as each team member has input in the planning of patient care.

During the treatment team meeting when Sharon's case was first discussed, the psychiatrist shared that Sharon had decided to work on her relationship issues. She stated that during the last couple's session, Sharon and her partner, Denise, had decided to end their relationship. A number of team members appeared to become quite uncomfortable, and nervous chatter erupted. The chemical dependency counselor stated that he had seen Sharon "in a lip-lock with another woman." The psychiatrist attempted to refocus the team by asking if anyone could describe Sharon's partner, in order to determine if the woman observed with Sharon was Denise.

The CTRS stated that he had met Denise and that she was a slender, blond woman appearing approximately 28 years of age. In response to this, the chemical dependency counselor laughed and remarked, "She looks like a dyke!" The registered nurse added, "I guess she's the man in the relationship." Next, the psychiatrist chuckled and stated "I wouldn't want to be alone with either one of them in a dark alley, if you know what I mean." Research has shown that only a small percentage of lesbians appear to fit society's stereotype, and that an equal number of heterosexual women have what is considered a masculine appearance. The treatment team, including the CTRS, became quiet after the exchange amongst the psychiatrist, the nurse, and chemical dependency counselor, and the team proceeded to discuss the next case.

Later that day, the CTRS went to his supervisor to report his discomfort over what had taken place in regard to Sharon's case. He shared that he was aware of his own feelings and level of comfort in working with lesbian and gay patients, but that he was experiencing guilt feelings over his inability to confront those individuals whose biases were obviously affecting their abilities to work with sexual minority populations, and in particular a current patient, Sharon. He and his supervisor decided to follow hospital policy and report the incident to each team member's proper supervisor. If this did not seem to effect change, they would follow the chain of command and report the incident to the authority at the next highest level within the organization.

Discussion Questions

1. Do you believe that the statements made by the chemical dependency counselor, nurse, and psychiatrist during the treatment team meeting were inappropriate? Why or why not?
2. What do you think of the CTRS's behavior during the treatment team meeting? If you had been in this situation, what would you have done?

3. How do you believe you would have reacted if you had witnessed Sharon and Denise kissing good-bye on the unit? What do you think about their behavior?

4. If you are uncomfortable working with lesbian or gay patients, how would you likely react to being assigned to a sexual minority patient's treatment team?

5. Thinking about how you answered question 4, which of your feelings would you hope to change? How? Why?

6. Identify ways that you can contribute to acceptance of diversity in your organization.

7. Make a list of ethical issues pertinent to this case. Discuss ways to address these issues.

In-Class Exercises

1. Invite speakers from a local lesbian, gay, bisexual, or transgendered organization to discuss their life experiences as a member of a sexual minority and the importance of creating a healthcare system that is accepting of diversity. If a speaker(s) cannot be found, obtain a video on gay, lesbian, bisexual, or transgendered issues and discuss reactions to the information afterwards.

2. Have each student prepare an editorial that will appear in the organization's monthly newsletter as to how all staff members have a responsibility to create an accepting environment for sexual minority clients. Consider how to communicate in written form attitudes, values, skills, knowledge, and the need for change. Read each other's editorial and provide ideas for improvement.

Role-Playing

1. Assign individuals to the roles of psychiatrist, psychologist, registered nurse, chemical dependency counselor, and CTRS. Role-play the situation that took place in Sharon's treatment meeting utilizing different means of dealing with the situation.

2. Your editorial on creating accepting environments for sexual minority clients just appeared in the organization's monthly newsletter where you work (see In-Class Exercises, number 2, above). You overhear two co-workers, standing in the cafeteria line, talking. One says, "I suspected he was gay. Now we know." You are gay/lesbian, how would you respond? You are not gay/lesbian, how would you respond? Include males and females in your role-play.

Field Experiences

1. Attend a meeting of a lesbian, gay, bisexual, or transgendered organization, such as Parents and Friends of Lesbians and Gays (PFLAG), a gay chapter of Alcoholics Anonymous, or a predominately lesbian, gay, bisexual, or transgendered religious organization (e.g., Metropolitan Community Church, Dignity, Amtikvah).

2. Spend a week wearing a pink triangle pin on your coat. (Homosexuals were forced to wear pink triangles in the Nazi concentration camps during World War II. The pink triangle is worn today as a sign of solidarity for the ways in which lesbians and gay men face prejudice and discrimination.) Keep a journal of your reactions and perceptions. Share these experiences with others in class.

Selected References for Case Study

American Therapeutic Recreation Association. (1990). *Code of ethics.* (1990). Hattiesburg, MS: Author.

Blumenfeld, W. J., and Raymond, D. (1993). *Looking at gay and lesbian life.* Boston, MA: Beacon.

Corey, G., Corey, M. S., and Callanan, P. (1993). *Issues and ethics in the helping professions.* Pacific Grove, CA: Brooks/Cole.

Gay and Lesbian Resources. [On-line]. Available: http://www. 3wnet.com/rainbow/gnl.html

Falco, K. L. (1991). *Psychotherapy with lesbian clients.* New York, NY: Brunner/Mazel.

Masters, W. H., Johnson, V. E., and Kolodny, R. C. (1995). *Human sexuality* (5th ed.). Menlo Park, CA: Addison-Wesley.

McFarlane, N., Keogh Hoss, M. A., Jacobson, J. M., and James, A. (Eds.). (1998). *Finding the path: Ethics in action.* Hattiesburg, MS: American Therapeutic Recreation Association.

National Black Lesbian and Gay Leadership Forum. [On-line]. Available: http://www.nblg/f.org

National Latina/o Lesbian and Gay Organization. [On-line]. Available: http://www.LLEGO.org

National Museum and Archive of Lesbian and Gay History. (1996). *The lesbian almanac.* New York, NY: Berkley.

National Therapeutic Recreation Society. (1990). *Code of ethics.* Alexandria, VA: National Recreation and Park Association.

Parents, Families, and Friends of Lesbians and Gays. [On-line]. Available: http://www.pflag.org

Pope, K. S., and Vasquez, M. J. T. (1991). *Ethics in psychotherapy and counseling: A practical guide for psychologists.* San Francisco, CA: Jossey-Bass.

Queer Resource Directory. [On-line]. Available: http://www. qrd.org/qrd

The Gay, Lesbian, and Straight Education Network. [On-line]. Available: http://www.glsen.org

Audiovisual Resources

Homophobia in the Media and Society. [videotape]. Available from Barker Media, Room 10-500, MIT, Cambridge, MA 02139.

Sexual Orientation: Reading Between the Labels. [videotape]. Available from NEWIST/CESA #7, Studio B, University of Wisconsin, Green Bay, WI 54311.

We Are Not Invisible. [videotape]. Available from Indianapolis Youth Group, P.O. Box 20716, Indianapolis, IN 46222.

CASE 8 - BERNIE

Bernie, who you first met in chapter one, case 9 (page 54), is a nine-year-old, White male with spina bifida. He is attending Camp Rolling Thunder, a camp for children with spina bifida, for the first time. Bernie is obese for his age, uses a wheelchair for mobility, and uses diapers to control his incontinence. He has a shunt in his head to maintain drainage for hydrocephalus. Bernie requires help in dressing with everything except his shirt, help with activities of daily living, especially toileting/diapering, and some assistance with transfers. Bernie is in a cabin consisting of four other boys and three counselors. This is the first time Bernie has been around others with spina bifida aside from visits to the clinic.

Discussion Questions

1. What types of difficulties, fears, or anxieties might Bernie be feeling as a first-time camper at a camp for children with similar disabilities? How could you help Bernie to eliminate or work through those fears?

2. Within his cabin, Bernie is the only camper who still uses diapers as a primary form of incontinence control; the other boys use a catheter independently. How could you encourage Bernie to become more independent with his hygiene needs?

3. How could you help Bernie deal with the social issues of being teased for snoring or being over-

weight? What advice could you give to his counselors in this situation?

Role-Playing

1. Bernie is willing to try new activities, but frequently
   waits for a counselor to reassure him about the
   safety of an activity. He is also often self-conscious
   about his participation in the activity. Role-play a
   scenario in which Bernie is hesitant to go swimming
   even though he has expressed an interest in swimming. As his counselor, how will you address his
   concerns and encourage his participation in swimming?
2. Assuming that Bernie did eventually participate in
   swimming, role-play how you would follow up with
   Bernie later that day. When preparing for the role-
   play, consider learning strategies and client motivation issues.

Selected References for Case Study

Austin, D. R. (1999). *Therapeutic recreation: Processes and techniques* (4th ed.). Champaign, IL: Sagamore.

Goldberg, B. (Ed.). (1995). *Sports and exercise for children with chronic health conditions*. Champaign, IL: Human Kinetics.

Levine, G. R. (1996). Neuromuscular disorders. In D. R. Austin and M. E. Crawford (Eds.), *Therapeutic recreation: An introduction* (pp. 184–212). Needham Heights, MA: Allyn & Bacon.

Paciorek, M. J., and Jones, J. A. (1994). *Sports and recreation for the disabled* (2nd ed.). Carmel, IN: Cooper.

Sherrill, C. (1998). *Adapted physical activity, recreation and sport: Crossdisciplinary and lifespan* (5th ed.). Boston, MA: WCB McGraw-Hill.

CASE 9 - A FAMILY IN CRISIS

To most people, Blake Peterson seems like a typical American teenager. Blake is a male, 15-year-old White high-school freshman. He plays football, basketball, and baseball, is popular with his teammates and fellow students, and is recognized in his small hometown as a talented athlete. He is considered to be of above average intelligence, and until the last two report cards were issued, he had been on the "A" and "B" honor roll and liked by his teachers. However, his last two report cards included mostly "Ds" and "Fs." During the summer before his freshman year, Blake began to run around with some of the older athletes, partying with them and experimenting with alcohol. At first he was only drinking after the game on Friday night and then again on Saturday. Within a month, though, he began using marijuana as well. It was not long until he began to use more frequently and experiment with other substances.

Blake is from an upper-middle class, well-respected family. Tom, Blake's father, is a 40-year-old accountant, and Susan, his mother, is a 38-year-old elementary school teacher. They attend church every Sunday at the First Baptist Church, where Susan is the children's director and Tom is the church treasurer. They have been married for 20 years. Blake has an older sister, Sarah, who is 18 and attends college, and a younger brother, Josh, who is nine.

The family appears to be a very strong, happy one. They are known to take vacations during the summer. They attend church and community activities together. They enjoy having other families over for meals and games. They even eat dinner together every night. They seem to enjoy spending recreation time together.

Despite all these positive influences, substance abuse is common in Blake's family. His father is a recovering alcoholic and his grandfather was also an alcoholic. There is also a history of drug and alcohol abuse and dependency among Tom's siblings and their families. Tom began attending Alcoholics Anonymous (AA) about

24 years ago. He has been sober for the past 22 years. Tom no longer feels the need to attend AA meetings on a regular basis. Occasionally, when he feels under a lot of stress, he will attend a meeting. Tom's alcoholism is common knowledge in the town, and his children know about it. It is seldom mentioned or even thought about. He is respected by his family, the town, and the church.

About a year ago, Susan was diagnosed with breast cancer. She underwent chemotherapy and was not able to participate in the same type of active lifestyle that the family had been accustomed to; family activities began to disappear. Susan is no longer going through chemotherapy, and the doctors believe that the cancer is gone. She is getting her strength back and is able to do more with the family.

Susan's cancer took its toll on Tom. He began attending more and more AA meetings and working later hours in order to escape the pain he felt at home. Sarah has been away at college and is no longer able to be there for family events. Blake was involved in sports after school and on Friday nights. When he was not playing sports, he was out with his friends. Thus, it was harder to plan and carry out family activities.

Meanwhile, Blake was beginning to use drugs and alcohol more frequently. He had increased his weekend use to almost daily. His grades had dropped drastically, he was getting into trouble at school, his attitude at home was poor, and he had dropped out of sports. Tom and Susan did not know what was going on with Blake; they had decided that these changes were a result of Susan's cancer. They began to reach out to Blake to find out what was going on. Finally, they took him to a psychiatrist.

Blake was very open with Dr. Gaby. He told her about his drug abuse and the problems he was having at school and at home. He also told her that he had gotten into some trouble with the law. Dr. Gaby determined that Blake was abusing chemicals and suffering from depression. She convinced Blake to admit to his parents that he was using drugs and that he had been arrested, which he did. He explained to his parents that he had been using alcohol and marijuana regularly, and that he had experimented with cocaine and speed. He also told them about the arrest. The family discussed their options with the counselor and Blake was admitted to Sunrise Adolescent Treatment Center (SATC), a residential treatment center that provides family services as well.

At SATC, Blake was cooperative during his assessment. He was honest about his drug use and his depression. He told the therapist that he was on Prozac for his depression. He stated that he was willing to do what he needed to do to get help.

Blake's family, however, is struggling with Blake's issues. Tom is blaming himself because addiction is often passed from one generation to the next. Susan is blaming herself because she believes that her cancer caused his depression and drug abuse. Sarah feels guilty because she is away at college and has not been there for her brother. Josh misses his brother and is worried that Blake will not get to come home. The family agrees to attend counseling at SATC on a weekly basis.

During the assessment with the CTRS, Blake stated that he is looking forward to going back to high school and getting involved in sports again. He also expressed an interest in spending more time with his family. He explained that his family used to spend a lot of recreation and leisure time together, but since his mother's illness, they have not been able to do as much. He stated that he misses doing these things and hopes that once he is discharged, they can do things as a family again.

Discussion Questions

1. Refer to the *Diagnostic and Statistical Manual of Mental Disorders* (4th Ed.) (DSM-IV) to review the descriptions of substance abuse and depression. Describe Blake's symptoms relating to each diagnosis.
2. Based on what you know about substance abuse and depression, discuss how or why the two disorders surfaced or occurred almost simultaneously with Blake. Based on what you know about substance

abuse, Blake, and his family, should the family be included in Blake's treatment process? If so, to what extent should they be involved?

3. Some time has passed. The Petersons have been extremely helpful to you, the CTRS, in establishing a family leisure program at SATC. Blake is back in school and has been drug-free. Tom has agreed to serve as chair of your family leisure program advisory board. You and Tom have spent several Monday nights planning and working together. You ask Tom to have dinner with you one evening. You realize that you are very attracted to Tom, and you know that he is not happy in his relationship with Susan. What should you do?

In-Class Exercises

Family therapeutic recreation is not common in treatment facilities today. However, the SATC offers family therapy through the counseling staff. You are aware of Blake's desire to participate in leisure with his family upon discharge. In order to have the Petersons participate in the therapeutic recreation program with Blake, you must explain the importance of this to the clinical director and treatment team. As a group, brainstorm a number of points that would help to convince the director to begin a program that will involve the families as well as clients. Address the following:

a. Significance of having the family participate;
b. Goals for the program;
c. When/how families will participate;
d. Design of program–number of families per group, what they will do, staff involvement; and
e. Examples of similar programs (e.g., community therapeutic recreation, play therapy).

Role-Playing

Based on the brainstorming session above, role-play a scenario in which one or more students play the part of a CTRS and several other students act as the clinical director and members of the treatment team. Through effective communication, convince these individuals to begin a family treatment program. As an adaptation, include Blake and his parents as part of the discussion. How could they be effective self-advocates in this scenario?

Selected References for Case Study

American Psychiatric Association. (1994). *Diagnostic and statistical manual of mental disorders* (4th ed.). Washington, DC: Author.

Bell, T. (1990). *Preventing adolescent relapse: A guide for parents, teachers, and counselors*. Independence, MO: Herald House/Independence Press.

Center for Substance Abuse Prevention. (1992). *The fact is alcoholism tends to run in families* (DHHS Publication No. [ADM] 92-1914). Rockville, MD: U.S. Department of Health and Human Services.

Daley, D., and Raskin, S. (1991). *Treating the chemically dependent and their families*. Newbury Park, CA: Sage.

Deiser, R. B., and Voight, A. (1998). Therapeutic recreation and relapse prevention intervention. *Parks and Recreation, 33*(5), 78–83.

Faulkner, R. W. (1991). *Therapeutic recreation protocol for treatment of substance addictions*. State College, PA: Venture Publishing, Inc.

Jackson, T. (1993). *Activities that teach*. Cedar City, UT: Red Rock.

Jaffe, J. (1995). *Encyclopedia of drugs and alcohol*. New York, NY: Macmillan Library Reference.

McFarlane, N., Keogh Hoss, M. A., Jacobson, J. M., and James, A. (Eds.). (1998). *Finding the path: Ethics in action*. Hattiesburg, MS: American Therapeutic Recreation Association.

Monroe, J. W. (1987). Family leisure programming. *Therapeutic Recreation Journal, 21*(3), 44–51.

National Clearinghouse on Alcohol and Drug Information. [On-line]. Available: http://www.health.org

National Institute on Alcohol Abuse and Alcoholism. [On-line]. Available: http://www.niaaa.nih.gov

National Therapeutic Recreation Society. (1990). *Code of ethics.* Alexandria, VA: National Recreation and Park Association.

Nelson, D., Capple, M., and Adkins, D. (1995). Strengthening families through recreation. *Parks and Recreation, 30*(6), 44–47.

Rainwater, A. (1992). *Therapeutic recreation for chemically dependent adolescents and adults: Programming and activities.* Reston, VA: American Alliance for Health, Physical Education, Recreation and Dance.

Rifkin, L. G. (1994). The importance of leisure to the recovery process. In D. M. Compton and S. E. Iso-Ahola (Eds.), *Leisure and mental health, volume one* (pp. 191–201). Park City, UT: Family Development Resources.

CASE 10 -

HAROLD AND SARAH WILSON

You met Harold Wilson, a 79-year-old African American male with Alzheimer's disease, and Sarah Wilson, his 76-year-old wife, in chapter two, case 4 (page 114). The couple was referred for assessment by their daughter. Mr. Wilson was diagnosed with Alzheimer's disease four years ago when he started showing signs of confusion. Since that time, he has become increasingly dependent on his wife, who provides 24-hour care.

One of the concerns of the Wilson's daughter was her mother's health. Sarah Wilson provides round-the-clock care for Mr. Wilson without any assistance. She is reluctant to allow in-home service providers to come into her home due to concern about the quality of care they provide. She only lets a family member stay with Mr. Wilson once a week while she goes to the store. Financial constraints also are an issue related to in-home services. The couple has limited financial resources and cannot afford to pay for services.

A case manager from the local Area Agency on Aging recently interviewed Mrs. Wilson and concluded that she is depressed. During the interview, Mrs. Wilson indicated that caregiving had become tremendously burdensome. She cried several times during the interview and indicated, "I never expected it would be like this."

Sarah's doctor is also concerned about the lack of respite Sarah has from caregiving. Her blood pressure is dangerously high and the doctor is fearful of her having a stroke. When Sarah is asked about taking some time for herself, she indicates that she feels guilty for going out when she knows Mr. Wilson cannot.

While Mrs. Wilson is adamant about not placing her husband in a nursing home, the burden of providing 24-hour care has reduced her quality of life and contributed to a decline in her physical and mental health.

Discussion Questions

1. What planning and/or ethical issues might the CTRS be concerned with regarding home healthcare in this case? With any case of home-based healthcare?
2. What are the areas of concern for a CTRS regarding Mrs. Wilson?
3. What approaches might be used during leisure education with Mrs. Wilson?
4. How can Mrs. Wilson's daughter and son-in-law assist in improving her quality of life?
5. What options are available for Mr. and Mrs. Wilson to enhance their quality of life?
6. "Harold is hopeless since he has Alzheimer's disease," reported Mrs. Wilson's son-in-law to you.

How would you respond to the son-in-law, how could you provide leadership in this situation, and how could you support the son-in-law in this situation?

7. Are there any activities that Mr. and Mrs. Wilson could do together to meet his and her needs? Analyze the activities to see if they will produce the desired outcomes.

In-Class Exercises

In small groups, discuss the role of therapeutic recreation with older adult caregivers. Develop a model for home-based services with this population.

Field Experiences

Invite a representative of the local Alzheimer's Association to your class to discuss caregiving issues. Try to determine strategies that caregivers can use to cope with their stressful situations.

Selected References for Case Study

Aronson, J. (1992). Women's sense of responsibility for the care of old people: "But who else is going to do it?" *Gender and Society, 6*(1), 8–29.

Bedini, L. A., and Bilbro, C. W. (1991). Caregivers, the hidden victims: Easing caregiver's burden through recreation and leisure services. *Annual in Therapeutic Recreation, 2,* 49–54.

Bollin, S., Voelkl, J. E., and Lapidos, C. (1998). The at-home independence program: A recreation program implemented by a volunteer. *Therapeutic Recreation Journal, 32*(1), 54–61.

Butin, D. N. (1991). Helping those with dementia to live at home: An educational series for caregivers. *Physical and Occupational Therapy in Geriatrics, 9*(3-4), 69–82.

Caregivers Resource Homepage. [On-line]. Available: http://www.caregivers911.com

Couper, D. P. (1989). *Aging and our families: Leader's guide to caregiver programs*. New York, NY: Human Sciences.

Hagan, L. P., Green, F., and Starling, S. (1997/98). Addressing stress in caregivers of older adults through leisure education. *Annual in Therapeutic Recreation, 7*, 42–51.

Hughes, S., and Keller, M. J. (1992). Leisure education: A coping strategy for family caregivers. *Journal of Gerontological Social Work, 19*(1), 115–128.

Keller, M. J., and Hughes, S. (1991). The role of leisure education with family caregivers of persons with Alzheimer's disease and related disorders. *Annual in Therapeutic Recreation, 11*, 1–7.

Robinson, K. M. (1988). Social skills training program for adult caregivers. *Advances in Nursing Science, 10*(2), 59–72.

Rogers, N. B. (1999). Family obligation, caregiving, and loss of leisure: The experiences of three caregivers. *Activities, Adaptation and Aging, 24*(2), 35–49.

Sommers, T., and Shields, L. (1987). *Women who take care: The consequences of caregiving in today's society*. Gainesville, FL: Triad.

The ALZHEIMER Page. [On-line]. Available: http://www.biostat.wustl.edu/ALZHEIMER

Voelkl, J. (1998). The shared activities of older adults with dementia and their caregivers. *Therapeutic Recreation Journal, 32*(3), 231–239.

CASE 11 - KATIE AND LILLY

Katie and Lilly are two biracial females ages 6 and 8, respectively, who are involved in Camp Horizon (introduced in chapter three, case 6, page 192). They are sisters who had previously been removed from their home and placed in foster care. They were returned to their home prior to their involvement in Camp Horizon. The family is being monitored weekly by Child Protective Services (CPS) to ensure that the girls are being cared for adequately.

Katie and Lilly are sweet, thoughtful, and caring girls. Katie loves to sit in a leader's lap during story time and Lilly likes to wrap her arms around the leaders. They both love to give and receive hugs. They thoroughly enjoy camp.

One of the camp activities was "Edible Creatures," in which the campers made a zoo out of food, and then ate it for snack. Each camper was asked to bring something for the activity. Katie and Lilly volunteered to bring peanut butter. On the day of the activity, Katie approached the camp director and stated, "I brought the new one (peanut butter) because the opened one had roaches in it." She was so proud of herself that she brought in the new one, but the director didn't have the heart to use it. The camp director told her to keep the peanut butter and eat it at home.

Later in the camp, it was discovered that the girls were infested with head lice and that they had been coming to camp wearing the same (soiled) clothes. The camp director documented these findings in weekly progress notes and talked to the case manager about Katie and Lilly. It was suggested by the case manager that the girls be excluded from camp until their head lice had been treated. They missed one day of camp. When they returned, they told the camp director that they had treated their hair and that their mother had discharged a "roach bomb" in their room. The girls' mother, however, had neglected to treat their mattress and pillows, so the lice came back. They were sent home again.

The CPS case manager then asked the camp director to write a detailed letter outlining her observations of the girls. The director's letter and weekly progress notes would be used, along with other CPS findings, to again remove the girls from home and place them in foster care.

Discussion Questions

1. If you, as the camp director, know that Katie and Lilly want to stay with their family, do you minimize the severity of the information you have discovered? In answering this question, consider these points:
   a. In your opinion, should the children stay with the family or be placed in foster care? Who should make this decision?
   b. You have evidence that CPS will use the information you provide to place Katie and Lilly with people who will care for their needs. Yet, you know it will upset the girls to be separated again from their family.
   c. To what extent should Katie and Lilly's wishes to stay with their family be honored? What are their rights in this situation?

2. Katie and Lilly's mother calls you, the camp director, and tells you how much the girls enjoy camp. She explains she is trying to get rid of the various insects in her apartment, but the apartment complex in the housing project is so infested that it will take time. She asks you not to report the children's situation until she has had a chance to get it under control. What is your response to Katie and Lilly's mother?

3. You are in a store and another former Camp Horizon participant approaches you and begins to tell you that she is being physically and emotionally abused again. What are your professional responsibilities? Moral responsibilities? Is there any difference in these two perspectives?

4. How important is it to maintain "professional distance" in scenarios such as these? What can you do if you find yourself becoming too emotionally involved with participants in your program?

In-Class Exercises

Invite a representative from CPS to class to discuss signs of child abuse and neglect and what to do, professionally

and personally, if you suspect that one of your participants is being abused.

Selected References for Case Study

American Therapeutic Recreation Association. (1990). *Code of Ethics*. Hattiesburg, MS: Author.

burlingame, j. (1998). Confidentiality. In F. Brasile, T. K. Skalko, and j. burlingame (Eds.), *Perspectives in recreational therapy: Issues of a dynamic profession* (pp. 265–285). Ravensdale, WA: Idyll Arbor.

Corey, G., Corey, M. S., and Callanan, P. (1993). *Issues and ethics in the helping professions*. Pacific Grove, CA: Brooks/Cole.

McFarlane, N., Keogh Hoss, M. A., Jacobson, J. M., and James, A. (Eds.). (1998). *Finding the path: Ethics in action*. Hattiesburg, MS: American Therapeutic Recreation Association.

National Clearinghouse on Child Abuse and Neglect Information. [On-line]. Available: http://www.calib.com/nccanch

National Therapeutic Recreation Society. (1990). *Code of ethics*. Alexandria, VA: National Recreation and Park Association.

Witt, P. A., and Crompton, J. L. (Eds.). *Recreation programs that work for at-risk youth: The challenge of shaping the future*. State College, PA: Venture Publishing, Inc.

Audiovisual Resources

Professional Ethics. [videotape]. Available from Indiana University, Department of Recreation and Park Administration, HPER Building, Room 133, Bloomington, IN 47405-4711.

Chapter Five

Client Evaluation in Therapeutic Recreation

Evaluation information is used in at least three different phases of the therapeutic recreation process: when conceptualizing and designing interventions, when monitoring program implementation, and when assessing program effectiveness and efficiency. In this chapter, evaluation will refer primarily to impact assessments—"a measurement of client progress in reaching the predetermined goals of the treatment plan within the therapeutic recreation program" (Beddall and Kennedy, 1985, p. 63). Thus, specific client goals and objectives, formulated in advance, provide the standard for determining the extent to which desired behavioral or functional changes are obtained, with both anticipated and unanticipated outcomes being considered.

There is a close link between the evaluation of clients' progress and the intervention strategies or therapeutic recreation programs established to address clients' goals. Since such programs are considered successful when participants develop skills and behaviors needed to obtain the global outcome of optimal health and well-being, inevitably an evaluation of one involves an evaluation of the other. It follows that ascertaining clients' progress toward optimal interdependent functioning enables therapeutic recreation specialists to determine indirectly the effectiveness of therapeutic recreation intervention strategies. Intervention strategies are evaluated to determine if they were implemented as planned, and if the selected processes and content were appropriate relative to accomplishing client outcomes or goals.

In order to evaluate clients' progress, therapeutic recreation specialists must establish specific goals and objectives and develop a plan that will identify the type of information needed and specify how this information will be systematically and routinely collected, analyzed, reported, and used to improve the individual therapeutic recreation program plan.

Understanding Evaluation in the Therapeutic Recreation Process

Evaluation is the last step in the individualized therapeutic recreation process. Since evaluation implies measurement against predetermined criteria, it actually begins during individual therapeutic recreation program planning, when the goals and objectives are formulated from input information, and continues until both short-term and long-term goals are achieved (O'Morrow and Reynolds, 1989). Basic systems theory provides a theoretical framework for understanding the individualized therapeutic recreation process as it has been presented thus far and for appreciating the role of evaluation in this process. The input, process, output model is illustrated in Figure 5.1.

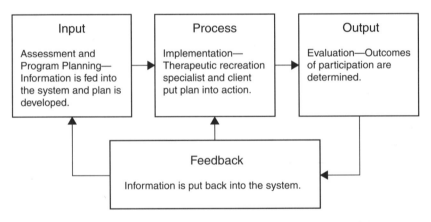

Figure 5.1 The Therapeutic Recreation Systems Model

The assessment and individual program planning phases of the therapeutic recreation process are in fact *input* phases during which information is fed into the system. This information documents clients' baseline abilities (i.e., attitudes, skills, and knowledge existing at the beginning of treatment) against which clients' progress will be measured. In the language of quality assurance, this phase represents the standard of *structure*. Structure reflects the antecedents to quality service, referring to both the setting and location where therapeutic recreation services are provided, as well as the resources (O'Morrow and Carter, 1997; Riley, 1991). *Process* refers to what goes on between the therapeutic recreation specialist, the client, and the service delivery system. During this phase, therapeutic recreation specialists and clients implement the individual program plan as they engage in activities and interactions designed to bring about desired outcomes. In the *output* or *outcome* phase, the consequences of participation are discovered. Thus, evaluation continues when therapeutic recreation specialists and clients compare the actual participation results with the original goals and objectives. Analysis of participation produces information that is put back into the system and may lead to a modification somewhere within the system. This phase is known as the "feedback loop." Input, process, and outcome variables are used to draw inferences about the quality of care.

Outcomes may verify that the system is meeting its objectives, that is, the therapeutic recreation program plan is able to facilitate the achievement of individual intervention goals. In this case, the system is updated, that is, new goals/objectives are selected, new target activities or functional domains are determined, and/or compensatory strategies for ongoing engagement in desired activities are adopted (Wilhite, Keller, and Caldwell, 1999). If outcomes do not meet the goals or objectives of the system, the system changes. Modification may be needed to adjust objectives, cues, reinforcement, specific content, processes, activities, and/or leadership techniques.

Evaluation information collected and analyzed during therapeutic recreation program planning and implementation enables therapeutic recreation specialists to make necessary changes in an individual program plan while it is being designed and in the early stages of delivery (while corrections can still be made). This approach, referred to as process or *formative* evaluation, involves more than an ongoing comparison between objectives and results (effectiveness), however. It also seeks to determine if the level of effort or cost of the program is appropriate in light of the outcomes (efficiency). Formative evaluation focuses on what actually has occurred as opposed to comparing what has occurred with what *should* have occurred— program auditing (Rossi and Freeman, 1993). Such analysis involves reviewing the type and extent of interventions employed by specialists as well as the total cost of resource utilization. Areas that might be evaluated include policies, procedures, and administrative issues; human and physical resources; program benefits; and whether regulatory and professional standards were met. Such evaluation may lead to a consideration of alternate, more effective and efficient approaches. Examples of formative evaluation questions include (Patton, 1997):

1. What's working as expected? What's not working as expected?
2. What are the primary activities of clients? What do they experience?
3. How do actual resources, staff competencies and experiences, and time lines compare to what was expected?
4. What do participants like and dislike? What are their perceptions of what's working and not working?
5. How well are staff functioning together? What are their perceptions of clients? Of administrators? Of their own roles and effectiveness?
6. What has changed from the original design and why?

Evaluation information collected at the end of an individual program plan, or at preselected intervals, enables therapeutic recreation specialists to determine whether clients have achieved intended benefits and to assess the appropriateness of therapeutic recreation programs and services. How successfully is the therapeutic recreation intervention providing clients with the resources, services, and benefits desired? This approach, referred to as outcome or *summative* evaluation, asks the basic question, "To what degree have clients or their environment changed as a result of the program's interventions?" During this phase of evaluation, therapeutic recreation specialists make decisions regarding individual program continuation, modification, and/or termination. Present approaches are compared with alternative strategies that may be more effective and efficient. Examples of summative evaluation questions include (Patton, 1997; Stumbo, 1996):

1. Did clients achieve targeted outcomes? If not, why?
2. Did clients learn a skill, or change a behavior, or improve their health, or change an attitude?
3. To what extent and in what way was the intervention program feasible? What was not feasible? Why?

4. What were the start-up and continuing costs of implementation?
5. Has the intervention program proved sufficiently effective and efficient that it merits continuation?
6. What has been learned about implementation of the intervention program that could inform other similar efforts?

When clients' goals have been achieved or when agencies' services are no longer appropriate for clients, a discharge or transition plan is developed (Carter, Van Andel, and Robb, 1995). This phase of evaluation should lead to necessary referral and follow-up services.

Environmental characteristics should be considered when determining the contribution that selected processes and content have made to the achievement of clients' transition goals and objectives. For example, evaluations of possible environmental barriers, such as inaccessible facilities, lack of adapted or special equipment, or absence of natural helpers and companions could be one aspect of measuring clients' progress toward transition to natural environments such as home or community.

Value is another important concept to consider when assuring quality. According to burlingame and Skalko (1998), the perceived worth of individualized therapeutic recreation services may be described economically, by their usefulness or importance, or by more symbolic terms such as optimal well-being, health potential, and quality of life. Shank, Kinney, and Coyle (1993) suggest that evaluating the direct outcomes of therapeutic recreation interventions needs to be followed by determining how these outcomes influence broader health and human service concerns. The most important outcomes of therapeutic recreation services may be their ability to help clients preserve both immediate and long-term health and well-being (Breske, 1995). For example, high levels of recidivism are extremely costly to clients, insurers, and health and human services care systems (Wilhite et al., 1999). Can these costs be avoided or reduced if therapeutic recreation services are provided? What is the value of learning to be an active, interdependent member of the community? Of maintaining health and well-being over the life course?

Evaluation information can be either quantitative or qualitative. Quantitative information provides statistical answers to evaluation questions. For example, such items as the number of times a client participated in activities, the length of time a client is post-injury and/or discharge, the amount of time a client spent in a specified activity, or a client's score on a functional independence measure constitute quantitative data. Quantitative information is more significant when placed in the context of other factors such as location of the activity, staff-to-client ratios, and qualifications of the staff. Qualitative information is more inclusive and provides a detailed description of people and/or situations. Qualitative data could include the nature and extent of a client's disability, a client's opinions, a client's attitudes toward and/or interest in specific activities, and a client's acquisition of specific skills. Both types of evaluation information are important and should be used.

Purposes of Evaluation

As earlier stated, measuring and documenting the extent of clients' progress in therapeutic recreation requires that the content and process of a program plan must be evaluated. It is important to ensure that clients are receiving effective services delivered in an efficient manner. Accordingly, therapeutic recreation specialists seek evaluation information to judge the merit of the planned intervention relative to achieving client goals and objectives and identifying ways of improving it. For example, evaluation might be used to assess the appropriateness of goals and objectives, to determine program content or process strengths and weaknesses, to measure the effectiveness of program resources such as equipment, materials, supplies, and facilities, to determine if initially authorized services still seem justified, to ascertain client satisfaction, to learn about unintended effects, to measure staff effectiveness, or to compare program impacts with their costs.

Evaluation is also necessary to demonstrate accountability in therapeutic recreation. It confirms the efficacy of therapeutic recreation intervention, justifies program content and process relative to clients' needs and desired outcomes, and in general demonstrates that desired outcomes are being achieved in the most effective and efficient manner. Evaluation may also be used to justify budget expenditures as they relate to individual therapeutic recreation program plans, or to verify the need for additional staff, supplies, and equipment, as well as expanded facilities or increased access to existing facilities.

Finally, because it monitors and records the quality of therapeutic recreation as perceived by both service providers and recipients, evaluation serves the important purpose of providing general documentation of therapeutic recreation programs. Criteria and standards for quality of care in therapeutic recreation have been developed by professional organizations, such as the National Therapeutic Recreation Society and the American Therapeutic Recreation Association, and by various external accrediting groups such as the Joint Commission on Accreditation of Healthcare Organizations and the Commission for the Accreditation of Rehabilitation Facilities. Therapeutic recreation specialists and clients must add to these standards by identifying other important aspects of service delivery based on their experiences and expertise. In other words, how is quality therapeutic recreation intervention best achieved for their specific situation? Therefore, evaluation serves to document the quality of therapeutic recreation programs and provides information for continuing, refining, or discontinuing existing techniques and service delivery methods.

Evaluation Models and Techniques

Using the systems analysis of input (structure), process, and output (outcome) phases of the therapeutic recreation process, the *Discrepancy Evaluation Model* (Provus, 1971; Yavorsky, 1976) provides a useful approach to individual evaluation. The Discrepancy Evaluation Model (DEM) relies on the assumption that measurable objectives or outcomes serve as standards for clients' success. In this approach, actual outcomes are compared with desired outcomes, and any discrepancy between clients' performance and predetermined standards is examined. Feedback from this investigation leads to suggestions for revising the individual therapeutic recreation program plan in order to resolve discrepancies. Questions to be answered include: If there is a discrepancy, why? What corrective actions are possible? Which corrective alternative is best?

DEM can be employed at any stage of the system, but it is often used primarily as a summative evaluation technique. In contrast,

Utilization Focused Evaluation (UFE) approaches emphasize formative evaluation concerns, useful evaluation findings, and flexible methods. UFE is done for and with specific, intended primary users (e.g., key decision makers, stakeholders) for specific, intended uses (Henderson and Bialeschki, 1995; Patton, 1997). According to Patton (1997), these users should be identified as real people, and evaluators must work with them to make decisions about the evaluation process. Connolly (1984) points out that it is inadequate merely to measure whether objectives were met. It is necessary to examine the context of the individual therapeutic recreation program along with demonstrated behaviors. Input and process characteristics that might have influenced program outcomes, either negatively or positively, must be identified. UFE emphasizes the usefulness of evaluation information as it relates to individual therapeutic recreation program revision and improvement. Thus, a

desired approach to evaluation is one that compares actual outcomes with desired outcomes, during and after program implementation, and uses this information as a basis for improving intervention.

Triangulated evaluation is a systematic, multifaceted approach that uses a variety of methods, sources of data, or evaluators (e.g., interviews, questionnaires, tests, observation, records review, client portfolios) to gather both qualitative and quantitative information. It encourages therapeutic recreation specialists to use the full range of evaluative methods and resources to produce an in-depth portrayal of a client and program and provides both an evaluative description and a judgment of worth or merit (Howe, 1982). Also, using multiple evaluators, where more than one person is developing instruments, collecting data, and interpreting results, makes it more likely that comprehensive information will be obtained (Henderson, 1995). Howe (1982) suggests that triangulation has much practical utility because the model's evaluation design is simple and does not require a high degree of "numerical" measurement. "Human concern and the potential relevance of unanticipated outcomes are of great impor-tance" (Howe, 1982, p. 91). Howe and Keller (1988) further explain that triangulation evaluation emphasizes clients' perspectives and makes possible a greater understanding of their needs. In addition, the use of multiple methods is desirable because it helps to confirm findings, thus permitting a more accurate interpretation and applica-tion of the results.

A Suggested Evaluation System

Continuous and systematic evaluation is facilitated by an evaluation system (Henderson and Bialeschki, 1995). A five-step approach to client evaluation, adapted from Gunn and Peterson (1978, pp. 265–267), is applicable to the process of client evaluation in therapeutic recreation regardless of the specific model used. This approach includes:

1. stating the evaluation questions and subquestions;
2. determining sources of data;
3. identifying methods for collecting data;
4. planning when data are to be collected and by whom; and
5. indicating how data will be treated.

Step 1. Stating Evaluation Questions and Subquestions

The purpose of this step is to focus the evaluation. Therapeutic recreation specialists should consider for whom the evaluation is being conducted and for what reason(s) (i.e., what do specialists want to know?). Audiences of the evaluation could include clients, parents or guardians, therapeutic recreation staff, treatment team members, administrators, accrediting bodies, and program funders. Examples of basic evaluation questions include:

1. What were the outcomes of the program, both anticipated and unanticipated?
2. Was the program implemented as designed?
3. Were activities and interactions appropriate in light of goals and objectives?
4. Were goals and objectives valid, realistic, and appropriate?

Each evaluation question may then be factored into subquestions. These are specific questions that must be asked in order to answer the broader evaluation questions. For example, subquestions for the evaluation question concerning implementation might include the number and qualifications of staff involved, the number and characteristics of participants, the availability and characteristics of supplies, equipment, and facilities, and the number, length, and content of activity sessions. Austin (1999) points out that any subquestion is appropriate if it addresses the primary concern expressed in the broad evaluation question.

Programs can be judged by a variety of indicators; however, some will be more valid than others. For instance, therapeutic recreation specialists may use attendance figures as an indicator of a program's worth. Attendance figures indicate how many clients were served. Yet, they cannot describe what actually happened to the clients participating in the program (Henderson and Bialeschki, 1995; Rossman, 1995). Additionally, coordinated client evaluations are being conducted in which treatment team members focus on their area of expertise, resulting in minimal overlap in the type of data collected by each discipline.

Step 2. Determining Sources of Data

In this step, therapeutic recreation specialists first determine what information will be needed to answer the evaluation subquestions, and then identify from what source(s) this information can be obtained. The questions under investigation will influence the identification of appropriate information sources. For example, the number of program participants might be obtained through program registration or attendance records, and the characteristics of participants through individual records, files, charts, test data, staff reports, family, and previous evaluation reports. Information about clients' achievements may be obtained from progress notes, discharge summaries, and portfolios. Therapeutic recreation specialists must also determine the validity and reliability of potential sources of information. Ideally, evaluation data should present a balanced and comprehensive view of the program or service and its impact (Rossman, 1995).

Step 3. Identifying Methods for Collecting Data

Once sources of data are determined, specialists must select the actual techniques they will use to obtain evaluation information. This selection involves determining what types of resources, human and physical, are needed to conduct the evaluation, as well as the availability of these resources to therapeutic recreation specialists. As discussed earlier, the use of multiple methods of collecting data, and multiple evaluators, is recommended.

Very practical concerns influence methods of collecting data. For example, designing and conducting individual evaluations may require much staff time, thereby affecting the amount of interaction among program participants. External evaluators may sometimes be used, but in most cases therapeutic recreation specialists are responsible for evaluating the progress of clients and the efficacy of individualized activities and approaches. The evaluation methods used must, therefore, be assessed relative to the amount of time and cost required. In addition, certain evaluation techniques require specialized training, skills, and experience.

A particular evaluation technique may be deemed inappropriate because of the characteristics of the clients being evaluated. For instance, an interview would not be the best evaluative method to use with a client with severe mental retardation who is both easily distracted and nonverbal. On the other hand, this method would be very appropriate for obtaining evaluative information from this client's parent, guardian, teacher, or caseworker. Certain methods may also produce undesirable or unnecessary intrusions into a client's affairs or activities. Keeping these factors in mind, therapeutic recreation specialists have a variety of techniques from which to choose. These include questionnaires and surveys, standardized tests and measures, attitude and interests scales and inventories, interviews and conversations, structured and unstructured observations, rating scales and checklists, case studies, and anecdotal journalistic logs or narrative writings. These various forms of data collection require a variety of physical resources including audiotape recorders, standardized test instruments, videotape recorders, computers, and biofeedback machines. Generally, data collection should be kept as simple as possible (Landrum, Schmidt, and McLean, 1995).

The collection of data requires recording and storing information as it is gathered. This process usually involves a filing and storage system for the various evaluation forms and narratives being completed and possibly the entering of data into a computerized classification and retrieval system. As discussed in chapter three, computer-assisted management information systems allow evaluation information to be accumulated, analyzed, and displayed in a variety of ways. Typically, data are inputted directly into the computer, or recorded first on a paper-and-pencil form and then inputted into the computer. In the future, database systems such as RehaSys will be able to analyze data indicating target outcomes that have been met and to what degree (Landrum et al., 1995). Associated with each target outcome will be a treatment protocol delineating specific objectives. The protocol will state how objectives will be measured, and what criteria will be used to determine success. These systems will also be able to estimate how long it will take to achieve global or overall outcomes (Landrum et al., 1995). Additional client data that may be provided by management information systems include routine intake data, participation levels, program completion rates, caseloads, client characteristics, and program costs (burlingame, 1998; Patton, 1997).

Step 4. Planning When Data Are to Be Collected and by Whom

Different evaluation subquestions require different times and/or frequency of collection. For example, attendance records require continuous collection; characteristics of program participants probably need to be collected only once, at the beginning of the planned intervention; and data relating to program outcomes are collected at the end of the intervention and during previously determined interim points. In addition, specific responsibility for collecting data must be defined for treatment team members and therapeutic recreation specialists.

Step 5. Indicating How Data Will Be Treated

In this step, therapeutic recreation specialists must determine how the information pertaining to each subquestion will be used to answer the evaluation questions and how results will be reported to the various evaluation audiences or stakeholders. Quantitative evaluation results may be analyzed and reported in terms of frequency, percentage, measures of central tendency, and measures of dispersion. More sophisticated statistical analysis, such as correlation, difference, and variance also may be used. Qualitative analysis, on the other hand, usually necessitates organizing, analyzing, and synthesizing words and text and then answering the evaluation questions. Basic descriptions, critical reviews or narratives, case studies, and content analysis may be aspects of qualitative analyses.

Methods of delivering evaluation reports vary and may include case studies, graphs, tables, charts, slide shows, videotapes, questions and answers, executive summaries, progress notes, and discharge plans. The reports can be both written and oral. The method of reporting is determined by the purpose of evaluation and its intended audience. Therapeutic recreation specialists may prepare a general report for all evaluation audiences. Or, they may prepare specific reports for different evaluation audiences. These reports are individually tailored and focus on the audience's perception of priority concerns.

Obviously, evaluation information is going to be helpful only to the extent that it is used to interpret the strengths and weaknesses of an individual therapeutic recreation program plan, determine the overall effectiveness and efficiency of interventions, and make revision decisions. The five-step approach described here provides a framework for implementing a system of evaluation that will substantiate the accomplishment of outcomes and permit results to be applied toward revision and improvement of clients' therapeutic recreation program plans.

Summary

Individual evaluation, a vital component of program planning and implementation, is a continuous, ongoing process used to determine clients' progress toward the development of optimal well-being through healthy, interdependent leisure lifestyles. During individual program planning, therapeutic recreation specialists specify what information needs to be collected, and how, in order to substantiate clients' progress toward goals and objectives. During and after program implementation, evaluation serves to document outcomes and demonstrate that these are a function of therapeutic recreation interventions. Areas for possible revision and improvement of services are also indicated.

Bibliography

Austin, D. R. (1999). *Therapeutic recreation: Processes and techniques* (4th ed.). Champaign, IL: Sagamore.

Beddall, T., and Kennedy, D. W. (1985). Attitudes of therapeutic recreators toward evaluation and client assessment. *Therapeutic Recreation Journal, 19*(1), 62–70.

Breske, S. (April, 1995). In come outcomes: Strategies to help you in the climb to stay on top. *Advance for Directors in Rehabilitation, 4*(4), 14–8.

burlingame, j. (1998). The role of information technologies. In F. Brasile, T. K. Skalko, and j. burlingame (Eds.), *Perspectives in recreational therapy: Issues of a dynamic profession* (pp. 463–486). Ravensdale, WA: Idyll Arbor.

burlingame, j., and Skalko, T. K. (1998). Managing quality to meet and exceed standards. In F. Brasile, T. K. Skalko, and j. burlingame (Eds.), *Perspectives in recreational therapy: Issues of a dynamic profession* (pp. 39–62). Ravensdale, WA: Idyll Arbor.

Carter, M. J., Van Andel, G. E., and Robb, G. M. (1995). *Therapeutic recreation: A practical approach.* Prospect Heights, IL: Waveland.

Connolly, P. (1984). Program evaluation. In C. A. Peterson and S. L. Gunn, *Therapeutic recreation program design: Principles and procedures* (2nd ed.) (pp. 136–179). Englewood Cliffs, NJ: Prentice Hall.

Gunn, S. L., and Peterson, C. A. (1978). *Therapeutic recreation program design: Principles and procedures.* Englewood Cliffs, NJ: Prentice Hall.

Henderson, K. A., and Bialeschki, D. (1995). *Evaluating leisure services: Making enlightened decisions.* State College, PA: Venture Publishing, Inc.

Howe, C. Z. (1982). Some uses of the multi-modal method of curriculum evaluation in therapeutic recreation. In L. L. Neal and C. R. Edginton (Eds.), *Extra perspectives: Concepts in therapeutic recreation* (pp. 87–98). Eugene, OR: Center of Leisure Studies, University of Oregon.

Howe, C. Z., and Keller, M. J. (1988). The use of triangulation as an evaluation technique: Illustrations from regional symposia in therapeutic recreation. *Therapeutic Recreation Journal, 22(1),* 36–45.

Landrum, P. K., Schmidt, N. D., and McLean, A. (1995). *Out-come-oriented rehabilitation: Principles, strategies, and tools for effective program management.* Gaithersburg, MD: Aspen.

O'Morrow, G. S., and Carter, M. J. (1997). *Effective management in therapeutic recreation service*. State College, PA: Venture Publishing, Inc.

O'Morrow, G. S., and Reynolds, R. P. (1989). *Therapeutic recreation: A helping profession* (3rd ed.). Englewood Cliffs, NJ: Prentice Hall.

Patton, M. Q. (1997). *Utilization-focused evaluation* (3rd ed.). Newbury Park, CA: Sage.

Provus, M. (1971). *Discrepancy evaluation*. Berkeley, CA: McCutchan.

Riley, B. (1991). Quality assessment: The use of outcome indicators. In B. Riley (Ed.), *Quality management: Applications for therapeutic recreation* (pp. 53–67). State College, PA: Venture Publishing, Inc.

Rossi, P. H., and Freeman, H. E. (1993). *Evaluation: A systematic approach*. Newbury Park, CA: Sage.

Rossman, B. (1995). *Recreation programming: Designing leisure experiences* (2nd ed.). Champaign, IL: Sagamore.

Shank, J. W., Kinney, W. B., and Coyle, C. P. (1993). Efficacy studies in therapeutic recreation research: The need, the state of the art, and future implications. In M. J. Malkin and C. Z. Howe (Eds.), *Research in therapeutic recreation: Concepts and methods* (pp. 301–335). State College, PA: Venture Publishing, Inc.

Stumbo, N. J. (1996). A proposed accountability model for therapeutic recreation services. *Therapeutic Recreation Journal, 30*(4), 246–259.

Wilhite, B., Keller, M. J., and Caldwell, L. (1999). Optimizing lifelong health and well-being: A health enhancing model of therapeutic recreation. *Therapeutic Recreation Journal, 33*(2), 98–108.

Yavorsky, D. K. (1976). *Discrepancy evaluation: A practitioner's guide*. Charlottesville, VA: University of Virginia.

CASE 1 - TOM GOES FOR TWO

In chapter three, case 2 (page 176), you attempted to integrate Tom into the city recreation department's competitive basketball league for children of all ages. Traditionally this program had been limited to nondisabled players. Tom, who is eight years old, has a spinal cord injury, and uses a wheelchair for mobility, wanted to participate in the league.

Discussion Questions

1. How would you evaluate your efforts to functionally and socially include Tom in the basketball league? Your response should consider specific evaluation questions you want answered, what information (data) will be needed to answer these questions, potential sources of this data and methods of collecting, times and frequency of collecting data, and how the results of evaluation will be used.

2. How could you use triangulation to improve the process of evaluation? Consider various methods, sources of data, and evaluators that could be used to generate an in-depth picture of Tom's and the program's success.

3. If you discovered that the program was not as successful as it was prior to your efforts to include Tom, what would you do?

In-Class Exercises

Invite CTRSs from community-based and institution-based programs to participate in a panel discussion on program and client evaluation in therapeutic recreation. Ask each class member to prepare a question or two for the panel.

Selected References for Case Study

Devine, M. A., McGovern, J. M., and Hermann, P. (1998). Inclusion in youth sports. *Parks and Recreation, 33*(7), 69–76.

Green, F. P., and DeCoux, V. (1994). A procedure for evaluating the effectiveness of a community recreation integration program. *Therapeutic Recreation Journal, 28*(1), 41–47.

Gunn, S. L., and Peterson, C. A. (1978). *Therapeutic recreation program design: Principles and procedures.* Englewood Cliffs, NJ: Prentice Hall.

Henderson, K. A., and Bialeschki, D. (1995). *Evaluating leisure services: Making enlightened decisions.* State College, PA: Venture Publishing, Inc.

Moon, M. S. (1994). *Making school and community recreation fun for everyone: Places and ways to integrate.* Baltimore, MD: Brookes.

Schleien, S. J., Ray, M. T., and Green, F. P. (1997). *Community recreation and persons with disabilities: Strategies for inclusion* (2nd ed.). Baltimore, MD: Brookes.

CASE 2 - CRAWFORD CORRECTIONAL INSTITUTE

Crawford Correctional Institute (CCI) was described to you in chapter two, case 1 (page 98). In chapter four, you revisited CCI when reviewing the case of James (case 2, page 232). It is a maximum security prison housing approximately 1,000 male inmates. The median age for this population is 35 years, and the majority of inmates are serving their second or third term. A variety of inmate needs were discussed in these cases including psychosocial, physical, and cognitive deficits. In chapter two, you, as a new CTRS, were challenged to establish a therapeutic recreation program.

Discussion Questions

Describe what you consider to be the value or relevance of providing therapeutic recreation services in this setting. How would you describe this value or relevance to various stakeholders? In your discussion, identify the stakeholders and the specific outcomes that help to document therapeutic recreation's value and relevance.

In-Class Exercises

1. Classically, quality of care has been defined by measures of structure, process, and outcomes. Using these measures, brainstorm a list of structure, process, and outcome criteria that could be used to determine the efficacy of the therapeutic recreation program at CCI. Brainstorm a second list of structure, process, and outcome criteria that could be used to determine the efficiency of the therapeutic recreation program at CCI.

2. As discussed in chapter two, about 250 of the inmates are involved in therapeutic recreation. Develop a system of evaluation that a CTRS could implement to cover such a large caseload. Include a description of the specific documentation system you could employ. Consider how you could use

formative and/or summative evaluation procedures. Likewise, consider how you could use qualitative and/or quantitative data.

Selected References for Case Study

American Therapeutic Recreation Association. (1993). *Standards for the practice of therapeutic recreation and self-assessment guide.* Hattiesburg, MS: Author.

burlingame, j., and Blaschko, T. (1997). *Assessment tools for recreational therapy: Red book #1* (2nd ed.). Ravensdale, WA: Idyll Arbor.

Mayfield, S. (1992). Quality assurance and continuous quality improvement: Tools for assessing "quality" in therapeutic recreation settings. In R. M. Winslow and K. J. Halberg (Eds.), *The management of therapeutic recreation services* (pp. 137–162). Arlington, VA: National Recreation and Park Association.

Munson, W. (1991). Juvenile delinquency as a societal problem and social disability: The therapeutic recreator's role as ecological change agent. *Therapeutic Recreation Journal, 25*(3), 19–28.

Nikkel, R. E. (1994). Areas of skill training for persons with mental illness and substance use disorders: Building skill for successful community living. *Community Mental Health Journal, 30*(1), 61–72.

Peterson, C. A., and Stumbo, N. J. (2000). *Therapeutic recreation program design: Principles and procedures* (3rd ed.). Needham Heights, MA: Allyn & Bacon.

Riley, B. (Ed.). (1991). *Quality management: Applications for therapeutic recreation.* State College, PA: Venture Publishing, Inc.

Stumbo, N., and Bloom, C. (1990). The implications of traumatic brain injury for therapeutic recreation services in rehabilitation settings. *Therapeutic Recreation Journal, 24*(3), 64–79.

Wankel, L., and Berger, B. (1990). The psychological and social benefits of sport and physical activity. *Journal of Leisure Research, 22*(2), 167–182.

Audiovisual Resources

Documentation and Behavioral Observation. [videotape]. Available from Indiana University, Department of Recreation and Park Administration, HPER Building, Room 133, Bloomington, IN 47405-4711.

CASE 3 - ONIE KEENE

Onie Keene, a 72-year-old African American female, had taken care of her husband of 50 years during his long-term illness. During this time of caregiving, she gave up many of her previous activities. She was no longer an active member of her church, she stopped growing roses, and discontinued most of her elaborate baking. Six months after Mrs. Keene's husband's death, she fell, breaking her right hip, right arm, and right shoulder. After 10 days in an acute care facility, she was transferred to your rehabilitation center. Although a bit anxious, she began her physical (PT) and occupational (OT) therapies. As the CTRS, you visited Mrs. Keene, explained what therapeutic recreation was about, and completed an initial assessment. While at the center, Mrs. Keene worked on mobility, dressing, eating, and toileting goals during PT and OT.

Mrs. Keene's therapeutic recreation goals were to increase social interaction by leaving her room daily and attending group activities, increase ambulation with a walker by participating in a daily walking program, and increase fine-motor skills of her broken arm and shoulder by playing board games five times each week. After 21 days, Mrs. Keene was ready to go home.

Even though Mrs. Keene had engaged in all her therapies and met basic goals, her ambulation was still poor. She needed a walker to ambulate independently, and then could ambulate only for short distances. She could use a cane with a person assisting. She would not be able to drive, she lived alone, and she had limited use of her right arm. She had a daughter who lived in another state who had asked Mrs. Keene to stay with her. Mrs. Keene was ready to go to her own home and felt that she could manage alone.

In-Class Exercises

1. Brainstorm a list of discharge or transition options for Mrs. Keene. Consider the perspectives of Mrs. Keene, her daughter, and various members of the treatment team (e.g., TR, PT, OT). How are discharge or transition plan options you select influenced by Mrs. Keene's original goals?

2. After completing the following role-play, develop a discharge or transition plan for Mrs. Keene. As recommended by Carter, van Andel, and Robb (1995), include a progress summary, a functional abilities assessment, transition recommendations, and a follow-up plan (p. 142).

3. In your discharge plan, you recommend weekly in-home visits for six weeks. Mrs. Keene's insurance company has requested documentation on specific outcomes and their impact. Using the five-step approach to client evaluation discussed in this chapter as a guide, identify the outcomes expected to be attained during various intervals within the projected six weeks and how these outcomes will be monitored. When addressing the impact of these anticipated outcomes, make a convincing case for how they will help Mrs. Keene preserve both immediate and long-term health.

Role-Playing

Role-play a discharge or transition team meeting for Mrs. Keene. Mrs. Keene, her daughter, a CTRS, a physical therapist, and an occupational therapist should be among the team members participating.

Selected References for Case Study

American Therapeutic Recreation Association. (1993). *Standards for the practice of therapeutic recreation and self-assessment guide.* Hattiesburg, MS: Author.

Austin, D. R., and Crawford, M. E. (1996). *Therapeutic recreation: An introduction* (2nd ed.). Needham Heights, MA: Allyn & Bacon.

Carter, M. J., Van Andel, G. E., and Robb, G. M. (1995). *Therapeutic recreation: A practical approach.* Prospect Heights, IL: Waveland Press.

National Therapeutic Recreation Society. (1995). *Standards of practice for therapeutic recreation services and annotated bibliography.* Arlington, VA: National Recreation and Park Association.

Peterson, C. A., and Stumbo, N. J. (2000). *Therapeutic recreation program design: Principles and procedures* (3rd ed.). Needham Heights, MA: Allyn & Bacon.

Petryshen, P. M. (1993/94). Managed care: Shaping the delivery of healthcare and creating an expanded role for the caregiver. *Annual in Therapeutic Recreation, 4,* 108–114.

Audiovisual Resources

Documentation and Behavioral Observation. [videotape]. Available from Indiana University, Department of Recreation and Park Administration, HPER Building, Room 133, Bloomington, IN 47405-4711.

Individual Program Planning. [videotape]. Available from Indiana University, Department of Recreation and Park Administration, HPER Building, Room 133, Bloomington, IN 47405-4711.

CASE 4 - KENJI

Kenji, an 11-year-old Japanese American male you met in chapter two, case 10 (page 136), is comatose secondary to a brain injury. In Kenji's case, you were asked to develop a sensory stimulation program and a program documentation flow sheet. Review the details of Kenji's case, and then respond to the following.

Discussion Questions

1. The need for verifying the efficacy of therapeutic recreation interventions is well-established. What is less certain, however, is how one should determine measures of efficacy through outcomes. In Kenji's case, what are the most important outcomes to be achieved? As outlined by Shank and Kinney (1991), consider:
   a. Effectiveness and efficiency of outcomes,
   b. Reasonable expectation of achieving the outcomes,
   c. Time frame for viewing the outcome (short-term vs. long-term expectation), and
   d. The political and personal value of the outcome (p. 76).
2. With the above discussion in mind, is sensory stimulation an appropriate intervention? Why or why not? What other therapeutic recreation intervention might prove efficacious in meeting specified outcomes?
3. Shank and Kinney (1991, p. 79) describe three levels at which the value or relevancy of therapeutic recreation outcomes can be considered. The first level indicates outcomes that are specific and unique to therapeutic recreation service (e.g., personal behaviors, leisure skills). The second level indicates outcomes that are specific and immediate to clients (e.g., improved mobility, enhanced alertness). The third level indicates outcomes of value to health and human services care systems and society in general (e.g., reduced recidivism, employability). Using

Kenji's case, describe how therapeutic recreation interventions in general, and sensory stimulation, specifically, will be of value and relevance to Kenji, his family, the treatment team, and the larger health and human services community.

In-Class Exercises

1. The team's discharge goal for Kenji is that he will be discharged to his home with continuing academic and rehabilitation support provided. Formulate at least two long-term goals related to this discharge goal. For each long-term goal, develop at least two short-term goals written in behavioral terms (i.e., behavior, conditions, criteria). Refer to chapter two for a review of writing goals.

2. For each short-term goal developed above:
   a. List several evaluation questions;
   b. Determine evaluation subquestions;
   c. Determine sources of evaluation information;
   d. Designate methods of collection, evaluation, and information;
   e. Specify when data will be collected; and
   f. Determine how evaluation information will be used.

Selected References for Case Study

Gunn, S. L., and Peterson, C. A. (1978). *Therapeutic recreation program design: Principles and procedures.* Englewood Cliffs, NJ: Prentice Hall.

Niemeyer, L. O., and burlingame, j. (1998). Outcomes. In F. Brasile, T. K. Skalko, and j. burlingame (Eds.), *Perspectives in recreational therapy: Issues of a dynamic profession* (pp. 221–245). Ravensdale, WA: Idyll Arbor.

Shank, J. W., and Kinney, W. B. (1991). Monitoring and measuring outcomes in therapeutic recreation. In B. Riley (Ed.), *Quality Management: Applications for therapeutic recreation* (pp. 69–82). State College, PA: Venture Publishing, Inc.

Audiovisual Resources

Individual Program Planning. [videotape]. Available from Indiana University, Department of Recreation and Park Administration, HPER Building, Room 133, Bloomington, IN 47405-4711.

CASE 5 - WALTER BYRD

Walter Byrd's case was first presented in chapter one, case 11 (page 60), and then again in chapter two, case 12 (page 142). He has a diagnosis of right cerebral vascular accident (CVA) with left hemiparesis. Review the details of Mr. Byrd's case and then respond to the following.

Discussion Questions

1. Do you think Mr. Byrd has good potential as a rehabilitation candidate? Why or why not?
2. Discuss goals that are relevant to Mr. Byrd's treatment. Consider a global or discharge goal, several long-term goals, and at least one-short term goal for each long-term goal.
3. It has been determined that Mr. Byrd should be discharged to his home with appropriate homecare follow-up. According to the National Therapeutic Recreation Society's *Standards of Practice for Therapeutic Service* and/or the American Therapeutic Recreation Association's *Standards of Practice for Therapeutic Recreation and Self Assessment Guide*, what should Mr. Byrd's discharge and transition plan include?
4. Since Mr. Byrd is being discharged to his home, what would the CTRS want to know about his home, including the marina camp site and community prior to developing a discharge and transition plan?
5. What type of communication and discharge planning could the CTRS at the rehabilitation center initiate with recreational professionals working in the community?
6. What approach(es) would you use to determine the effectiveness of the discharge/transition plan? How

would Mr. Byrd's satisfaction with his achievement and maintenance of treatment goals be incorporated into your evaluation?

Role-Playing

Invite a CTRS, occupational therapist, physical therapist, speech therapist, nurse, and a person who has experienced a CVA to role-play an interdisciplinary discharge planning session. Discuss the issues that are raised during the session. Reflect on the role of the CTRS as a member of the interdisciplinary team.

Selected References for Case Study

American Therapeutic Recreation Association. (1993). *Standards for the practice of therapeutic recreation and self-assessment guide.* Hattiesburg, MS: Author.

Hogberg, P., and Johnson, M. (1994). *Reference manual for writing rehabilitation therapy treatment plans.* State College, PA: Venture Publishing, Inc.

Landrum, P. K., Schmidt, N. D., and McLean, A. (Eds.). (1995). *Outcome-oriented rehabilitation: Principles, strategies, and tools for effective program management.* Gaithersburg, MD: Aspen.

Melcher, S. (1999). *Introduction to writing goals and objectives: A manual for recreation therapy students and entry-level professionals.* State College, PA: Venture Publishing, Inc.

National Therapeutic Recreation Society. (1995). *Standards of practice for therapeutic recreation services and annotated bibliography.* Arlington, VA: National Recreation and Park Association.

Peterson, C. A., and Stumbo, N. J. (2000). *Therapeutic recreation program design: Principles and procedures* (3rd ed.). Needham Heights, MA: Allyn & Bacon.

CASE 6 - GETTING BACK ON HER FEET

Zami Alou, born in the Dominican Republic, emigrated to the United States with her husband. She is 26 years old and has two children. She left her husband four months ago because of his alcoholic fits of rage and verbally and physically abusive behavior toward herself and her children. Some instances were so severe that she or a child would be rushed to the emergency room for concussions, broken bones, and lacerations. She would say that she or her children were just clumsy and fell or tripped to avoid the angry recurrence again at home.

Money was also an issue. Living in a lower socioeconomic area of town brought about extra hardships and stressful burdens from which she tried to shield her children. She was only 15 when she first became pregnant and left home. Through the years, and particularly since emigrating to the United States, she has had limited contact with her family. Government assistance has helped her buy food and find more affordable housing. Unfortunately, the assistance just never seems to be enough.

Alone and on the streets, Ms. Alou felt she had nowhere to turn. She had to provide for herself and her children, but did not want to resort to prostitution or stealing to survive, so she sought help at a homeless shelter for abused and battered women and children.

According to Ms. Alou, she has many interests. During high school, she participated in athletics on her high-school swimming and track teams. Another passion of Ms. Alou's is her love of music. She is a talented pianist, but has not played the piano since leaving her childhood home. She understands the importance of education and regrets that she never graduated from high school or studied English more extensively. Now, however, she feels that her children come first.

Ms. Alou appears depressed, with low self-esteem and poor self-confidence. She states that she sometimes thinks about hurting herself. She tries to avoid social situations and interactions, stating that anytime her husband went out with friends, he came home drunk and abused her. She thinks that anyone who is around group settings gets drunk and becomes abusive.

Discussion Questions

1. What are some of the characteristics of people who are homeless? What are the specific concerns of Ms. Alou (e.g., lack of education)?

2. Discuss whether therapeutic recreation services are appropriate in nontraditional settings such as a shelter for abused and battered women and children who are homeless. If so, what would be the purpose of therapeutic recreation in this setting? How might therapeutic recreation services be conceptualized and delivered?

3. Thinking about how you answered the first two questions, what specific outcomes or benefits would be desirable for individuals in this setting? For Ms. Alou? How could therapeutic recreation services contribute to these desired outcomes? List several examples of therapeutic recreation outcomes.

4. Many of the services provided at the shelter are provided as group activities. Professionals often evaluate group activities by the degree to which *program* objectives were met. How do program objectives (or outcomes) differ from individual objectives or outcomes?

5. Periodic evaluation of individual progress must also take place at the shelter. Suggest a variety of methods for measuring the achievement of outcomes like those identified in question three. How would the techniques and strategies used for individual evaluation differ from those used for program evaluation?

6. How are you going to use your evaluation data? How will your interpretation of the meaning of your results relate to decisions regarding resources, policies, procedures, and/or individuals?

In-Class Exercises

1. For each of the therapeutic recreation outcomes you identified in question three, brainstorm a list of possible programs and activities you could use to achieve them. Consider both shelter-based and community-based options.

2. For each of the programs and activities you identified above, brainstorm a list of affordable community-based resources Ms. Alou and her children might use to pursue leisure choices.

Field Experiences

1. Keep a journal or scrapbook throughout the semester about one specific aspect of a social trend that concerns or interests you (e.g., homelessness, poverty, hunger). Write a reflection paper describing that trend in terms of changing definition and causes, proposals made or steps taken to deal with it, and how the trend affects the people with whom you may work. Prepare to discuss the trend in class.

2. Visit a shelter for people who are homeless. While there, spend time visiting with some of the residents and workers. Consider volunteering for the shelter.

3. Invite someone who works at a shelter for people who are homeless to come to speak in class. Invite some of the residents of the shelter to accompany the worker to speak about their individual experiences.

Selected References for Case Study

Dail, P. W. (1992). Recreation as socialization for the homeless: An argument for inclusion. *Journal of Physical Education, Recreation, and Dance, 63(4),* 37–40.

Kunstler, R. (1991). There but for fortune: A therapeutic recreation perspective on the homeless in America. *Therapeutic Recreation Journal, 25(2),* 31–40.

Kunstler, R. (1992). Forging the human connection: Leisure services for the homeless. *Parks and Recreation, 27*(3), 42–45.

Kunstler, R. (1993). Serving the homeless through recreation programs. *Parks and Recreation, 28*(8), 18–22.

National Coalition for the Homeless. [On-line]. Available: http://nch.ari.net

Patrick, G. D. (1994). A role for leisure in treatment of depression. In D. M. Compton and S. E. Iso-Ahola (Eds.), *Leisure and mental health, volume 1* (pp. 175–190). Park City, UT: Family Development Resources.

Roberts, A. R. (1998). *Battered women and their families: Intervention strategies and treatment programs.* New York, NY: Springer.

CASE 7 - VISIBLE LOVE

Visible Love is an organization serving at-risk youth. Services are targeted toward youth ages six through 19. Visible Love's services are available Monday through Saturday from 6:00 a.m. to midnight. The organization is nonprofit and receives funding from various groups and individuals in the community. All staff, except for the director, are volunteers. Goals of Visible Love are to provide youth with a safe environment away from home and off the streets, to provide positive role models, to provide opportunities for personal growth and development, and to provide intervention strategies for negative behavior. On a typical day, 20–25 children and young adults participate in various activities and programs offered at the Visible Love facility. A CTRS, who works in community recreation at a nearby center, volunteers her time in this program from 3:30 p.m. to 7:30 p.m. every other day. She is responsible for leading small group therapy sessions. Two of the participants in her groups are described below.

Duncan is a 15-year-old male of Italian ancestry, whose father is an abusive alcoholic. Duncan has shown up under the influence of alcohol three times since he first came to Visible Love four months ago. He is often hostile, and tends to act out violently toward younger males. He is irritable and quickly agitated. He dominates conversations and uses profanity regularly. He makes inappropriate sexual comments directed toward the females in his group. He is impatient with the other group members, but has controlled his negative comments toward them during the past two group sessions.

Duncan is a C- student in school and shows no interest in improving his academic standing. However, he finds great pleasure in playing soccer. His schoolmates say he has also displayed amateur talent in a variety of track and field activities. The CTRS has noted that Duncan almost instantaneously becomes calm, even friendly, when talking about soccer. Because of their common interest in soccer, Duncan has befriended a 17-year-old boy who also participates at Visible Love.

Cassie is a 12-year-old White female who has a tendency to inflict pain on herself. While at Visible Love, she is not allowed in the kitchen alone, or anywhere else a stray, sharp object may be found. She is extremely thin and does not keep up her physical appearance like most other girls her age. She could be at risk for anorexia, as evidenced by her habits of eating very small portions of food, if she eats at all, while at Visible Love. She has very low self-esteem and does not interact with others unless they approach her. Even then, she often chooses to remain alone. She has stated that she feels awkward around other youth, including her schoolmates and the children at Visible Love. Her clothes reek of cigarette smoke and she has been caught smoking outside the facility several times over the past two months. Cassie says that smoking helps her to relax and that she enjoys the buzz it gives her.

Cassie carries a sketch pad with her at all times, but has never allowed anyone at Visible Love to look in it. Sometimes, while she is outside and thinks no one is listening, she is heard singing. The children report that she has a nice voice. She has not talked about either drawing or singing in the sessions with the CTRS, although she does talk about her feelings and behavior.

Discussion Questions

1. What global outcomes or benefits would be desirable for the youth who attend Visible Love? For Duncan? For Cassie? How could therapeutic recreation services contribute to these desired outcomes? List several examples of therapeutic recreation outcomes.

2. Is it desirable for CTRSs to volunteer their expertise and time in settings where therapeutic recreation services do not currently exist? Why or why not?

3. In the case of the Visible Love program, what evaluation audiences would be interested in determining the worth of the therapeutic recreation program? For each evaluation audience you identify, discuss specific evaluation questions that would be of interest to them.

4. What information, in addition to what is provided in the case, would help you identify and evaluate long-term and short-term goals and intervention strategies for Duncan and Cassie?

5. What type of evaluation system could be used to track Duncan's and Cassie's achievement and maintenance of desirable goals over time? Why would this be important? How could you use this information?

In-Class Exercises

1. Half of the class select Duncan, and the other half, Cassie. For each, formulate at least two long-term goals related to one of the global goals identified in question 1 above. For each long-term goal, develop at least two short-term goals written in behavioral terms (i.e., behavior, conditions, criteria). Refer to chapter two for a review of writing goals.

2. Identify the programs and activities you will use to help Duncan (or Cassie) achieve the short-term goals you developed.
3. For each long-term goal, develop a list of formative and summative evaluation questions that might be used to determine the effectiveness and efficiency of the therapeutic recreation intervention.

Role-Playing

The United Way is a primary funder of the Visible Love program. A series of budget hearings are being held during which beneficiaries are asked to provide evidence of the worth or merit of their program and thus ensure the United Way's continued support. Role-play a scenario in which the director of the Visible Love program, and additional individuals selected by the director, update the United Way's board of directors concerning how the achievement of individual and program goals is impacting the clients, their family and friends, and the community served by the Visible Love program. Who might the director enlist to help present the information? Why?

Field Experiences

Many park and recreation agencies are serving at-risk youth. Visit an agency and learn about its programs and services. Discuss with agency personnel how they evaluate their programs and services. Learn about funding sources for these programs and services and how evaluation data are used to ensure continuation of this funding.

Selected References for Case Study

Caldwell, L. L., and Smith, E. A. (1994). Leisure and mental health of high-risk adolescents. In D. M. Compton and S. E. Iso-Ahola (Eds.), *Leisure and mental health, volume one* (pp. 330–345). Park City, UT: Family Development Resources.

Center for Substance Abuse Treatment (1998). *Recovery from substance abuse and addiction: Real people tell their stories.* Washington, DC: Author.

Colley, J. (1998). Risky business: Innovative at-risk youth programming. *Journal of Physical Education, Recreation, and Dance, 69*(1), 39–43.

National Clearinghouse on Alcohol and Drug Information. [Online]. Available: http://www.health.org

Witt, P. A., and Baker, J. (1999). Making a R.E.A.L. difference. *Parks and Recreation, 34*(3), 70–80.

Witt, P. A., and Crompton, J. L. (1996). *Recreation programs that work for at-risk youth: The challenge of shaping the future.* State College, PA: Venture, Publishing, Inc.

Witt, P. A., and Crompton, J. L. (1996). The at-risk youth recreation project. *Journal of Park and Recreation Administration, 14*(3), 1–9.

CASE 8 - HARRISON

You met Harrison in chapter two, case 11 (page 139), and saw him again in chapter three, case 8 (page 197). Harrison, a 32 year-old White male has been living with human immunodeficiency virus (HIV) related myopathy for about one year. His condition is deteriorating rapidly and his prognosis is poor.

Discussion Questions

1. In chapter three, you were asked to identify the indicators or outcomes that Harrison and his friends and family could use to evaluate his quality of life as his physical condition deteriorates. Thinking again of these outcomes, discuss whether therapeutic recreation interventions are appropriate when individuals are not expected to get better and can no longer achieve rehabilitation goals. Why or why not?

How would Harrison's treatment plan goals be modified under these circumstances? What new goals could be formulated for Harrison?

2. Discuss the value of therapeutic recreation interventions with clients who are dying. Using the *Optimizing Lifelong Health and Well-Being* therapeutic recreation model, discuss how Harrison and the CTRS could use the evaluation component of the model to reexamine desired goals and related activities.

In-Class Exercises

1. Brainstorm a list of goals of therapeutic recreation interventions that would be appropriate for clients who have a terminal illness. For each goal, specify how these goals are important for clients, their family and friends, and/or the larger health and human services community.

2. Develop a questionnaire on death. The local Cancer Society or hospice program might have one available to serve as a guide. Included could be such questions as: What is your experience with death? How would you tell a child about death? What are your family customs concerning death? What type of living legacy (e.g., a book, cassette, video, piece of artwork, poem), which reflects who you are, might you share with your family and friends? Discuss these responses in class.

Selected References for Case Study

Caroleo, O. O. (1988). AIDS: Meeting the needs through therapeutic recreation. *Therapeutic Recreation Journal, 22*(4), 71–78.

Hodges, J. S., and Sorensen, B. (1998). Quality during the end of life. *Parks and Recreation, 33*(5), 72–76.

Kubler-Ross, E. (1969). *On death and dying.* New York, NY: Macmillan.

National Association of People with AIDS. [On-line]. Available: http://www.napwa@napwa.org

National Hospice Organization. (1996). *You matter to the last moment of your life*. Arlington, VA: Author.

Scimeca, L., and Buggs, R. (1996). *Therapeutic recreation for the terminally ill: Interventions and illness specific recommendations*. Paper presented at the American Therapeutic Recreation Association Conference, San Francisco, CA.

Turner, N. H., and Keller, M. J. (1988). Therapeutic recreation practitioners' involvement in the AIDS epidemic: Rationale and implications. *Therapeutic Recreation Journal, 22*(3), 12–22.

Wilhite, B., Keller, M. J., and Caldwell, L. (1999). Optimizing lifelong health and well-being: A health-enhancing model of therapeutic recreation. *Therapeutic Recreation Journal, 33*(2), 98–108.

Index

Other Books by
Venture Publishing, Inc.

The Evolution of Leisure: Historical and Philosophical Perspectives (Second Printing)
by Thomas Goodale and Geoffrey Godbey
Experience Marketing: Strategies for the New Millennium
by Ellen L. O'Sullivan and Kathy J. Spangler
Facilitation Techniques in Therapeutic Recreation
by John Dattilo
File o' Fun: A Recreation Planner for Games & Activities—Third Edition
by Jane Harris Ericson and Diane Ruth Albright
The Game and Play Leader's Handbook: Facilitating Fun and Positive Interaction
by Bill Michaelis and John M. O'Connell
The Game Finder—A Leader's Guide to Great Activities
by Annette C. Moore
Getting People Involved in Life and Activities: Effective Motivating Techniques
by Jeanne Adams
Great Special Events and Activities
by Annie Morton, Angie Prosser, and Sue Spangler
Hands on! Children's Activities for Fairs, Festivals, and Special Events
by Karen L. Ramey
Inclusive Leisure Services: Responding to the Rights of People With Disabilities
by John Dattilo
Internships in Recreation and Leisure Services: A Practical Guide for Students (Second Edition)
by Edward E. Seagle, Jr., Ralph W. Smith, and Lola M. Dalton
Interpretation of Cultural and Natural Resources
by Douglas M. Knudson, Ted T. Cable, and Larry Beck
Intervention Activities for At-Risk Youth
by Norma J. Stumbo
Introduction to Leisure Services—7th Edition
by H. Douglas Sessoms and Karla A. Henderson
Introduction to Writing Goals and Objectives: A Manual for Recreation Therapy Students and Entry-Level Professionals
by Suzanne Melcher
Leadership and Administration of Outdoor Pursuits, Second Edition
by Phyllis Ford and James Blanchard
Leadership in Leisure Services: Making a Difference
by Debra J. Jordan
Leisure and Leisure Services in the 21st Century
by Geoffrey Godbey
The Leisure Diagnostic Battery: Users Manual and Sample Forms
by Peter A. Witt and Gary Ellis

Leisure Education: A Manual of Activities and Resources
 by Norma J. Stumbo and Steven R. Thompson
Leisure Education II: More Activities and Resources
 by Norma J. Stumbo
Leisure Education III: More Goal-Oriented Activities
 by Norma J. Stumbo
Leisure Education IV: Activities for Individuals With Substance Addictions
 by Norma J. Stumbo
Leisure Education Program Planning: A Systematic Approach—Second Edition
 by John Dattilo
Leisure in Your Life: An Exploration—Fifth Edition
 by Geoffrey Godbey
Leisure Services in Canada: An Introduction—Second Edition
 by Mark S. Searle and Russell E. Brayley
Leisure Studies: Prospects for the Twenty-First Century
 edited by Edgar L. Jackson and Thomas L. Burton
The Lifestory Re-Play Circle: A Manual of Activities and Techniques
 by Rosilyn Wilder
Marketing for Parks, Recreation, and Leisure
 by Ellen L. O'Sullivan
Models of Change in Municipal Parks and Recreation: A Book of Innovative Case Studies
 edited by Mark E. Havitz
More Than a Game: A New Focus on Senior Activity Services
 by Brenda Corbett
Nature and the Human Spirit: Toward an Expanded Land Management Ethic
 edited by B. L. Driver, Daniel Dustin, Tony Baltic, Gary Elsner, and George Peterson
Outdoor Recreation Management: Theory and Application, Third Edition
 by Alan Jubenville and Ben Twight
Planning Parks for People, Second Edition
 by John Hultsman, Richard L. Cottrell, and Wendy Z. Hultsman
The Process of Recreation Programming Theory and Technique, Third Edition
 by Patricia Farrell and Herberta M. Lundegren
Programming for Parks, Recreation, and Leisure Services: A Servant Leadership Approach
 by Donald G. DeGraaf, Debra J. Jordan, and Kathy H. DeGraaf
Protocols for Recreation Therapy Programs
 edited by Jill Kelland, along with the Recreation Therapy Staff at Alberta Hospital Edmonton

Quality Management: Applications for Therapeutic Recreation
edited by Bob Riley

A Recovery Workbook: The Road Back From Substance Abuse
by April K. Neal and Michael J. Taleff

Recreation and Leisure: Issues in an Era of Change, Third Edition
edited by Thomas Goodale and Peter A. Witt

Recreation Economic Decisions: Comparing Benefits and Costs (Second Edition)
by John B. Loomis and Richard G. Walsh

Recreation for Older Adults: Individual and Group Activities
by Judith A. Elliott and Jerold E. Elliott

Recreation Programming and Activities for Older Adults
by Jerold E. Elliott and Judith A. Sorg-Elliott

Recreation Programs That Work for At-Risk Youth: The Challenge of Shaping the Future
by Peter A. Witt and John L. Crompton

Reference Manual for Writing Rehabilitation Therapy Treatment Plans
by Penny Hogberg and Mary Johnson

Research in Therapeutic Recreation: Concepts and Methods
edited by Marjorie J. Malkin and Christine Z. Howe

Simple Expressions: Creative and Therapeutic Arts for the Elderly in Long-Term Care Facilities
by Vicki Parsons

A Social History of Leisure Since 1600
by Gary Cross

A Social Psychology of Leisure
by Roger C. Mannell and Douglas A. Kleiber

Steps to Successful Programming: A Student Handbook to Accompany Programming for Parks, Recreation, and Leisure Services
by Donald G. DeGraaf, Debra J. Jordan, and Kathy H. DeGraaf

Therapeutic Activity Intervention With the Elderly: Foundations & Practices
by Barbara A. Hawkins, Marti E. May, and Nancy Brattain Rogers

Therapeutic Recreation: Cases and Exercises
by Barbara C. Wilhite and M. Jean Keller

Therapeutic Recreation in the Nursing Home
by Linda Buettner and Shelley L. Martin

Therapeutic Recreation Protocol for Treatment of Substance Addictions
by Rozanne W. Faulkner

A Training Manual for Americans With Disabilities Act Compliance in Parks and Recreation Settings
by Carol Stensrud